Bellies and Bullseyes

This book is dedicated to the South Parade Mafia: Irene, Nicholas, Lucy, Emma, Charlotte and Daniel. They gave me the springboard to turn my trials and tribulations into ultimate triumph.

Bellies and Bullseyes

The Outrageous True Story of Darts

SID WADDELL

EBURY
PRESS

5 7 9 10 8 6 4

Published in 2007 by Ebury Press, an imprint of Ebury Publishing

A Random House Group Company

The Random House Group Limited Reg. No. 954009

Addresses for companies within the Random House Group
can be found at www.randomhouse.co.uk

A CIP catalogue record for this book is available from the British Library

Mixed Sources
Product group from well-managed
forests and other controlled sources
www.fsc.org Cert no. TT-COC-2139
© 1996 Forest Stewardship Council

FSC

Printed and bound in Great Britain by Clays of St Ives PLC

ISBN 9780091917555 (hardback)
ISBN 9780091923358 (paperback)

To buy books by your favourite authors and register for offers visit www.rbooks.co.uk

First picture section: p2 © ITV; p3 top-left and top-right, p4, p5,
p6, p7, p8 bottom used courtesy of *Darts World*

Second picture section: p1 bottom, p2 top and bottom-right, p5 bottom, p6 top used
courtesy of *Darts World*; p2 bottom-left, p4 top, p5 bottom, p7 middle, p8 top
© Empics; p7 bottom © Getty Images; p8 bottom © Ben Duffy/swpix.com

All other pictures taken from the author's personal collection or are copyright
unknown. Every effort has been made to contact and clear permissions with relevant
copyright holders. Please contact the publisher with any queries.

CONTENTS

PROLOGUE

From Pub to Parliament

As a little boy growing up in the Ashington coalfield in East Northumberland, I was a sensitive, often sickly, child. I was so highly strung that the approach of important exams at grammar school threw me into a complete funk. Just the fear of not being top in all the subjects meant that I would often worry myself into a chronic asthma attack.

These began in the summer of 1954 when I was fourteen, but by the time I was due to sit my A Levels in June 1958, I had an antidote. To calm the jangling nerves and relax the wheezy tubes the recipe was a game of darts, a bit of banter with some pals and a couple of pints of rough cider. Yes, you've got it in one – booze and bullseyes.

On the night before an exam I would sit hunched on a stool in the bathroom of our tiny pit cottage in the village of Lynemouth, a light year away from my parents who were lapping up telly in the main room. With my dad's dirty pit clothes in one corner, a pile of mucky bed sheets in the other and our scruffy Bedlington terrier, Whisky, lying across my feet, I would learn, parrot-fashion, great gobbets of information about History and English till around eight o'clock. Then I would race to the bus stop, travel the six miles to

Morpeth, our local market town, and dive into the brightly lit back room of the Black and Grey pub.

For the next two hours my bulging brain was on hold; I would not try to recall a single academic fact. Instead I would sip the cloudy, sweet scrumpy and play darts against a bunch of lads who worked on local farms. I did not like to play singles because I have never really liked the competitive aspect of sport. I captained the school rugby team and got international schoolboy trials and I was a finalist in the England Schools 100 yards in 1957, but I was ever the dilettante. I wanted to drop goals like Cliff Morgan or run like the great Jesse Owens. Darts was my own private theatre. I loved the bright spotlight above the board, the feel of the goose feathers on the bomber darts in the old George V Coronation mug beside the blind charity stocking. In a pairs darts match I relished the sarcastic banter when we put the whitewash on our opponents. I loved the meaty thunk of brass into flock. I loved the gut jolt when a double flew in. It was instant therapy for the grammar school's biggest swot, Bighead Sidney. I loved just the mere fun of chucking, boozing, chatting and not thinking.

It worked. My marks got me a scholarship to Cambridge University. And I reckon that my obsessive drive to get darts on to telly and later to commentate on the sport really started in that tatty Morpeth boozer all those years ago.

It was in a Cambridge pub, The Mill on Mill Lane, that I had my most traumatic darting experience ever. First, though, we need a bit of back story. I was a pints and pub lad when I arrived in Cambridge. I had graduated from odd games of darts to regular visits to

Ashington workingmens' clubs for a few pints of Federation Special. At St John's College I drank and sang after rugby matches in The Mitre and hit the college Buttery bar outside the dining hall after dinner each night. That's where, on a gloomy damp February night in 1960, I met Phil Coates and the college darts team.

'Mister Waddell, Scholar of the College, would you care to represent John's tonight at darts against Downing at The Cricketers?' The words were clipped and formal, as if uttered by a senior member of the MCC rather than a tubby bloke in tweeds aged no more than twenty.

I agreed. The next two or three people into the bar were invited to play and a jolly evening ensued. A year later I was the captain and had made the organisation much more professional. So much so that the St John's Killers reached the university four-man darts final.

Which brings us to The Mill, home pitch of the Selwyn College team. The four of us entered the premises at 6.30, eager to have a drink and warm-up throw before the 8 p.m. start, our faces set like a Panzer division. The board was well lit and the Greene King ale went down a treat. The landlord swanned over and had a chat. 'You lot look pretty good. Our team from Selwyn are trainee vicars. They hardly drink and they hardly ever practise.'

Trainee vicars, I thought, smashing in a double top. Taking on the Killers. Bring 'em on. We ordered more ale.

They came in like a bunch of extras from *All Gas and Gaiters*, all grey flannels and hacking jackets. Their leader wore a dog collar and was smoking a bendy Meerschaum pipe. Their drinks order was three half shandies and a glass of orange.

I was always our lead-off man and was normally deadly on double 13 to start in a game of 301. I missed by miles. Meerschaum hit double 20 first dart … and things just got worse. Over the next hour they took us to the cleaners. Our heaviest scorer, John Champion, managed only 23 next trip to the board and in no time we were white-washed in leg one. In the next leg we got away on the double but could not score well: John Champion got a measly 41 and did not like our groans. We did not improve. We began swearing at each other and the landlord told us to pack it in. The gentlemen of the cloth swanned on with beatific smiles. They beat us 7–3 in legs to become the champs. We shook hands limply and then got really bladdered.

We avoided our home pub, The Mitre, for a week. Imagine the scorn of the rugger buggers. 'Beaten at darts? By a bunch of sky pilots? Jesus!'

A couple of years later, in the Premier workingmen's club in Ashington, I first played darts for money and learned another life lesson. Since my night of shame with the trainee vicars I had not played or indeed bragged much about my darts prowess. But from the start Cliff Howe, a chunky ex-Para, and I could do no wrong. There was a spinner by the board and you had to start the game of 301 with the double it spun to. Whatever the double, I got it with my first visit to the board. Cliff backed me up with steady tons.

We won three legs straight for one pound a go and were ready for anybody – except Dick Wilkie. He was a burly sea-coal collector and was in the uniform of the trade – flat cap, tartan muffler, muddy waders. He was watching a domino game on which he had a side bet. His chalk mark was next on the board. We called him over to play.

'I'll throw for Tot, till he finishes,' he said, pointing to a domino player. We shrugged casually. I spun the spinner and it landed on my favourite, double 13. I got it third dart.

'Piece of piss,' murmured Cliff.

Wilkie, half an eye on the dominoes, tossed three darts well wide of the bed. Cliff plundered the treble 19. Wilkie missed again. In another six darts we wanted double 20 and Wilkie had not started. He stepped up to the oche and paused. 'On a whitewash, eh? Will you give me three in a bed?' he smiled. The domino players stopped to watch. We nodded. Surely not …

Wilkie loosened the raggy muffler. He tilted the greasy cap up a notch, clearing his eye-line. He plopped all three darts in the double 13. 'Double or quits lads?' he asked cheekily. We sloped off to the dance room like whipped dogs.

My obsession with darts was deepening. Trainee vicars in Cambridge. Sea-coal Charlies in Ashington. Some experiences you just can't buy. It was on that night I sensed the sheer visceral drama of darts; the oche as the Armageddon of the rampant male ego. Like Hamlet and Iago, Wilkie was a hero figure in pure theatre.

Which brings me to my most significant early encounter with the world of darts. For this we must fast forward to April 1972 when I was very happily working as a documentary producer at Yorkshire Television in Leeds. I had just finished making a documentary about Bobby and Jackie Charlton, when Donald Baverstock, the mercurial Welsh director of programmes, called me into his office. When I got there I found waiting for me, along with Donald, was Peter Jones, also a Welshman and brilliant sports director. 'Right, boyo, we want you to stop thinking about football for a bit and think about darts,' said Donald with a light in his eyes. 'I've told Lew Grade and the boys that we are working on a pub games show and that darts will be its main focus. Peter here is covering the *News of the World* championship finals for *World of Sport* this weekend and I'd like you to go along to observe.'

Peter nodded. 'Twelve thousand darts fans turn up at the Ally Pally as drunk as skunks. They cheer on their heroes just like a football crowd. They have banners, gonks, rattles, the lot. It will be great telly.'

I must admit I had my doubts, but they did not last long.

At eleven o'clock the following Saturday morning I was sitting behind Peter in the scanner of the ITV outside broadcast unit at Alexandra Palace. Brilliant pale light sprayed down through the glass roof and the dartboard oche area was as impressive as a marble altar. But there was no sign of the darting hordes. The phone rang and Peter answered it. It was *World of Sport* asking for shots of the merry fans to use on a trailer. 'They are not here … yet.' Peter was apologetic.

At two minutes to twelve he was back on the phone. 'You can have those shots now. The lads are here.' Twelve thousand men and boys, sporting cardigans, T-shirts and tattoos, some carrying six-packs and many with leeks and dragon flags, swirled into the arena. Commentator Dave Lanning interviewed some of them.

'Where have you been all morning?' asked Dave.

'In the pubs,' came the universal reply, as if to a simpleton.

On the lips of many was the name that was soon to become synonymous with professional darts: Alan Evans.

Alan, real name David, was not exactly a hero in the mould of Owen Glendower. He was small, even in Cuban heels, tubby, had gappy teeth and played in a blood-red sweatshirt that did little to hide his prominent belly. With his fans going crazy, he took the stage in the semi-final against the reigning champion Dennis Filkins. Dennis, looking like a friendly butcher, sported a nervous grin before the match started, while Alan shouted silently to himself and kissed the red dragon flights on his darts.

Evans's delicate style, poised like Eros, was in marked contrast to his chunky appearance. There was a balletic quality to his throwing action and he held his arrows like a surgeon about to slice – ever so delicately. His dark Celtic features snarled at a miss, soon to be followed by a war whoop that Cochise would have been proud of when he shot well. He leapt in the air giving Denis Law-style salutes to his fans. He clinched the match against Filkins with treble 18, double 16 and jumped two feet off the floor. His fans mobbed him off the oche.

It did not seem to matter that he lost the final to Brian Netherton of Cornwall.

When Dave Lanning, Peter Jones and I spoke to Evans shortly after his defeat in the final, it was clear that he had used several pints of lager as 'fuel'. His tiny eyes slitted with emotion and he punched his chest. He was almost in tears that he had not 'done it for Wales'. Around us the fans chanted his name.

Dave, Peter and myself, the trio who were to become the backbone of the *Indoor League* darts team, retired to a Wembley hostelry. Dave, who was Britain's leading speedway commentator, was convinced that televised darts was the coming thing. Peter sipped whisky and waxed lyrical about technical wonders he could envisage: super slow mo on the flight of the missile, split screen on the face and the target. I sat back and drank it all in. My scepticism had vanished. I was convinced that Evans and lads like him would soon be stars. Inside my working-class brain was this nagging revolutionary idea. Wouldn't it be great if darts got on to television alongside football, rugby, tennis and cricket. Inverted snobbery? Massive chip on Geordie shoulder? You bet. A few days later we learned that seven million people had watched the darts on *World of Sport*, one of their biggest audiences of the year.

Thirty-three years later, a bright April day found a motley collection of darting people in the Terrace Marquee of the House of Commons. Edward Lowy, his brother Richard and his father Stanley, the founder of Unicorn Darts, were there. Dick Allix, event director of the Professional Darts Corporation and Tommy Cox, PDC tournament organiser, busied themselves around a very fancy oche. Phil Taylor, twelve times world champion, practised menacingly, while world number one Colin Lloyd and veteran Bob Anderson accepted a cheeky Chablis from a flunky. I had a wee swallow myself.

We were eagerly awaiting the start of an 'Exhibition for the Sport of Darts' hosted by darts daft Bob Russell, MP for Colchester. The plan was to do our thing with tungsten and tonsil to convince members of both Lords and Commons that darts was a sport. Sport UK had a list of approved sports that featured baton-twirling but not tungsten tickling. Disgraceful! I wondered if maybe a dozen or so Honourable Members might show up and was amazed when over seventy trooped in, eager for a throw and a bevvy.

First in and first on the practice board was a four-man team of Lords, led by Lord Tom McNally, Lib Dem leader in the Lords, who pulled out a set of much-used 25-gram tungsten arrows and let fly with purpose. I was impressed. Their opponents, a team of sharp-suited Tories, exchanged pleasantries, sipped wine and it was Game On! I started fairly soft and sensible on the commentary, but then let rip. 'I've heard of four lords a-leaping, but this the first time I've seen four lords a-tossing'. There were belly laughs from all corners. To the Tories: 'I'll bet you lads would not be down here supping and slotting if Missus Thatcher had still been in charge!' I got them all going by apologising for the lack of red wine: 'That Roy Jenkins played havoc with the stock of claret.'

The politicos had a ball. The Tory shadow Minister for Sport hit a ton, and Richard Caborn, Minister for Sport, went out in two darts from 97. At around half past three the lads reluctantly went back to running the country. Dick, Tommy and I sipped the last of the free wine and cosily looked back over the years. Both had managed great players in the past: Dick was with Eric Bristow and Tommy had Jocky Wilson and Phil Taylor. We recalled the harsh days of the great darts dispute with the British Darts Organisation. Our nostalgia was garnished with the triumph of a great day. Tommy summed it up: 'Whoever thought us three would end up on the terrace of the House of Commons?'

The next day's news was even better. Sport England announced that it would recognise darts as a sport, and it was certain that Sport UK would follow suit soon. And to think that a snotty BBC bigwig once told me that darts would go on the Beeb 'over my dead body'.

1

'Skills at the Arrows of Outrageous Proportions'

In the middle of 2003 the *Observer* newspaper printed a list of the ten funniest sports television programmes ever invented. Top of the list by a mile was the *Indoor League* presented from 1972–78 by Freddie Trueman and produced for most of that time by me. The brash, raucous show was our tribute to the unsung heroes, male and female, of shove ha'penny, table football, bar skittles, arm-wrestling, bar billiards, pool and darts. In 1973, the television critic of *The Times*, Stanley Reynolds, was amazed that over three million people tuned in at lunchtime to watch a show he described like this: 'It has all the recherché values of *It's a Knockout* and the heady atmosphere of floodlit rugby league.'

We were well chuffed by this backhanded accolade. The massive pool of working-class viewers was exactly what we were aiming at. In fact, series four of the show got figures of nearly eight million when it went out in early 1975. It was a custard pie flung in the face of the viewers and they licked off every scrap. Freddie walked out in a suede cardigan, smoking a pipe and toting a pint of ale. He greeted the viewers like pals: 'Na' then lads and lasses are yer ready for pottin' and slottin', tossin' and bossin' to win a hundred quid?' He always signed off with his catchphrase 'I'll sithee', and, till he died in mid-2006, people kept coming up to him and saying the line with a wink.

The show was mapped out in May 1972 in a posh office at Yorkshire Television in Kirkstall Road, Leeds, and four people were involved. Donald Baverstock, the programme controller, had developed the title and the general idea when watching his rather staid father get all worked up playing bar skittles. Peter Jones was a very good darts player and was well aquainted with the top players in South Wales. I was the reigning all-Yorkshire shove ha'penny champion and had served my apprenticeship at the sport in the red-hot Durham City Super League. John Fairley, head of local features, was to be the executive producer, and he, like all of us, played skittles and shove ha'penny for a couple of hours and helped consume a full crate of Double Diamond. The meeting ended with Peter and I reporting enthusiastically on the atmosphere and fan mania at the *News of the World* darts finals. We all agreed that the darts would be the jewel in the crown of the *Indoor League* and that the great Freddie Trueman, lately embarked on a career as a stand-up comedian, would be the perfect presenter.

Next day, in my role as producer of the new show, I briefed a team of researchers and set them the task of finding local stars in the various sports. We hoped the show would eventually go national, but our first batch of champions was from the north. We held the heats of the *Indoor League* on the YTV nightly news show *Calendar* and some real characters walked in through the studio door. A very young Willie Thorne, destined to become a snooker star, showed us his skill at pool and presenter Richard Whiteley could hardly stop laughing at one of our shove ha'penny players. He called himself Buffalo Bill and he dressed in full cowboy regalia. In one holster he had a six-gun – and in the other his five shiny shoving ha'pennies! Mind, on the shiny wooden pitch, Bill was no laughing matter.

Then it was time for our big weekend. In mid-October 1972 I walked into the Queen's Hall in Leeds and was gobsmacked. Even before a dart was tossed or a skittle toppled, the atmosphere was superb. Our champions prowled and took liberal swigs of the free ale. The set was a three-ring circus with sports going on simultaneously. Giant figures of Andy Capp and his wife Florrie and their pals looked down on the action like working-class gods. Once the action started, Freddie Trueman, pipe and pint in hand, kept tabs on the games like an anxious concert secretary hoping the 'turns' were up to scratch. They were.

Without any disrespect to the other sports and their stars, I have to say that our darts competition was something else. The contestants had none of the first-night nerves of some of the skittlers and bar billiards players. The darters practised with icy precision. Many of them knew each other and exchanged edgy banter. They all drank, some copiously.

They also had form. John Walker of Hull, fresh-faced and aggressive, had been to the finals of the *News of the World*. Charlie Ellis from Wyke near Bradford was the favourite. He had craggy features and pure white-blond hair. Dave Lanning dubbed him 'The Viking War God'. Charlie had his own special darts room in his local pub where he often played money matches for up to £250. But in the end a twenty-seven-year-old lad called Colin Minton from Easingwold near York took the title and the £100 first prize. He told Freddie that he had been playing since he was about eight in his dad's pub. They had to put a beer crate under the board so he could climb up and pull his arrows out. We had stumbled on a sporting subculture.

Over the next few weeks we edited the tapes and sent some of the material to the ITV bosses in London. They thought the show was wonderful and it was agreed to make a second series for a national audience. I drafted the scripts and Freddie was due in the studio soon afterwards to record the links. We had a meeting with John Fairley and John Wilford, the editor of *Calendar*, and had a read-through of my scripts: 'Hello and welcome to the first television show to break the huddle round the dartboard and the pool table and bring you the champions of the tap room.' I was aware of a feeling of concern in the room. Fairley and Wilford were shaking their heads.

'It doesn't sound like Freddie,' said John W.

'It sounds like bloody *Panorama*,' said John F.

I did not know what to say. Fairley did. He called down a secretary and told her to stand by with her shorthand pad. He looked hard at me. 'Right, Sidney, talk exactly like you tell your stories in the bar about Alan Evans and Co.'

I twigged immediately – and Fredspeak was born. 'Hey up lads and lasses. I hope tha's got a soft seat 'cos you'll be trampolining on it soon when you see the lads and lasses we've got ruckin' and chuckin' arrers here at *Indoor League*...'

It was one thing getting the script right but quite another getting Freddie to deliver it. It did not help that at ten o'clock on the first morning of recording links our star turned up with the hangover from hell. He had done a successful stand-up gig at the Fiesta night club in Stockton and had celebrated late and large. Still, after ten minutes in make-up and a shot of black coffee, he looked OK. He raised his pipe and began rehearsing the links. 'I don't talk like this,' he wailed.

'You do now,' said Fairley dryly.

To be honest, Freddie rehearsed the lines with some aplomb and the odd bit of self-mocking mugging. But just as we went for a take, somebody mentioned continuity. On tape Freddie always had a partially filled glass of ale, which we had to match in the studio. But where to get beer? I dived into the YTV bar and pleaded with the steward to let me have something, anything. The result was that Freddie was supplied with Newcastle Brown Ale as 'continuity' and was topped up and slurring by noon. We had to call it a draw.

Series one went out in the North in spring of 1973 and was well received. For series two, we moved the venue to the Leeds Irish Centre, one of the biggest workingmen's clubs in Britain. We gathered there on the last weekend in August 1973 with great expectations and the potters and slotters did us proud. A bar staff of about a dozen, in wellies and aprons, began pulling pints for players and punters at 10.30 a.m. Half an hour later they pushed up the grilles on serried ranks of ale. It was free to players and, as usual, the darters were first in the queue. Six hours later the staff called a one-hour time out on serving beer and a voice behind me said 'Eighty-one pints.' I turned to look at a little Irish lad in a suit. He shrugged at me and said: 'There's nine of us.'

The two days fulfilled my every dream. In the women's darts, the world number one player was Jean Smith who played in a Para's beret! She was also certified blind; not allowed to work with machines because of defective eyesight. In the bar billiards, headmaster Taffy John was dapper and dignified and every inch a star. In the shove ha'penny, Neil Cleminson, a biology researcher under David Bellamy at Durham University, out-Lanninged Dave Lanning by describing the Huddersfield champion as 'the Spassky of the sliding small change'. Fraser Davey also excelled in the arm-wrestling commentary by describing a posy Chelsea lad as 'the Narcissus of the knotted knuckles'. I pleaded with table football commentator, Keith Macklin, to try to match the zany nature of the other commentators, but my pleas fell on deaf ears. I was not just playing 'Mr Producer'; then, as now, the commentary on 'sport in miniature', like darts and table football, which can be repetitive, must have vibrancy and attack in the patter. It is why the Dave Lanning style, littered with puns, became the benchmark and why Dave is still in business.

However good the other sports were, the men's darts competition was the Prix d'Honneur. Reigning champion Colin Minton was back and so was Charlie Ellis, his hair a deeper shade of gold as befitted a 'Viking War God'. Alan Evans prowled the practice boards in his blood-red shirt, exuding menace and supping lager purposefully. Near him was twenty-year-old Tony Ridler from a famous darting clan, who had won the all-Newport Singles at the age of thirteen. Tony's mouth twisted on release and seemed to blow the darts into the treble 20. On another board a snaggle-toothed Cockney giant slurped beer at an alarming rate and pounded the doubles. He was Ron Church, 'The Leaning Tower of Shoreditch', and was clad in a holey cardigan that was new during the Great Fire of London.

On a corner board was probably the most interesting bunch of all the darters. After the first series had gone out, I received a very cocky letter from very cocky Cockney. A bloke called Olly Croft announced himself as supremo of London, and indeed England, darts and offered to bring three star players north to show the rest how to play. I introduced myself to Olly, who was wearing a maroon blazer with a darty badge and looked a ringer for Mr Pickwick. He had mutton-chop whiskers that met under his chin. He introduced me to a stout lad called Tony Bell and to Willie Etherington, who was built like a rugby league forward. He pointed at his third champion, who was practising, and said: 'That's Tommy. He's going to win.'

I knew a bit about Tommy O'Regan. He was an ex-jockey and had been national darts champion three times. He was drinking large gin and tonics and in twelve attempts at double top hit the target eleven times. 'Best of luck, gents,' I muttered, meaning 'cocky Cockney bastards'.

What happened over the next two days on our championship oche is still a joyous blur. The standard was marvellous, the banter between the players, especially Evans and the Cockneys, inspired, and the commentary great. I had alongside me as my assistant John Meade, recently hired from a Scarborough newspaper, and in the middle of a brilliant semi-final between Evans and Ridler he scrawled a note for Dave Lanning. Suddenly Evans banged in a 180, the first of the competition, and Dave read out John's line: 'This Taff hath skills at the arrows of outrageous proportions.' We laughed and danced around the scanner. We knew we were on to a real winner.

The Evans/Ridler match was our zenith. Alan won the first leg in 15 darts and hit a 180. Tony replied with 17 darts and also a 180. Alan won the decider in 18 darts. We were so excited that we sent a tape of the match to *World of Sport* and they ran it. It was a great trailer for series two, which went out in October 1973 and got well over three million viewers.

The final did not live up to our expectations. A confident Tommy O'Regan beat a nervous Alan Evans. Olly Croft shook my hand and smiled. I was not sure what to make of him. He spoke with a rough Cockney twang and was reckoned to be the owner of a profitable tile company. He told anybody who would listen that he wanted to be the 'Alf Ramsey of Darts'. His dictatorial attitude to the players when he did become darts supremo was to be at the heart of the dispute that ripped darts apart twenty years later.

Series two of the *Indoor League* went out nationally at lunchtimes for thirteen weeks from October 1973 and was a smash hit. It got around three million viewers and the ITV network committee asked for more. The team celebrated in fine style. A few days before Christmas, Peter Jones, John Meade and I took a train to London from Leeds for one mighty boozy jolly, the *TV Times* Television Pro-Am Darts Spectacular at the Taverner's Bar at Lords. We got on the train at about 11 a.m. and headed straight for the buffet car. Given that it was going to be a long day, Peter and I stuck to cans of trusty old McEwan's Export. But John started on brandy and sodas just after Retford and was pretty fresh, as we say in Yorkshire, by the time we got to London.

The bash was brilliant, with a host of stars like Acker Bilk, no mean chucker, and Anita Harris pairing up with the darts stars. Freddie Trueman joined us and Dave Lanning was the host. Acker Bilk paired up with Alan Evans and won the tournament. By the final, John Meade was pretty pissed but well in control. Suddenly boxer Joe Bugner joined our company and John greeted him effusively, slurring just a smidgeon.

'Little guy, you are drunk,' said Joe with a smile.

John pulled himself up to his full height of five foot four. His moustache bristled and his left eye rolled. He turned to Freddie and shouted: 'Pick me up Freddie, I want to hit him.'

Freddie obliged. He held up John like a puppet and John threw pretend punches at Joe. The usual après-darts fun had started. Cliff Inglis of Plymouth, an England international darter, decided to raise the bar. Cliff asked Freddie to stand up against the board, turn sideways and put a cigarette in his mouth. Freddie obliged again. We were all agog. Cliff had taken drink and now cranked up the tension by downing a good half of a pint of bitter. He then let fly and whipped the fag from Freddie's lips. Before the applause died, Cliff asked one of the hostesses, a busty lass, to step up. She did and at Cliff's suggestion took off her bra.

Cliff asked somebody to put a one pence coin on her left breast. We all gasped. Cliff lined up the arrow, let it rip and it clipped off the coin. Cue genuine appreciative applause. I'll draw a curtain over the rest of the proceedings.

'Never mind the programme, get the publicity,' is an old telly adage and soon after the Christmas bash I went to London for a meeting with Dave Lanning and Peter Jackson, the editor of *TV Times*. My brief from Donald Baverstock was to get Freddie Trueman's photo, bare-chested and with our winners' gold medals round his neck, on the magazine cover. It helped no end that Dave was a senior member of staff at *TV Times* and the deal was cracked within fifteen minutes.

Dave and I celebrated at two of his favourite watering holes. First we went to the headquarters of the Bilk Marketing Board, a club owned by Acker Bilk and brother Dave. There we had a swally and discussed Acker's considerable prowess with the arrows with his proud brother. Next stop was the Capricorn Club in Goodge Street, which Dave jokily referred to as 'an upholstered sewer'.

The 'Cap' turned out to be not so bad. It was a place where committed topers, tired journalists and general low-lifes went when the pubs closed at three in the afternoon. OK, the carpet was a bit tatty and it was a bit dingy but the clientele, regulars and out-of-towners, looked pretty well heeled. As we edged our way to a table by the small stage, one or two people greeted Dave. Soon we were supping of Fuller's best bitter, deep in discussion of great darts matches. The music should have given us a clue – it was 'Green Onions' by Booker T and the MGs, but we were far away on the oches of the mind.

Then a shapely black female leg clad in a mesh stocking and attached to a black suspender belt wiggled and flexed between us and our pints. We took no notice, continuing to fling phantom darts and debate why Evans did not use the bull route out from 82. There was a gasp from the audience and we looked up. A red G-string was dangling inches from our noses. Dave raised his drink. 'Cheers, Susie, darling. Buy you a drink in just a tick. We're discussing business.' To me he added: 'Friend of mine.' He returned to the darts match but the statuesque Susie was not to be denied. She tossed her G-string on to our table and presented her ample breasts to us. We got the message and sat back to enjoy her show. I looked around the room and blokes were shaking their heads at the poor sad pair at the front. Gays? Blind men? No, simply two darts nuts. After her act Susie joined us for a drink then shot off into the Soho maze to do another job. By now Dave and I were feeling no pain; he was on white wine and I was on whisky. Dave recalled some of his best speedway lines such as this gem he flung in when Barry Briggs was just leading a race: 'Come on Barry my son, there's two Aussies *up your pipe*.' Then he looked me right in the eyes and said: 'You know, Sid, you could commentate.' I hoped it was not just the booze talking.

A few weeks later and we were back at the Leeds Irish Centre for more potting and tossing. This time I really had to earn my corn as producer. The first day went well until about 4 p.m. when my female personal assistant came up to me in tears and said she was quitting. She had fallen in love overnight with an arm-wrestler and was leaving her husband and heading South to set up a love nest. I swallowed hard and wished her all the best. I did not predict the riot…

It began around the table football area. Two black players, favourites for the tournament, were playing two white lads whose fans were a bit the worse for drink. The black lads scored the winning goal, one of them gave a victory air punch and it connected with the chin of a fan of the opposition. Cue an almighty ruck. Several of our giant cardboard figures were sent toppling and so was a camera. I rushed to the table football area and rapidly hustled Leeds United's Terry Yorath – acting as our referee without the knowledge of Don Revie – away from the fracas. Just as I got Terry into the green room, things got worse. A fight at an Irish wedding upstairs joined our fight and soon the scene was like a saloon brawl in a western. As Dave Lanning quipped from his eyrie above the darts: 'We seem to have a new sport here at *Indoor League*.'

There was no course of action open to me as producer but to stop proceedings for the day. We cleared the premises and I checked out the damage. It was minimal: a camera casing had a slight crack and our standing figures were fine. I had a chat with director Peter Jones and he suggested I ring our boss John Fairley, while he asked round about alternative venues for the next day's action. John told me to set in motion any moves I saw fit. Peter had been successful in finding another large local workingmen's club. It was the Belle Isle club in Beeston, about four miles from the Irish Centre. I rang them, and the club arranged a special committee meeting for eight that night.

It was like a scene from the *Wheeltappers and Shunters*. I sat across a table from the committee wearing my best dark pinstripe suit. They wore solemn expressions, waistcoats and watch-chains. I started my plea with the words: 'I have been a fully affiliated Club and Institute Union member for sixteen years.' I proudly waved my membership card of Lynemouth and District Social Club, which my dad renewed every year. It hit just the right note. Faces relaxed and a deal was cut. We would start moving the outside broadcast equipment in there and then, and there would be no fee. I convinced them that their bar takings would go through the roof. I shook hands all round and left.

The men's darts was won by a Welsh giant called Leighton Rees, who had a Bobby Charlton comb-over, a giant beer belly and a thirst to match. By the end of the final Leighton had drunk at least eight pints of lager and a couple of large brandies. After the match a group of us sat with him and his bosom pal Alan Evans and Leighton lit up a huge cigar. 'You'll be ready for a real drink now, but,' said Alan. He was. As producer I had a hospitality kitty and the Welshmen tore a hole in it. It was worth every penny. As we staggered out, a committee man and the club steward stopped me. The bar takings had gone through the roof, they told me, and added that I could bring my 'circus' back any time.

Back at Yorkshire TV I was flavour of the month, despite my riot. A week before the new series of *Indoor League* was due to go out, Alan Whicker himself stopped me in the corridor. I had produced half a series of *Whicker's Women* with him in 1972 and we'd got on reasonably well. 'I see you managed to get Freddie Trueman's picture on the cover of *TV Times*. That's more than you ever did for me,' he said. I shrugged and mumbled something about that being showbiz. He winked and strode on, dapper as a penguin heading for a garden party.

A couple of weeks after the recording of the *Indoor League* series three, Alan Evans came to Leeds to film some trailers. We had a liquid lunch and met the film crew at the Irish Centre at about 2.30. The plan was to shoot Alan hitting 180s and giving his famous Denis Law victory salute. There was only one problem: Alan chucked a few darts that were nowhere near the treble 20, and said he needed more booze. He'd had four pints of lager over lunch, but I went to the bar and got four more! He swilled most of the first new pint down in one. He proceeded to hit 140s at will, but no 180s. On the eighth pint, almost weeping with effort, he planted three darts in the 60 bed. We all cheered madly – except the cameraman. He looked up sheepishly from his eyepiece and sighed: 'Sorry, Sid, we ran out of film just before the last dart!' I gritted my teeth and went back to the bar. We tried for two pints longer, had no luck and packed in. There was a silver lining though. Alan and I went to Batley Variety club where he signed twice as many autographs as the headline act, singer Lovelace Watkins.

Looking back on that exciting time puts the standard of today's players into perspective. In 1973, 180s were as rare as rocking-horse droppings. Now they are like flies in a farmyard. At the 2006 Stan James World Matchplay tournament in Blackpool, the thirty-two players notched up 232 in seven days' play. But just look what we started.

I was now totally fascinated by the subculture that we had uncovered in the world of darts. So it was with eager expectation that I attended the first ever World Masters Individual Darts Championship at the West Centre Hotel in Fulham in late August 1974. Olly Croft, by this time honorary secretary of the British Darts Organisation, which was running county and international darts, was the main organiser and the sponsors were Phonogram, the record company. On offer to the selected twenty-two world stars was the biggest cash prize in the game – £400, plus a hi-fi set! The *News of the World* winner up till that time won a car, and not a cash prize.

And what a line-up of players there was. There was the bearded, wild-eyed Ceri Morgan from Glamorgan, who had very religious parents but was very fond of the ale. Warming up, I spotted Harry Heenan, a bar manager from Glasgow, taking a dram as he caned the doubles. The soft Devon voice of Cliff Inglis rippled from a corner, and I wondered if he'd celebrate here, win or lose, by knocking coins off pert nipples like he had done at the Christmas Pro-Am. Representing the Isle of Man was John 'The Jug' Craine who I had seen sink enough pints to fell an ordinary mortal at the last *Indoor League*. But by far the most focused bloke around was the teetotal George Lee of Surrey. Evans and Rees had described him as a 'hustler' and coming from them that was a massive compliment.

Despite being a big bloke, Lee was beautifully balanced on the oche. In his first match against Fred Turner of Hertfordshire, he won the first leg with a 100 finish, treble 20, double top. He never looked at his opponent, spending the time between his own shots staring at his flights or nodding to pals in the crowd. This was the most hyped and beer-fuelled crowd I had yet come across in darts. I was told there was a lot of big side-betting, and the fans were certainly very vocal. Cries of 'Light 'em up George' and 'Get him off your back' punctuated the respectful silence that fell when the players threw. I was impressed that the shouts only happened *after* a throw. There was an unwritten code of sportsmanship observed by players and spectators. I was starting to feel like Hemingway at the *corrida*, trying to appreciate every nuance.

In the event, Lee did not make the final. It was contested between Heenan and Inglis. Heenan had a done a 13-darter in his first round match and Cliff had held off a charge of five 60s in seven darts by Barry Luckham of London. The pair matched each other, hitting scores over 100 at will. Both drank copiously but the standard did not drop. In the end Cliff, the more relaxed throughout, won and the players collapsed in each other's arms. For an encore, Cliff got out his sharpened builders' nails and threw them like knives into the treble 20. He offered to knock a coin off my tongue, but even though I'd had a few, I politely declined.

Evans and Rees kept mentioning money matches or 'chasers'. Neither was a full-time darts professional, and playing county or international darts gave them plenty of pride but actually left them out of pocket. So they had taken to challenging all-comers for fifty, a hundred or two hundred pounds, with side-betting as well. And just by chance, at the end of 1974, a big 'chaser' was on the cards. Two Manchester businessmen, Alan Kay and Nat Basso, both big wheels in the boxing world, had decided to sponsor George Walsh of Stockport, the reigning National Darts Association of Great Britain champion. They promised that George would drive around in a Rolls-Royce, wear three-piece mohair suits and never drink or smoke – though nobody seemed to tell George the latter stipulation. They announced in the national papers that they were looking for challengers in a £500 match. They very quickly got one – Alan Evans, in his tatty red Welsh top, primed with strong lager and cheered on by hundreds.

The match was played at the Poco-a-Poco club in Stockport on 24 November, 1974. John Meade and I sat among the crowd of over a thousand excited fans like kids at a Christmas party. Alan was rapidly becoming a household name and had just been mentioned on *Coronation Street*. We'd had a drink with him in the players' practice area and he had been bouncing. When he and Walshy left to go onstage, I reckon Alan was on his sixth pint of lager and his opponent well down a bottle of gin.

Alan went off like a train in the best of seven legs of a 1,001 match. He was hot from a 105 average in a leg of a similar match in Hull, and went into a 2-0 lead. His northern base was the Midland Hotel in Stockport and fans from there waved leeks and red rattles. Walshy was red-faced and seemed to have no other plan than to drink more gin. He loosened his tie, won a gritty leg three then drew level in leg four with this amazing sequence of shots: 180, 100, 100, 140, 100, 180, 41, 42, 48, 58, 60 shot-out. OK a bit gin-affected at the end, but it scuppered Alan. His head dropped and the bounce disappeared. Walshy coasted the next two legs to win 4-2.

As the two men exchanged brief, almost sullen, handshakes, half the crowd stood and applauded. Dozens of people ran down to the stage and flung money. The players walked through a carpet of fivers and tenners as they thanked the board officials.

That was the moment I really realised that the humble sport of pub darts was about to explode all over our telly screens. Not for the first time, John Meade and I got happily pissed with the gallant loser. Alan only got maudlin towards the end of a long night. 'I'm playing great but why do I always come second?' It was all about to change dramatically.

I was determined to make a television documentary about Evans and the volatile, boozy sporting world he lived in. The material for this scheme began flooding in soon after the Stockport match. On 27 December, I got a phone call from the steward of the Ferndale

Labour club in the Rhondda Valley. The club was in Alan's home village and he traditionally played a Boxing Day exhibition there for charity. Alan had played twenty-six local players, hammered nearly all of them, but excelled his own outrageous standards in the final game. He deliberately left 150 to finish the game and shot out on THREE BULLS! A week later he took the biggest championship prize in world darts – £750 for the Watney's British Open. Then, in a money 'chaser' match against Yorkshire star Brian Langworth, he averaged 105.

That summer Alan went professional. He had been on the dole for long periods and for a while was a brewery drayman. 'But after we'd put the barrels in the cellar, they couldn't get me off the dartboard!' he explained. Now he bought a mauve Daimler Sovereign and did a five-month tour of Butlin's holiday camps. He averaged eight 180s a week. 'I wanted to be a footballer and had trials with Cardiff City, but rheumatic fever put paid to that dream when I was sixteen,' he said at the time. 'But I am now at the start of a new dream.'

I myself had taken my television career to pastures new. I left Yorkshire Television early in 1975 and moved over the Pennines to the BBC's new northern headquarters in Manchester. I began working with my old friend and mentor Donald Baverstock on highbrow current affairs programmes. But I was allowed the odd day off to pursue my lowbrow obsession, the Alan Evans documentary

One October evening that year I stepped out of Alan's Daimler at Brickcroft Social Club in Rochdale and had my first taste of one of his exhibitions. He walked into the concert room and four hundred people gave him a standing ovation. How I wished I'd had the cameras along, but I reminded myself that this was basic research. I sat down at a table reserved for Alan's guests near the stage and was given a pint of John Willie Lee's best bitter. It had a touch of wild nettle in the flavour, but went down a treat, and the committee kept them coming. Alan joined me, by now wearing a white Elvis outfit, tight shirt and flares, with a couple of badges that said 'Proud to be Welsh'. He drank three pints of lager quickly, signed autographs and then bounced on to the stage. After ten minutes sharp patter, in which he suggested all Lancashire men were puffs and all the women ugly, he began his night's work.

It was magic to watch. Alan played twelve local stars and usually shot out while they were still 200 behind. He finished one leg by hitting two double 20s and another on the bull. He did this despite increasingly drunken heckling from a big ginger lad in a granddad shirt and bright red braces. 'You're nothing but a sheep shagger' and 'Taffies are all thieves' were two of Ginger's witty offerings. Alan left his reprisal till the very end. As he began his closing chat, Ginger shouted again and Alan pounced on him. He dragged the bloke on to the oche and gave him three darts. 'Now put those darts where your big mouth has been all night.'

The crowd were in hysterics.

Ginger squinted at the board, shuffled his drink-affected legs and tossed a dart out of the board. Alan clapped. As Ginger wound up for his second go, Alan walked behind him and began plucking his red braces as if they were the strings of a double bass. This brought the house down and Ginger shook Alan's hand.

'Without prats like that, I wouldn't have an act,' said Alan as he collected his £100 fee in readies from the concert secretary. 'And the hecklers are twice as bad in London.' I scribbled down in my note-book that an Evans exhibition was a must for my film.

Before I could get started, Alan had his biggest darting achieve-ment to date. A few days after the Rochdale exhibition, he won the World Masters title against a great field of top players. The first prize was £1,000 and he danced round the stage in his Welsh Elvis outfit, brandishing the cheque in one hand and a giant leek in the other.

In April 1976 I began filming *The Prince of Dartness* for BBC Northwest. I started on the morning before the *News of the World* Grand Finals in a Queensway pub where Tommy O'Regan, already well gone with the gin at noon, did his party piece of hitting nomi-nated doubles hidden by a sheet of newspaper. Alan Evans had a quick high-scoring match against Tommy, then off we went to Ally Pally. Apart from great atmospheric shots of the twelve-thousand-strong crowd I got wonderful teary-eyed drama as Alan watched his pal Leighton Rees, favourite for the title, crumble on stage in the final. There had been a delay of forty-five minutes between the semis and the final due to the television coverage being altered, and this affected Rees much more than his opponent, Manchester lorry-driver Bill Lennard. Bill won and Evans wept. I rubbed my hands in glee; I was getting the agony as well as the ecstasy.

Our next stop was Weston-super-Mare and Wales versus the rest of Great Britain at the plush Webbington Country Club. Rees captained Wales and O'Regan captained Britain. There was a great atmosphere and Alan, with about six pints of lager down him, hit three 180s in winning his match. He played the crowd like Sinatra. And the match was notable for two other things. Firstly, at the end of his match a very drunk Tommy O'Regan dived off the stage and into the crowd and began punching a heckler. Great behaviour from the rest of Great British captain. Secondly, I got my first whiff of the Borgia-type politics abroad in darts. The event was the first international to be organised by the United Kingdom Darts Federation, whose driving force was Bristol businessman Eddie Norman. Sadly, Eddie and his organisation were seen as rivals by Olly Croft's British Darts Oganisation, which was running county and international darts themselves. O'Regau, Rees, Evans and Co. were criticised for taking part in the UKDF event. The BDO was determined to have a monopoly on darts. It was not long before the UKDF ceased to exist.

I finished shooting my documentary a week later at Liverpool, where Alan took on the pride of Merseyside at an exhibition. He was on splendid form and beat all-comers. But he was expected to have a job on in the last match. His opponent was a Scouse legend, Albie Brown, with a curly mullet and a droopy Zapata tash. Albie did not show till the very last minute. He practised in a nearby pub and came into the club at exactly half past ten. By then Alan was on his eighth pint of lager and was throwing brilliantly. The MC introduced Albie and the crowd went wild. This was the lad who had recently won the Merseyside singles on crutches after breaking a leg. It was a tight match and went to the deciding leg. Then Alan deliberately left the bull to win. Alfie gave him a knowing wink. Alan's first dart hit the button. Game to Alan Evans – and what a finale to my film. It went out locally in October 1976 and was so well received that it went out nationally on BBC2 the following March. I began getting word on the darts grapevine that South Wales and Lancashire were not the only hotbeds of darts for big money. The names of two blokes, one from South Yorkshire and one from North Derbyshire, kept cropping up: Brian Langworth and John Lowe. Langy was a legend in his home town of Sheffield and had developed his darts while in the army, boosting his pay with money matches. Lowe was a late starter in the game; Evans, Ridler and Bristow were playing when they were hardly out of nappies, but Lowe did not throw a dart till he was in his twenties. One night in 1966 in a village pub near Chesterfield a team player got taken short in mid-game, handed the darts to John and he scored 100.

By the middle of 1976 Langy and John were in their prime as money players. Langy was hot from two victories over George Walsh and challenged John, a star with Yorkshire and England, to a match for £400. By the time the two met at the Arundel Club in Sheffield, there was another £400 in side-betting. As usual in a 'money race', it was long-course darts – the best of nine legs of 1,001. John went off like a train in leg one and was averaging 123 after six visits to the board. He won the match easily by five legs to one. But, typically, John did not rest on his laurels or his bank balance. He immediately announced that he and Langy wanted to take on Evans and Rees 'for really big money'.

A few weeks later the Northern pair, accompanied by two busloads of supporters, entered the lair of the Welsh dragons, Maerdy Workman's Hall in the Rhondda. Hundreds of locals waved their blood-red scarves and their prize leeks, howling greetings to the

Englishmen. On the stage were two giant cardboard boxes and the MC told the crowd that they should go to one box if they were betting on the Welsh, and the other if they were betting on the English. There was an imbalance since most people were going for Rees and Evans, but this was sorted out when some of the locals had a second bet on the English. Ten minutes before John was due to play Leighton Rees, there was £1,500 in the boxes, of which the winning pair would take £700.

Lowe recalls the blatant gamesmanship that Rees tried on him in the practice room. Rees walked in with eight pint bottles of strong brown ale on a tray with two empty glasses: 'You've come a long way, John, you must be thirsty. Get a few of these down you.' Rees drank deep and John sipped politely. In fact John told me he was surprised that Rees did not offer him a brandy chaser like he did to some mugs.

On stage it was no contest. John beat Rees 4–0 in legs of 1,001 and Langy beat Evans 2–0 in legs of 3,001. 'And you've got to give it to the Welsh,' John told me. 'Rees and Evans shook our hands and the crowd gave us a standing ovation as we walked out with *their* money.'

A few days later Alan flew off over the Atlantic to be guest of honour at the Golden State Open in California. It was on this trip that he did something that endeared him to all true darts fans. He was invited on the prime time *Johnny Carson Show* and talked in good faith for several minutes about his love for darts and his pride in pulling on a Welsh shirt. Then with a smarmy grin the host asked him to go to the board and throw his darts *backwards – through his legs*. 'I am a serious darts player, not a circus clown,' was Alan's reply as he marched off the show.

I had one last area to explore to make my darts education complete. All the players and officials I had talked to in the last four years told me that I must attend an international match. That was where the pride, passion and drama came in buckets. And, as I found out, so too did the drink ...

In mid-February I went up to Newcastle from my home in Leeds for the England/Scotland clash. I attended the pre-match banquet and had a drink with some of the players before the meal. Alan Glazier, a star exhibition player like Evans, was courteous and shy. Tony Brown, also of England, looked like Desperate Dan and was drinking gin fast. Charlie Ellix, a small Cockney, also seemed to have a mighty thirst. Across the way, nineteen-year-old Eric Bristow toyed with a pint of lager. Later he told me that the *Indoor League* had inspired him. 'When I was sixteen me dad was teaching me darts and I used to sit on the settee watching *Indoor League*. I said to me mum and dad "I want to go on that".' He did, and he won it.

Next day the action and atmosphere at the City Hall lived up to expectation. The last time I'd been there was to see PJ Proby, and the support was a band called Nero and the Gladiators. The darts was gladiatorial and the Geordie crowd loved every minute. Two images live in my memory. Firstly, Bristow saluting the crowd after a 16-dart leg and going on to win. Secondly, a stocky mop-headed little bloke from Kirkcaldy who bounced around the stage in tartan trews and did a number on Charlie Ellix. He was described in the programme as 'Jocky' Wilson – 'one of the unemployed'.

A great cast was now assembled for a great show at the theatre of darts. I am often a pub bore, a wild-eyed bender of the ears of strangers with my latest enthusiasms, be they for pop or football stars. I would stand in the Beeb bar in Oxford Road for hours, chelping on about Evans, Lowe and Bristow and how their talents should be paraded on BBC television. Little did I know that I was not going to be sitting in the crowd when it all took off, but right in the heart of the spotlight.

2

The Geordie Lip

My call to the proud colours of darts commentating came totally out of the blue. In the spring of 1977 I began working with BBC producer John Miller on a series called *Roots of England*. It was to be an in-depth look at traditional English communities based on fishing, farming, coalmining and other jobs. By mid-July we had set up some strong material with fishing families in Whitby on the Yorkshire coast and with chainmakers in the Black Country. I had also made good headway with a farming family at Kersey in darkest Suffolk. After a long, and at times heated, family discussion over tea they had decided to let us film them. So, me being me, I had a few well-earned pints of Greene King bitter in the bar of my hotel in Ipswich by way of celebration. It was Wednesday 20 July.

After pint three I decided to call home and speak to my wife Irene. She was very excited. A couple of hours earlier Keith Phillips, number two to Nick Hunter in the BBC Manchester sports department, had called, wondering if I was available that Sunday to do an audition as a darts commentator. They were setting up the first ever world championship and Nick had seen my film about Alan Evans. His secretary Barbara Gibson had also mentioned my ear-bending sessions about darts in the bar; she had described me as: 'A curly haired Geordie who just goes on and on about bloody darts.' Would

I go to Sheffield that weekend and try some patter at the British Inter-County Knockout Cup finals? I told Irene to tell Keith I'd crawl there naked over molten tar. Then I went back to the hotel bar and had a large Johnny Walker Black Label, liberally laced with water. Commentator? World Championship? I was shaking like a novice whippet before its first handicap.

I did not touch alcohol for the next three days. I pored over the *News of the World* chart of the best shot-outs; 82 is either treble 14, double top or bull, or double 16, depending how you feel. It was a lot to try to take in; there are at least *four* ways out for all the odd shots between 105 and 135! What with trying to memorise the scores and fearing the sudden onset of an asthma attack, I hardly slept a wink.

On the Sunday morning Irene drove me down to Sheffield and I relaxed a bit when I entered the Club Fiesta. I saw on the practice boards some faces I knew, and they were top players. With Bill Lennard of England, Rab Smith of Scotland, Phil Obbard and John Assirati of Wales in the frame, there would be high-quality play, so I would not be making apologies in my commentary.

There were ten dartboards on the go and eight teams taking part. Glamorgan were the massive favourites, with several internationals in their team. Keith Phillips decided to wait an hour or so to let the action warm up. He was very calm and exceedingly soft-spoken and it helped. When he and I crouched down near our first match and he switched on his tape recorder, I felt fine. We were near enough the oche to see the hand-chalked record of the scores and I made a mental note to keep my voice down so as not to upset the players. Then I dropped really lucky. The match we had picked was a belter. It featured the reigning *News of the World* champion Mickey Norris of Kent, a ruddy-faced studious lad whose favourite shots I knew, and 'Bonner' Thompson of Crook, a Durham legend. I started out well by calling a couple of Mickey's shot-outs correctly but then got something to really get my teeth into. Bonner was inspired and it lit my touch paper. I whooped in pure Durhamese: 'Custy stuff, Bonner me laddo!' I got a couple of hard glances from the Kent team, but I did not disturb the players. And I did not go over the top when Bonner won. Keith didn't say much but I knew I'd made him smile a time or two.

I got into full flow on the final and once again my thanks to the lads from Durham. Nobody thought the Durham team stood a chance against the stars of Glamorgan, and the Welshmen raced into a 4–1 lead. But then Durham hit back and had a chance of drawing level if Ray Oxberry, a lorry-driver from Sunderland could beat World Number Four Phil Obbard. I knew that Obbard was a bundle of raw nerves; he had been inconsolable when losing the 1976 World Masters final to John Lowe. His face was drawn as he took on Oxberry, who threw big brass bomber darts rather than knitting-needle thin tungsten like everybody else. He also favoured treble 19, rather than treble 20, in his scoring phases. I popped in the odd colourful phrase like 'He's into that treble bed like Gareth Edwards on the blind side' and 'Those darts are thicker than Hamlet panatel-las but they are caning that treble 19'. The latter made Keith really laugh. I also picked up the mournful looks Obbard was giving his darts as they flew awry: 'Phil looking like the Black Prince on a bleak day on the battlefield.' I had a job keeping my voice down as Ray clinched the match with a bull finish.

Keith Phillips shook me by the hand, said he'd got enough on tape and we went to the bar for a pint. Irene, then as now, was happy to sit in the car and read the Sunday papers rather than keep tabs on the tungsten. I supped steadily and cheered on the Durham lads to a surprise 8–7 victory. I knew in my heart that I had done well.

The following Tuesday, at about 12.30 I was sitting in my tiny office at the BBC in Manchester, going through my notes on fishing families in Whitby and planning a research trip there soon, when the phone rang. It was Barbara Gibson asking if I could pop along the corridor to have a word with Nick Hunter. There was absolutely nothing in her voice to send me up or down. I had been in Nick's company in the bar a few times and been impressed. He was a few years older than me and in a way very public school, but he was witty, urbane and liked a drink. He was also incredibly powerful. Although he was answerable to the head of sport in London, Nick was the supremo of cricket, rugby league and bowls and had masterminded the Beeb's successful move into snooker, persuading the doubting London bosses to spend a fortune on OB (Outside Broadcast) coverage of the World Championships in Sheffield. He was just the man to do a proper job on darts.

I got a cheeky grin from Barbara as I passed through the outer office. Nick was sitting at his desk wearing a lurid Pringle golfing sweater and looking out of the window. He motioned me to sit down. My mouth went dry. Suddenly he shouted through to Barbara: 'Get your boy some paper and a pen – and grab us a couple of coffees.' My hand trembled as he eyed me up across the desk, smoothing his Van Dyke beard: 'Very good audition – bit too Geordie at times. But you've got the job.' There was no pause to gauge my reaction. 'You'd better write this down.' With shaking fingers I wrote down a list that I still have: 'October 9, Vernon's Treble Top team competition for *Grandstand*, at Charnock Richard, near Preston. Sid and David Vine to commentate. February 6 to 10, World Darts Championship at Nottingham. Again with David Vine.' I looked up open-mouthed with shock; for once in my life I was speechless.

'Not like you to be stuck for words, Sidney old chap. I think this calls for a spot of lunch.' I simply nodded and offered a silly grin. I had the feeling we were not heading for the Beeb canteen and over-cooked liver with doorstep chips. I was right. I also realised that the public school patter, all the 'old chap' malarkey, was put on for comic effect, or possibly was employed to cover nervousness.

It turned out that Nick Hunter was a man after my own throat. Within ten minutes we were walking into the secluded basement wine bar of the ultra-posh Midland Hotel. It was dimly lit and decorated with old wine bottles and plastic grape vines. I had once had a memorable night there with George Best and Mike Parkinson. It was definitely a step up from the Capricorn Club in Goodge Street. It was obvious right away that Nick was a regular.

'Nice sweater, Mister Hunter sir,' said a tall slim waiter with a hint of Italian in his voice.

'Fuck off, George, and bring us a bottle of something nice.' Nick winked at me to let me know he was joking. I had twigged as much; working with this bloke was going to be real fun.

Over the next couple of hours and three bottles of Bardolino, Nick and I put darts, sport in general, and eventually the world to rights. Nick had seen my Alan Evans film and thought it excellent. He had made a similar film some years earlier about the legendary Tommy Barrett, a quiet man from Middlesex who in the mid-1960s was the best dart player in the world. Tommy had achieved the amazing feat of winning the *News of the World* title two years on the trot, in 1964 and 1965. You have to remember that millions started out in the competition at pub level and the format was the best of only *three* legs of 501. Nobody has ever matched that achievement.

Nick told me how the idea for the first world championship had been developed. As part of his work on snooker, Nick had been involved with Mike Watterson, a bright Derbyshire lad who was involved in sports promotion. Mike was friendly with John Lowe, who had persuaded him that a world darts championship could be easily organised. John said that he, Eric Bristow and Alan Glazier from England should definitely be in the field as well as Alan Evans and Leighton Rees of Wales. John also suggested that Olly Croft and the BDO be called in to run the tournament. Imperial Tobacco, which sponsored the World Snooker Championships, had jumped at the chance to come aboard. Nick hoped to put out about nine hours of material.

He must have seen me gulp. 'You will have to do 95 per cent of the commentary and David Vine will spell you if you get tired. Remember, we will only ever be live on the final. All the rest will be recorded highlights. So if you swear, fart, cough or get the shot wrong – we can cut it out. Let me tell you what your role will be. I worked with the great Brian 'Ginger' Cowgill, an ogre with a legendary bad temper, but an expert on covering sport. He said that all you did was sit the viewer in the best seat in the house, give him a pair of binocu-lars and hand the microphone to somebody who knows a lot about the sport.' He paused and patted me on the leg. 'That's your role.'

He struck a chord when he said that certain BBC bosses did not think they should put darts on the telly. Just like myself Nick had no time for the snobs who saw the game as a pastime played by drunks in pubs.

We stopped talking shop shortly after that. We finished up with Nick telling all about his exploits playing cricket for Warwickshire second team and me telling him how I narrowly missed international schoolboy honours at rugby and athletics. Then we rolled down Oxford Road and back into the Beeb.

On the train back home to Pudsey I kept taking the sheet of paper out of my briefcase: *Grandstand*. World Championship. BBC Commentator. Sid and David Vine. Up there with my idol the great Eddie Waring, John Arlott and David Coleman. My wildest dream would have been to become a dogsbody on the production team. At long last the little lad from Lynemouth was going to be famous. Irene was delighted for me, despite my reeking of red wine, almost guaran-teed to bring on a bad dose of gout. Then I rang my dad, and his reaction was typical: 'I'm very pleased for you, son,' said Bob. 'But you know nowt aboot darts.' His tone was quizzical, almost pitying. The phrase was to come back at me over the next few years from many different lips and give me many sleepless nights.

Over the next four months I became a total darts obsessive. I bought a set of 25-gram nickel-tungsten darts and took them every-where. On research trips for the documentary series, I took on chainmakers, fishermen and farm hands – and was thrashed soundly. I kept a condensed version of the shot-out charts in my wallet and practised the big finishes in half the pubs in Pudsey. Then, on 9 December, 1977 I made my commentary debut. It was at a sports complex at Charnock Richard, and I remember feeling no nerves at all on the train ride over from Leeds. I knew the games would be recorded and any blobs edited out. Also, there would be no hanging around; I was due to meet a reporter from *Radio Times* to do a joint article on the upcoming world championship. In fact, I was so casual about the whole thing that I decided to play a joke on the production team. It was a time when many television sports department people wore bright sweaters with prominent logos, a subtle touch to show they were macho members of the sports fraternity. So, on the way to the venue I called in at Chorley market and paid £2.99 for a black acrylic pullover with a tatty golden bee on the breast. Sure enough, several of our team asked what it represented and where they could get one. I told them it was the badge of the Pudsey Buzzers, a gentlemen's touring cricket team.

At the venue I met the reporter and he told me he had got good interviews with John Lowe and Eric Bristow. Eric was still only twenty but was hot from winning the World Masters title and already seeded number one for the Embassy World Championship. The reporter from *Radio Times* was anxious to get Eric to pose in his England blazer for a picture in front of a silver screen and a couple of silver umbrellas. Eric wasn't keen. 'Silver brollies, mate, do you fink I'm Jean Shrimpton?' I tried to help. 'The photo will look better if you stand there – loads more light,' I said.

He frowned. 'Has John Lowe done this?' I lied that John had posed earlier. 'OK.' I got the strong impression that you took no liberties with this fellow, who looked for disrespect everywhere. I've known Eric for thirty years since that day and nothing about him has changed.

I might not have upset Brissy on my debut, but I did get up other people's noses. The Vernon's Treble Tops competition was between a dozen seven-man teams. As the first pair walked out on the stage and we began recording David Vine introduced me: 'With me on commentary is a young newcomer, Sid Waddell ...'

'Thanks, dad,' I said and got going.

David congratulated me at the end of the recording but asked me why the ageist crack. I replied that it was short for 'daddio', but he did not look happy at all. As I walked off at the end I heard him say into his microphone something about 'a right cocky sod'.

During my first performance I managed to upset some of the crowd and players. David and I did our thing on a first-floor balcony, about sixty feet up and back from the stage action. We were not soundproofed in any way, because, I assume, at the snooker, 'Whispering' Ted Lowe and the others operated at the table side and very much *sotto voce*. Not the style of the lad who was soon to become dubbed 'The Geordie Lip'. I got really excited and loud when a Geordie team, from Cramlington near Ashington, were going well. So much so that an angry voice from below threatened to 'come up and smack that bastard on the balcony'. Then I loudly predicted a player would try to go out from 128 with 60, 60, double 4. The bloke froze on stage, turned theatrically, looked up at me and bellowed: 'No I bloody won't' – then went out with 60, 18, bull! It brought the house down, not so much for winning the leg but mainly for putting me in my place. But, believe me, this was small beer compared to the stick that lay ahead.

I came down off that balcony feeling a million dollars. Nick Hunter had praised my efforts down the talkback and David Vine had forgiven my 'dad' crack and described the pair of us as 'a couple of hairy arses that suited darts down to the ground.' In the bar Nick got the drinks in and we were joined by Bill Lennard and a short stocky bloke in a sharp suit called Tony Green. Tony said he was Bill's manager and as we chatted it became apparent that he would be on Nick's team at the world championship, spotting shots for the cameras. Tony had played darts for Lancashire B team and was an experienced referee/caller. He talked in a thick Hull accent and I put him down straightaway as a fellow 'hairy arse'. Later, I sat with the winning Geordie team, who knew some of my darting pals from Ashington, and drank several pints of beer and a couple of whisky chasers. There were no hard feelings about the 'bastard on the balcony'. At about midnight I got a taxi the fifty-odd miles back to Leeds. It cost me £23 – my fee was only £80 – but I reckoned I deserved it for just getting through my first gig.

Next day I watched myself go out on *Grandstand*. I sounded enthusiastic – though nowhere near as manic as I later became – and seemed to know what I was talking about. At the end of the final match Frank Bough popped up and said with a sly wink: 'With David Vine there was Sid Waddell, a new lad determined to make a mark.'

The first Embassy World Professional Darts Championship was an unbelievable experience. Unlike my stint on *Grandstand*, this was to be a five-day haul, with the final going out live. I would have to commentate solo on all the matches, with David Vine doing only links and packages. The tournament was due to start on Monday 5 February, 1978 and the nerves began to jangle in the last week of January. I was by then observing a meticulous preparation regime. Round about noon on my day off from the Beeb, I would set off from home with my darts and the *News of the World* shot-out charts. In the taproom of the Park Hotel I would set up the charts on the mantel-piece beside my pint of shandy and I would then try to throw the big shots that the stars could hit at will. The regulars used to shake their heads at this strange bloke playing darts against himself – and commentating on the action: 'So here's the Geordie Lip, lean and lissom, poised and poisonous...' I never managed to learn the shot-outs parrot-fashion but just going through these bizarre motions stopped me worrying so much about the massive test to come. What if I got asthma? What if I got too excited and started gibbering in broad Geordie?

Came the day and, sitting on the train to Nottingham with a couple of cans of McEwan's Export, I studied the score charts, convinced I would make awful mistakes live on air in the final and be sacked on the spot. I had heard whispers that certain people in the game did not think a television producer who had never been a top player should be the commentator. There were indications that the BDO wanted to have say in who commentated. I remembered the orchestrated campaign by Lancastrians to get Eddie Waring, my long-time idol, sacked by the BBC for allegedly portraying a jokey image of the game of rugby league. In fact the campaign was proved to have a hidden agenda: to have Eddie replaced by Alex Murphy. As the train approached Nottingham through a blizzard my stomach churned. Thank God 90 per cent of our output will be recorded so my gaffes can be cut out, I thought. But what about doing the final … live … on my tod. I shuddered, supped up and bought another can.

Checking into the plush Albany hotel with some of the BBC team in their expensive casual clothes made me cringe. Irene and I were struggling to manage with five kids to look after. My wardrobe was a couple of Marks & Spencer sweaters – plus the 'Pudsey Buzzers' pullover – and some Farah stretch slacks. But once in the bar with the players on the Sunday night, I relaxed. Alan Evans and Leighton Rees pulled my leg about my accent. I swapped tales of Geordieland with Durham referee Sid Dowson. David Vine, immaculate in very expensive casuals, tried to force me to have a piña colada, his holiday tipple. Nick Hunter, urbane but very matey, grabbed a gin and tonic and a pint and settled in a corner. His first advice was just to enjoy myself. He said that I should not be afraid to let the matches 'breathe'; if six good darts flew true, there was no need for me to gild the lily. I should avoid stating the obvious: 'Let the picture be the flower and you add the colour' was the way he put it. He said that I should try not to speak over the three darts. 'Be succinct and vivid after or before the shot.' He laughed as he gave me his final rule: 'Don't swear and avoid any sexual innuendo.' I was now boosted and ready for anything. I was primed, focused but loose as a limbo dancer.

In mid-afternoon on the Monday there was a press conference at the venue, the Heart of the Midlands nightclub. There were about half a dozen reporters there and one of them really shocked the two Aussie competitors, Tim Brown and Barry Atkinson. 'Can I have a chat please?' he asked politely. 'I'm from the *Times of Australia*, London office.'

Barry was astounded. 'Blimey, your lot never send anybody along when we play at home!'

Soon it was showtime and once again David Vine and I were perched on a balcony like Statler and Waldorf – and once again there was no soundproofing. In the final minute before we started recording, Nick's voice came softly down the talkback: 'Now Sidney I want you to relax – just keep it nice and *tense*.' Beside me David Vine laughed heartily and so did half the crew. For me, it was a dream come true. Within a couple of hours my prediction that darts was excellent, dramatic television was proven right. Eric Bristow, the number one seed, was expected to stroll through his first-round match against Conrad Daniels, a chirpy, laid-back American. But Conrad, used to playing long games for big bucks, slowed the match down. He walked slowly up to the oche, took an age to aim, then meandered up to the board to pull his darts. Bristow prowled and fidgeted, sipping lager and snorting cigarette smoke from his nostrils like an unhappy dragon. The American won and pointed to the bar saying: 'OK turkey, losers pay.' The knowledgeable crowd applauded wildly.

My nerves had been no problem. But 'Whispering Sid' I was never going to be. One or two people in the crowd complained to the floor managers and were told that, like the heavy lighting round the board that made some players squint, it was the price you paid for television coverage. Over drinks that night in the Albany cocktail bar,

Nick Hunter told me to take no notice of any criticism. I had his backing and that of the BBC bosses; I had done well. But a day or two later, after I'd said: 'A big one here would be useful' for the umpteenth time, he did tell me firmly down the talkback not to say it any more. I did not need to ask why. Mind you, you often wonder who notices such things.

As I basked in the friendly atmosphere and, I'll admit it, the all-round praise that first night, there was one dark cloud on my horizon. I had not said a word to Nick or anybody, but John Miller had insisted that I be in Whitby, two hundred miles away, at one o'clock on the Friday of the final, which started live at seven. The forecast was of more snow, so it might be a hairy trip. Chatting to the fishermen would only take an hour, so with any luck I'd make it back. If not, David Vine and Tony Green would make adequate substitutes. Mind you, I had more sense than to tell Nick or any of his team my plan.

Next morning I joined Eric Bristow and his dad George at break-fast. They were in good spirits despite the defeat and had decided to stay the week. They needed some cash and so did I, so we went out and found a NatWest. I got my money no problem, but the Bristows were in heated debate. It appeared their account was short of funds, despite the fact that mum Pam should have put a winning cheque for £300 in. 'Surely she can't have cashed it and blown it,' said George, only half-joking. All turned out well after a phone call to their branch in Stoke Newington. The cheque was in, but not cleared. The bank let them have some cash. Eric and George told me about the early hours of one morning when, skint, they were making their way home through North London from a successful darts tournament on foot, carrying a large carriage clock and a canteen of cutlery. They were stopped by the police and asked where they had got the 'goods'. 'Won them at darts, mate,' said Eric. 'Of course you did, sir, kindly step this way.'

Day two of the tournament produced more great darts, but Nick Hunter was not happy. Despite his experience with snooker, rugby league and the Grand National, he was not satisfied that we were covering the darts action properly. Viewers were ringing in saying we were showing faces when they wanted to see scores. After deep discussions with the engineering staff and veteran director Ray Lakeland, Nick decided to split the screen – show the player and the target at the same time. It was a stroke of genius. You saw the agony or the triumph and the accuracy or lack of it at the same time. It became the standard shot for covering darts.

On Wednesday night we used split screen and it was a good job, because the quarter-final between Alan Evans and Leighton Rees had the lot. From the way they walked on in their red Welsh shirts, you would never have guessed they were bosom pals. They glared at each other and brushed a semi-polite handshake. Leighton slugged at his lager. Alan kissed his darts. Evans started with 180. My nerves dissolved and my voice went raw-edged with expectation. 'They first met in Tonypandy workingmen's club in 1970 and here they are, bosom pals and bosom enemies. Anything can happen now...' It did: the Welshmen played as if they'd dined on the bread of heaven. Evans won the first leg in 13 darts. The atmosphere was super-charged. All my bragging about the drama of the game, the colour and macho behaviour I had seen, was being proved right.

Rees took a pull on his sixth pint of lager since starting practice, and his third on stage. Later, David Vine was to voice over a montage of shots of Leighton rhythmically supping lager like it was going out of fashion, 'putting away nearly as many pints as doubles.'

Rees curled his lip in deep concentration and took the game to three legs to two with 137, 180, 180, double 2. Magic: a 10-dart leg delivered to order, the best ever seen on national TV up to that time; Evans had done a 10-darter on Harlech a few months before. The crowd roared their appreciation and so did I – I've listened to the tapes! Nobody told me to button it; no referee, crowd or production crew. 'In the valleys they'll be a-singing as his arrows go a-winging.' The scanner rocked with laughter. They all knew we were in at the birth of something special. Finally, Rees took the match 6–3 with a 161 finish: 60, treble 17, bull. It could not have been scripted better. The two pals hugged. Nick and the BBC bosses were delighted. 'Darts is exactly like snooker,' said Nick. 'They're both sport in miniature.'

There was nothing miniature about the celebrations in the hotel cocktail bar that night. We all felt we had cracked it. I arrived late because I had a couple of jars at the club with Rees and Evans. The joint was jam-packed and full of Embassy Regal fumes. The sponsors, Imperial Tobacco, had not only put up the £3,000 first prize, they also dished out two hundred free fags or twenty panatellas *per day* to all sixteen contestants and all BBC personnel. Despite my asthma I chewed a couple of the cigars and chatted to Tony Green. He had been on the balcony with David and me, 'spotting' the out-shots for the cameras. Tony praised my efforts but added darkly, 'You'll have to learn the out-shots, you missed a couple.' It hit a nerve; I knew it was my major weakness, but I would not brood on the matter. I suddenly became aware of a party of two dozen dolled-up young women whom I did not recognise. 'Who are you lot?' I enquired.

'We're from the battered wives' home up the road, duck, it's our night out.'

The girls certainly enjoyed themselves. Many of the darters were unattached and a real party ensued. In fact some of the lasses did not get back to the home until after breakfast on the Saturday.

Now I don't know how John Motson, Andy Gray or David Gower prepare to commentate on a world final, but I bet it's nothing like my boozy, manic, some would say lunatic, run-up to my first world darts effort. The play on Thursday night was not quite so dramatic but it was very exciting. The main feature was a totally professional performance by John Lowe in beating Sweden's Stefan Lord by eight sets to four. After the night's play, the promoter Mike Watterson took me aside and shook my hand. 'When I heard you on *Grandstand* I had my doubts about your voice,' he said. 'But now I reckon Nick picked the right man for the job.' The people from Embassy also said I was doing a grand job. So … I had three or four pints of Banks' bitter and a couple of large whiskies before bed, plus a freebie panatella. Bad move. When the alarm rang at seven the next morning I was not at my best for my trip to Whitby to see the fishermen we needed for our *Roots of England* documentary. But I knew I had to make the trip. I was only seconded to the sports department for one week. If producer John Miller thought I was swinging the lead, he could make life difficult for me. Being a darts commentator could be a flash in the pan. My day job was my main bread and butter.

My train to York was at 7.30. There was no time to shave. I had a quick wash, dressed, chucked on a thin nylon anorak and ran to Nottingham station. I coughed once or twice, nursing a baby hangover. It was foggy and freezing cold but not snowing. By eleven o'clock things were not looking too bad. British Rail coffee and sausage rolls had perked me up and the snow on the fields round Sheffield was only light. At York I whipped into the Royal Station Hotel, sipped a large medicinal brandy and rang John Miller, who was already in Whitby. I said I would meet him by the swing bridge at one. He said there were blizzards on the North Yorkshire Moors, but did not suggest I abort the trip. Fair enough; I had met the fishing families before and had chatted them up, but he could easily have sewn up the loose ends himself and let me to go back to Nottingham. I went to the taxi rank and the first driver in the queue was not optimistic. 'Whitby? We could get stuck in a snow drift.' He was not at all keen but I promised him a tenner tip and off we went.

The snow got really bad on the far side of Malton. It was drifting several feet high in the fields and you could not see the sides of the road. We crawled for about ten miles, then the sun came out and we could see the sea. I nearly cheered out loud. I got out at the swing bridge in Whitby at 1.15 and within seconds nearly died of exposure. An icy gale was coming off the sea. It cut through my anorak and my Farah slacks. The red pantiles of the fishermen's cottages matched my nose. Then above the shrieking of sea-gulls, there came a cry. 'Sid! Sid! Down here!'

I looked below the bridge into the harbour and saw five figures waving at me. One was John Miller, in duffle coat, scarf and wellies, and the other four were fishermen. They were standing in mud with the tide coming in around their feet and scraping barnacles off a boat. I looked down at my skimpy Lotus moccasins, shrugged and joined the lads, splashing through the mud and the wavelets. They were members of the Storr family and they had just agreed with John to take part in our film, so my journey had been totally unnecessary. But the documentary was not what they wanted to talk about.

'Should we bet on Rees or John Lowe for tonight's final?' one asked. They had been glued to the darts all week. My feet were soaked and freezing, but I tried to look wise.

'I reckon Lowe will win 11–8,' I said. They all rushed off to the bookies.

John had fixed for us to see the local vicar to arrange filming in St. Mary's church and its famous graveyard that features in Bram Stoker's *Dracula*. In ten minutes, over a cup of tea, it was fixed. It was now nearly two o'clock and there were reports of more snow. I was considering ringing Nick Hunter and telling him to get a substitute for the final. I decided to give it go. The final was not due to start till seven so, unless there was another blizzard, I had half a chance. In the taxi going to York I took off my wet moccasins and socks, put my feet by the heater and nodded off.

The snow was light, the trains were on time and I had a couple more brandies and a couple of sausage rolls. I walked into the lobby of the Albany at Nottingham looking like the ancient mariner just after 5.30, all around me people suited and booted for finals night. Time for a shave and a general spruce up, I reckoned. Leighton Rees and George Bristow accosted me. 'We're off to pub with a real fire, come with us,' ordered Leighton. I decided that watching Rees practise was more important than my image, so I tagged along.

Ten minutes later, apart from wearing no socks and with my moccasins still soggy, it was as if my trip to Whitby had been a bad dream. We were in a pub with a roaring coal fire and Leighton was having a pint of lager with a brandy chaser. The pub had no dartboard. Did this worry him? 'No. I've practised enough,' he said. 'I just want to get warm. It's freezing at the back of the stage where the practice boards are.' He had another brandy and, mindful of my upcoming duties, I toyed with a half of bitter.

At 6.15 we walked into the Heart of the Midlands and it was buzzing. Nobody seemed to notice that I was unshaven and sockless. David Vine and I sat on the balcony calmly waiting for the off. Doing an hour and a half live did not worry me at all. If I had rung John Miller and flatly refused to go to Whitby, I'd have been chewed up with worry. As it was, though not exactly sober, I was a long way from being drunk.

The match was the best of 21 legs. Rees purred into a 9–3 lead, throwing arm snaking out like a cobra. He pulled steadily at pints of lager. Lowe, looking like 'an extra from *Coronation Street*', as one paper put it, sipped bitter and hit back with a 15-dart leg. Rees replied in kind. It was superb sport and I enjoyed myself, slouched in my plush seat, my bare feet sticking out over the balcony. To the cheers of the Welsh fans led by Evans, Leighton hit a 100 shot to win. The prize was £3,000; very nice for the store man from the valleys. But the pride of being the first-ever world darts champion was the main thing.

I sat on the balcony totally fulfilled. Mike Watterson, the promoter, handed me a pint and again congratulated me on my efforts.

'Sidney, just one question. Why no socks or shoes?' It was Derek Brown of the *Daily Mirror*.

'Superstition, mate. I always do finals in my bare feet.' It was relayed as gospel truth to his readers. I made no mention of trains and taxis and tots of brandy …

I joined the Welsh contingent and the new champion who was smoking a cigar the size of a vaulting pole. He was in a generous mood. In all seriousness he suggested to one of the Welsh selectors that they drop him and blood a new lad at the next international. Evans brought over a tray of drinks. 'Phone call for you, Leighton,' he said. 'Pickfords want to be your chauffeur.' Later, back at the hotel Tony Green sang the dirty version of 'Old McDonald's Farm', took off all his clothes but his underpants and showed his tattoos. I sank into a gentle pool of Banks' bitter, feeling like the dog's bollocks.

I went to bed on the floor of Tony's room – I had moved there to save money – just as the party was getting going. I made a shakey-doon beside the single bed and shook off all my sweaty clothes. So it was that totally naked I answered the door in a stupor about an hour later. Outside stood a battered wife clad only in bra and panties holding the hand of Nicky Virachkul. The girl looked me up and down and was not impressed. 'Where's Tony?' asked Nicky. 'Card school probably,' I replied. Off they went. I thought of rejoining the fun, but thought better of it, put on my undies and went back to kip.

The reaction to our coverage of the world championship was excellent. The final got 2.7 million viewers, half a million more than *Pot Black*. *Private Eye* featured one of my lines in Colemanballs. 'Another maximum! Rees did not know if he was having a shave … or having his hair cut.' Now, I did say this when Lowe had Rees under pressure. Nick had said on cans that I should comment on how it affected Rees. It shot through my mind what Rees had said to me about Evans's barrage of 180s in their classic quarter-final: 'I didn't know if I was having a haircut, a shave, a shit or a shampoo.' I think my instant edit of this was pretty good.

A few weeks later a bright young Mancunian, Peter Youens of BBC North publicity put out a press release for *Bullseye*, a BBC invitation darts tournament that we were planning, in which he described me as 'The Geordie Lip'. I had taken to using the phrase about myself when describing my manic darts persona. The *Daily Mail* sent a photographer along to the BBC bar in Manchester, and reporter Paddy O'Neill had some props: an Andy Capp-style cloth cap, a muffler and a foaming pint of beer. Wearing the cap and muffler I put on a cheeky grin and posed by the dartboard. Towards the end of the session, Nick Hunter walked in and frowned heavily when he saw my get-up. He knew about the press call, but did not bank on it being so garish. He toyed with a glass of white wine as I burbled on to Paddy about darts being full of working-class folk heroes. By the time I had finished, Nick was nodding approval and offered me a drink. 'Make it a white wine will you, this Boddington's is a bit gassy and I've already had three,' I said.

He grabbed me by the muffler. 'I'm not building you up as The Geordie Lip to have the image shattered with a poncey glass of bloody Chablis. You'll have a pint of Boddy's and like it.'

I did – because that's show business. I am a natural born publicity-hound and I was loving every minute of it. But even I was gobsmacked when I saw the *Daily Mail* piece. It was a full-page job, with me bracketed with Eddie Waring, John Snagge, the voice of the

Boat Race, and Dorian Williams, from the posh world of show-jumping. I bought six copies and sent one to my mother! I recalled Nick's frown in the bar and I reckon it meant this: he was 99 per cent sure my impassioned Geordie tones were right for Beeb darts, but maybe some of the bosses at TV Centre in London were not as confident. I did not let the point worry me; I resolved to work harder at the scores, and at my diction.

It was not just the BBC mandarins who I had to worry about. There were critics much nearer home. A few nights later I went for a drink at The Golden Lion in Pudsey and had a few pints and a chat with Gerry the landlord. I still had a ticklish cough from my stint at Nottingham – and the Embassy panatellas – and I occasionally raised my cupped hand to my mouth to cover it.

'Been on the telly for a week with the darters and now the big-headed twat's blowing on his hands just like they do!' It was more than a stage whisper. It came from a big lad with a bobble hat and a severe case of builder's bum. I looked down the bar and met his piggy eyes, then looked away. It was a portent of worse things to come. What's that saying about being careful what you wish for?

Almost a year later I was back on the darts beat. The world championship was due to be played in early February 1979 and in the first week of the new year Nick Hunter asked me to direct a titles montage of Leighton Rees. The idea was to take all the flock and packing off the darts board, leaving just the wire and the 60 bed, and then shoot Leighton, face scrunched with menace and concentration, scoring a maximum. It was a tall order. First, a very expensive non-shatter lens had to be used so that the darts would not break it. Second, it would take hours for the world champion to land three perfect darts in the odd target. Third, and most salient, Rees turned up at the pub in Manchester looking like he really had festered big-time over the festive season. His face was fatter and redder than ever, and he was thirsty. After a couple of pints of lager he reached for his home-made darts and had a go. He was rubbish; in the first hour he got no more than one dart in the target bed. 'I haven't had a dart in my hand for two weeks,' he moaned. 'And believe it not, my arm hurts.' Soon, he was almost in tears with the frustration and the strain on his upper right arm. There was only one thing to do, I called a brandy break. Leighton downed a couple of large ones and told me a bit about his life at home in the mining village of Ynysybwl. He lived with his mother who kept him well fed and he worked as a storeman. There was talk of him giving up the job and turning professional, but out of loyalty for all the time off he had been given, he was reluctant to leave. His idea of a perfect night was a few pints with his pals at the United Services workingmen's club. I warmed to this working-class hero, from a pit village just like my own up in Geordieland.

Meanwhile Leighton had warmed to the brandy. Now on his fifth pint of lager, with me matching him on Boddy's for support, he did the business. He hammered in 180s and I coached him to squint his black Celtic eyes as they peered into the lens. When I looked at the rushes with Nick the next day, he was delighted. The glower would have done justice to Bela Lugosi and the darts were aimed right at your eyes. It hurt to watch. 'I'll bet that was a pissy-arsed shoot,' Nick laughed. I laughed too, even though it hurt my head. The things we do for art's sake.

3

Jollees, Jibes and Insults

For the second Embassy World Darts championship we moved from the Heart of the Midlands in Nottingham and went upmarket – but not by a million miles.

I had been told that Jollees nightclub at Longton, Stoke-on-Trent was really easy to find: 'Just go up the hill till you get to the bus station, my duck.' They did not say that the club was *part* of the bus station. As I dodged past throbbing engines, sucking in diesel fumes and mucking up my best tasselled moccasins with sump oil on the night before the tournament, I was not impressed. I did not know what to expect behind the small glass door with the grinning jester logo. But then I entered what I will always remember as Wonderland.

A gentle throb of disco beat replaced the engine roar, my feet danced up purple carpeted stairs lit by orange spangled spots. Bathed in a glow of heady optimism, I looked at the pictures on the walls of the acts that had graced the premises before me and Tony Green. Engelbert Humperdinck, Roger de Courcey, Clodagh Rogers and the incomparable Barron Knights all seemed to have special smiles of encouragement just for me.

Bellies and Bullseyes

The place was full of young Stokies having a belting night out. The girls mostly had big hair and posh frocks, while the lads went for mullets, spear collars down to their nipples and flared trousers. Pints of lager filled the tables and folk were wearing see-through plastic gauntlets to eat their chicken in a basket. I introduced myself to the management and they welcomed me like an old pal. The only trouble was, there was no seat for me. Suddenly one of the bouncers had a bright idea. He led me to the commentary box, which was in the middle of the hall near the back. He sat me down and I just caught bits of the comedian's patter as best I could through the open door. I was served with a bottle of Blue Nun and a basket of chicken goujons – on the house. I relaxed, aware of the tremendous, not to say raucous, atmosphere outside. If a local comic got them going this much, what would Bristow, Evans and Lowe do? The outbreaks of applause seemed to make the whole place bounce. Purple fairy lights on every table arrowed down to the stage, lighting eager faces like in an enchanted forest. People came to look at me through the glass as if I was a specimen in an aquarium. Some popped in for autographs; I signed with greasy fingers. I was so excited I clean forgot to put my gauntlet on.

At about eleven o'clock I decided to make a move. Irene had ordered me to go extra easy on the booze: 'It's a long week, Sidney, and you have to watch your voice.' But I was so jazzed that I could not just jump in a taxi and head for my bed at the swish North Staffordshire Hotel three miles away. So I walked down the hill to the Crown and Anchor pub where the players and officials were staying. I danced in very much in the mood of Pinocchio seeking

62

the free and easy lowbrow life: 'High-diddle-dee-dee, a darter's life for me.'

The scene is for ever emblazoned on my psyche. The large front bar had become The Darters' Arms. Alan Evans and Leighton Rees sat chatting over beers and shorts with Staffordshire women county players. I was greeted by the Geordie tones of Doug McCarthy of Durham, the man who played darts in a pub bar while his wedding reception carried on upstairs, and the reigning World Master, Ronnie Davis of Byker. 'Hey up Sidney, kidda, can you play? Or can you just blether?' asked Ronnie. I called on Cliff Lazarenko, who was down-ing pints of lager in three gulps, to partner me but could not muster a higher score than 43 and was soon sacked. I was happy to nurse a pint of the local Banks' bitter and soak up the atmosphere.

At around midnight I got my second glimpse of Jocky Wilson. Reports had been coming South for months of the shaggy, boozy Jock with the hot temper and the dynamite darts, and suddenly there he was shunting me aside to get to the bar. He had a straggly mullet and was wearing a cheap Millett's anorak, with a half-eaten cheese bap sticking out of the pocket. He swigged at a pint that was obviously not his first of the day, and would not be his last. Lazarenko was now the acting barman – a scheme introduced by the landlord so that the lads could call time when they liked, if at all – and he pointed to Jocky's tiny attaché case, which was about the size of a shoe box. 'Got a week's stuff in there, have yer, John?' 'Away and feck yersell,' was the answer. In fact, as I found out later, all Jocky had in the case was some socks and undies, his playing shirt and a spare pair of trousers.

Later, Jocky persuaded our spotter Tony Green to play darts for money and they went at it till after one o'clock in the practice room. I tried chucking more darts but was again completely humiliated. I decided to make a move and went to fetch Tony. Outside the glass door of the practice room I stopped. Something told me not to barge in. I waved to Tony and he waved back, with a fist full of fivers. I got the message: Tony was winning big-time against Jocky and had no wish to leave. I got a taxi back to our hotel.

Next day the first-round matches were due to start at two and I got to Jollees about an hour earlier, feeling no nerves at all. The friendly welcomes from the players the night before had calmed me down. Ten minutes before the first match, Billy Lennard against Wales's Tony Clark, I sat in the soundproof commentary box laughing at Tony Green's stories of whopping Jocky the night before. 'He was skint, desperate and a bit pissed,' said Tony. 'I went to bed on Doug McCarthy's floor about fifty quid up.' What Tony did not know was that the saga had just started.

The first session of four matches went well; I picked up on Tony's spotting of tricky shots and had plenty of shocks to talk about. Tony Clark beat Lennard, Rab Smith put out Conrad Daniels who had conquered Bristow a year earlier and Terry O'Dea, a giant Aussie, put out the much-fancied Cliff Lazarenko. So later on Cliff became the permanent barman in the twenty-four-hour players' bar, a role for which fate might have cast him.

There was great excitement among our BBC team as the hour arrived for the entry of the great David Coleman. Peter Purves was due to join the team in mid-week to do bits for *Grandstand* and

Sportsnight, and would front *Bullseye* later in the year, but the doyen of sports commentary was to be the main presenter/interviewer for the bulk of the week. And what a prima donna entry he made. David had done that day's *Grandstand,* jumped on a plane and been driven helter-skelter to Jollees. At about nine o'clock I was having a pint in the band room, one of the practice areas behind the stage, when one of the assistant producers came and grabbed me. 'David wants you and your notes, quick!' There was pure terror in the lad's voice. I grabbed my briefcase and my beer and followed the lad to the production office. I could hear the swearing ten yards from the door: 'Who the fucking hell typed this? It's a fucking mess ...' There was no doubting the raspy high-pitched tones; they had screeched at me from the box since my youth.

I went in to find people scrabbling everywhere. The typist was almost in tears and two assistant producers with the match logs looked terrified. Coleman was half-made up and a lady was desperately trying to finish the job, and a dresser bloke was trying to fasten his tie, both very difficult while he ranted. I sipped my beer and said nowt. Suddenly Nick Hunter appeared from an inner office. He took David by the arm and slipped me a wink. 'This is Sidney,' said Nick. The jet-black eyes stopped rolling and the voice changed to the major-domo at The Ivy: 'Sid, Sid, so good to meet you. You were in great form this afternoon, I loved it.' Again Nick winked. The great man went on: 'I wonder what you've got in your notes about Evans and Rees boasting that one of them will win. I'm interviewing John Lowe live. I'd appreciate any gen.' I dipped into my files and duly obliged. 'DC is always uptight before a first night,' murmured Nick.

Tell me about it, I thought. To give him his due, David was brilliant with the players, always matey, but giving them the same serious attention he gave to the football and athletics stars. He made the odd crack about the ale. And one night not long after, he even tried to match their boozing …

I was determined to have a really early night on Saturday, but Tony persuaded me to go back again to the Crown and Anchor. I did not go near the dartboard, but instead had a few pints with John Lowe and his pal 'Big Ez' Barnes, a Clay Cross publican. John had told David Coleman on air that he was in great form and would definitely 'trim the Welshmen'. His confidence was warranted, as I well knew. In October 1978 I had watched him slice through a tough field that included Evans, Bristow and Tony Brown – a boozer of Lazarenkian proportions – at Great Yarmouth to win the Ladbroke Matchplay and £1,500. His ton-plus scoring had been phenomenal. I noticed that John took his pints of lager very slowly.

Ez and John shot off back to Clay Cross about midnight and half-heartedly I went to try to pull Tony away from Jocky. Fat chance. I pushed open the glass door of the practice room and it squeaked loudly. Tony looked at me and frantically pointed to a pile of fivers near his gin and tonic. Jocky pulled out his darts and came at me like Mel Gibson seeking the blue paint. 'I've had e-feckin'-nuff of you ya Geordie bastard. You tried to feckin' put me off last night and you're up to yer feckin' antics again.' It was like being sworn at by a wild animal. Jocky made a bee-line for Tony, 'Is you two bastards in cahoots? Have you told him to keep coming in here?' Tony shrugged and began a bit of calming spiel. I went home alone.

This scenario continued till the Wednesday night when Jocky was knocked out of the tournament, went home and at last let Tony go back to our posh hotel. So out of a booking for nine nights, Tony only slept in the room on four occasions. As we checked out on the Sunday, he looked at his bill mournfully: 'One hundred and twenty quid, for use of a *wardrobe* ...' But it was not that bad; he'd ended up taking about £70 off Jocky.

The third day of the tournament belonged to the Welshmen; they managed to grab the glory and gain a fair portion of notoriety. I watched Leighton Rees practise for his match against fellow Welshman Tony Clark and was amazed at how much lager he put away. By my reckoning Leighton had five warm-up pints and a large brandy. During the match, Leighton downed another three pints and struggled to find fluency. But, cheered on by a couple of hundred Alan Evans' fans from the Stockport area, he managed a win. Then he repaired to the bar – for a proper drink. Just before the start of the Alan Evans match against Tyneside's Ronnie Davis, Nick Hunter asked me to pop down and fix for Leighton to do an interview live with David Coleman at eleven o'clock. I rushed in on a scene reminiscent of the last days of the Roman Empire. The reigning world darts champion was chasing pints of lager with large brandies and brandishing a cigar as big as a stick of rock. It was only half past eight. Leighton agreed to do the interview and seemed to clock my worried glance at the booze. 'Got to steady the nerves after a tough one like that,' he explained.

Back in the commentary box, I had no time to dwell on Leighton's sobriety or otherwise. With the Stockport Mafia screaming

'Oggi, Oggi, Oggi', Evans fell behind to the cool Geordie. Then Alan began his classic slowing down of the game, accompanied with smug dirty looks at his opponent. I explained to the viewers that this was gamesmanship that verged on cheating and that it often worked. It did: Ronnie began rushing his shots and drinking faster. Evans grinned and began pounding the sixty. Alan won and made immediately for the bar. I shuddered to think how many he and Leighton could sup by the end of the last match, which featured Bristow and Terry O'Dea of Australia.

It was now about 10.30 and I was due to deliver Leighton to the studio at eleven. Nick had praised me over the talkback for my verbal efforts, so I reckoned I was due a wee swallow. I joined Evans and Rees and a gaggle of fans and sank a couple of pints of Banks. I had no worries. Leighton was sipping brandy and sucking on a second King Edward and seemed totally mellow. Alan was pissed, excited and holding court: 'I'll rip the fucking head off that bastard Bristow, you tell 'em Leight,' were his parting words.

Carrying a full pint of lager and toting his cigar the world champ followed me up the stairs to the BBC studio. David Coleman shook his hand warmly and the pair settled down. The plan was to have a clip of the match and then do the interview. With two minutes to go the studio lights came up and Leighton went very red and very sweaty. As David was cued, Leighton pulled a Jollees brochure of coming attractions from his pocket and squinted at it. 'Welcome to yet more world darts action from Jollee's club in Stoke …' David was giving it all the hype of the Olympics or the Cup Final. 'With me, I'm delighted to say, is the reigning Embassy champion, Leighton Rees.'

Leighton looked up from his bit of paper and blinked, 'Good to be here David, happy still to be in – the way I played out there.' There was the merest suggestion of a slur in the polite melodic tones.

But the next phase in the proceedings gave the game away. David asked Leighton who he feared in the rest of the field. There was a lop-sided grin, a soft belch and up came the paper – sadly, upside down. 'I got here a little list of comedians due here soon.' Pause, squint, Coleman nervous in two-shot. 'Norman – er – Colli...er. Bob – er – Monkhouse. And that well-known Welsh boy... Alan – er – Evans.' Two things were certain: the world darts champion was as drunk as a skunk and we could not terminate the interview because it was our only buffer. It ran, or should I say, dribbled on for another three minutes.

Being a sensitive worrisome soul as well as self-appointed PR guru to the new cowboy stars of BBC television, I thought I'd be in for a bit of flak back at the Crown and Anchor. Not a bit of it: David Coleman was chortling with glee at Leighton's performance and Nick Hunter said it 'humanised' the sport in a way that would grab Joe Public. Sadly, this was not the message that came on the jungle drums from darkest South Wales the next morning. At about noon I was sitting in the lounge bar of the Rose and Crown chatting to some ladies from the Staffordshire county team, when Leighton made his entrance, gripping a pint of tomato juice which exactly matched the colour of his eyes. The glower on the mighty chops stilled all conversation. Eyes like piss holes in the snow fixed me like I'd perpetrated the whole boozy saga.

'Sid, you have known me a long time,' soft, lilting, at the same time menacing. 'Was I pissed last night?'

I cut from direct eye contact and engaged boogie left hand of the brain. 'Well, I've got to say you had a few, Leight. But I have seen you much worse.' Pale flush of relief on proud face. 'Fresh, definitely, but *pissed* – no!'

The giant frame crumpled in a heap next to me, and the voice became that of a little boy who'd peed his pants in front of the whole school. 'There is holy fuck let loose in Ynysybwl.' I imagined the narrow streets of miners' cottages in the shadow of stark mountains, seething with malicious gossip. 'I've just come off the phone with my sister Shirley and she has bollocked me rotten,' he was almost in tears. He mimicked his sister's high-pitched voice: 'You went on the telly when you was pissed. Mam is so ashamed she has vowed never to walk down the village again. She will not show her face in the street or at the shops. You have disgraced the whole family.'

Suddenly he perked up, thrust the tomato juice aside and called for a pint of lager for each of us. Then the chastised child turned into Rumpole of the Bailey.

'"Hang on," I said to Shirley, "Did I swear on telly?"'

'"No," admitted Shirley. "Did I show my arse on telly?" "No," admitted Shirley again. "Well, then, I was not drunk."'

Shirley took time to compose the reply. 'You did not swear or show your arse, Leighton Rees, but we have known you a long time and you was *pissed*.'

The prosecution rested its case.

A few hours later a new lad joined our on-air team, Peter Purves, star of *Blue Peter* and famous for falling foul of an incontinent elephant. After half an hour in the practice room at the pub being introduced to the lads, I'll bet he wished he had stayed with the animals and the sticky-back plastic. He was ribbed rotten about *Blue Peter* badges and collecting silver paper for charity. But then he won them over with a brilliant gesture. He pulled out a set of well-used tungsten darts and planted a ton first visit to the board. Pretty soon the stars were almost at blows over who would partner him. Peter told me that he'd once been a regular team player in the South London Young's Brewery League. We had a long chat that afternoon and I mentioned how nervous I got before matches. He told me that I should copy his relaxed style when he introduced *Sportsnight* live the following evening. I sat waiting to be introduced, admiring the warm grin and the relaxed posture. The red light flashed and ever-the-pro Pete was live to the nation. 'Hello and welcome folks to *Jolleries in the Potties...*' I could hardly commentate for giggling.

The night before saw the commentary debut of Tony Green. Both David Coleman and Nick Hunter had been showering me with praise – Coleman had called me a 'natural' – but David wisely advised Nick that my highly strung, volcanic style might be subject to burn-out. So it was suggested to me that Tony be my back-up. I thought it a great idea. So on the Tuesday night he was rostered to do a match. Coleman noticed Tony chain-smoking Marlboros outside the box with ten minutes to go and decided a spoof was in order to calm the lad down. I saw David hand Tony a piece of paper. Tony read it and the fag nearly dropped out of his hand. I rushed over and he showed me a telegram. 'YOU ARE THE GREATEST MAN. SHOW THAT GEORDIE BUM HOW TO COMMENTATE. SOCK IT TO THEM. MOHAMMAD ALI.'

Our eyes met and I could see that Tony thought it might just possibly be genuine. We went in the box and put on the cans just as David's voice came through: 'Tony, I've got a couple of tickets for the next Ali fight – ringside.' Tony turned the air blue. But the spoof did the trick.

Tony has made a career out of commentating in a style that certainly pleases the purists. And very soon after becoming my back-up man, he seemed to respond badly to the top billing the Beeb gave me and the attention I got from the national papers. Our initially matey relationship turned sour over the next couple of years. It did not help that David Coleman always introduced me as 'our lead commentator'.

I was certainly glad and proud to be the 'lead' on the night of Thursday, 8 February, when the clash of Eric Bristow and Alan Evans sent the ratings through the roof. In my documentary Evans had professed his hatred of all Cockneys in general and Eric Bristow in particular and, as I watched him practise, downing pints of lager rapidly, I could tell he was in a mean mood. He was swearing at himself and kissing the dragon flights on his darts a good half-hour before the match. I looked into the rival practice area where Eric was warming up, chewing a flat pint of lager and snorting fag smoke. He looked pale and by far the more nervous of the two.

What a reception the pair got when they came on stage. Alan Evans' coachloads from Stockport were back in force, waving leeks and cuddly dragons. Eric Bristow was now living in the Stoke area and playing county darts for Staffordshire and the locals brayed their encouragement. Evans, slit-eyed and bouncing with aggression, went off the better, hitting a couple of 180s early on and gesturing with his fist to Bristow. I reckon it meant 'I'm gonna thump you' in the figurative sense, but the foreshortened telly shot made it look like a punch. Bristow replied with harsh verbals and a spray of fag smoke over the sixty bed. Evans, a non-smoker, brushed the smoke away theatrically, curling up his nose as if Eric was giving off a bad smell. I said on commentary that it was a clash of 'thoroughbred cockbirds'. Evans gulped his lager and continued the gestures; Brissy hardly touched his drink, but his body language showed he had lost the psyching-out battle. The referee had to chastise each player.

Alan won the match by three sets to one and danced around the stage like a drunken Welsh dervish. Eric turned his beaky nose to the roof, nostrils streaming smoke like a shattered stallion. The ritual handshake was no more than a perfunctory tap. Evans was whipped to the studio for interview while Eric stormed out of Jollees in self-disgust. The drama did not stop there. In a wild-eyed interview with David Coleman, Alan jeered at the 'idiot' who had seeded Bristow above him: it was a clear jibe at Olly Croft. Within two hours it was announced that the Welsh Darts Organisation would fine Alan £250, 'for bringing the game into disrepute' – dissing the boss of the BDO. Alan immediately announced that he would not pay the fine, thus starting a chain of events that would lead to a year-long ban. But there was a lighter side. As I left the commentary box I was stopped by a solemn-faced Evans' fan with a red bobble hat and a papier-mâché leek: 'Hey Sid, how can Alan bring the game into disrepute? *We've always been in disrepute.*'

Whatever the image of the game, we had certainly made some Beeb suits eat their words. Darts had gone out over their dead body, and the viewers loved it. The viewing figures had risen from just under three million for day one to 8½ million for the clash of the cockbirds. As a result, we were given two extra highlights programmes on Friday and Saturday.

The two men left to fight out Saturday's final were Leighton Rees and John Lowe. I was told by Nick that I'd be doing all the match, which would be played in two parts, and surprisingly I had no nerves at all. My wife Irene had driven down from Leeds on the Friday night and we had a big English breakfast together at the North Staffordshire Hotel. As usual she was a calming influence, telling me to take my time and not get flustered if I got a score wrong. As it turned out later, she was the one who put her foot in it – with David Coleman no less.

The match was due to start at one o'clock and just over an hour before I went to Jollees to watch the two stars practise. I was surprised to find them sharing a practice board like two pals in a pub team. All week competing pairs had been assigned to separate prac- tice boards to stop wind-ups. But here were two blokes going for the sport's biggest honour and chatting like schoolboys.

'Sticking to orange for this one Mr Lowe?' asked Leighton, pint of lager in hand.

John lifted his glass. 'Yes, you know me Leight, not really a drink- ing man.'

'That's not what the cleaner told me,' winked Rees.

I watched them throwing for a bit. The only sign of nervousness I could detect was that John was wearing the same red shirt that he'd won his semi-final in, instead of alternating it with his blue one.

Superstition? With Mr Method? I asked. He shrugged and nodded, chin jutting an extra inch. I felt as though I was intruding, so I wished them both the best of luck and went off down the hill to the Crown and Anchor. I had a pint of shandy and tried to relax. Suddenly a Yorkshire voice shouted out 'Hey Sid, any chance of sneaking us in?' I turned to discover Anthony Moss and Ian Cocking from Pudsey St Lawrence Cricket Club looking at me with beseeching smiles. They'd got so excited by the event on telly that they'd driven down on spec. I was nonplussed. Then Jim Sweeney of the BDO came to my rescue. He came over, listened to the score then said: 'No problem. Follow us.' We did, up the hill, down an alley and into Jollees' *potato lift* – the one used to take in tons of spuds for the punters' chips. 'We've been bringing our pals in this way all week,' said Jim. So I made my big entrance on the big day shaking hands with the cooks. Over the years my biggest problem was to be not mugging up for Embassy finals, but wangling my pals in on the sly.

As it turned out, my job was a doddle. John Lowe was in prime form and blitzed Leighton by 3–0 in sets to take the first session. I explained to the viewing millions that one of the main reasons for this was the new longer throwing distance of 7 feet 9¼ inches. A year earlier Rees had been on song from 7 feet 6, the world standard at the time. Leighton had told me that the extra 3¼ inches had wrecked his rhythm; even though he was a colossus, the cobra wave of the arm was a delicate movement, perfected over many years. He was never the same player with the longer oche.

By half past four I was back at the hotel watching telly while Irene had a kip. I had the news on and watched the wild scenes as Ayatollah

Khomeini, back from exile, rode through Tehran greeting the revolutionary faithful. I had worked for Iranian television for three months in spring 1975 and knew what a hero the old gent was ...

'And when John Lowe gets back to Clay Cross there'll be a reception as if the Ayatollah Khomeini had walked into town.' Free association of ideas has always been a main plank of my act, and that's how I greeted John Lowe's five sets to nil victory in the Embassy final at 8.30. It tickled Nick, David Coleman and many of the national papers. People began expecting cracks like this from me every time I was on, and I tried to provide them. The next day there was my picture and a full-page story in the *Sunday Mirror*. I was no longer 'The Geordie Lip', I was now 'The Geordie Whippet' – presumably because I was fast off the mark and never short of a bark – the man who 'scores a bullseye every time'.

Sadly, the old class bias against darts raised its thick head in the London *Evening News*. Patrick Collins called the Embassy tournament 'a tawdry circus' that ought to 'carry a government health warning'. Collins has never missed an opportunity in the past twenty-eight years to knock our sport. Apparently he attended the *News of the World* Grand Finals circa 1973 and was splashed by the bad aim of boisterous boozers in the gents' loo. One small slip that produced one giant step of prejudice. Oh what a shame. Of course, that kind of thing never happens at Henley or Twickers.

At the post-final party at the Crown and Anchor, Coleman was in his element. He stood in a corner holding court and sinking large whiskies at a rate of knots. The players to a man adored him for his humour and his respect, which is more than can be said for one or two who followed him in the presenter's chair. His clear liking for a few scotches went down a bundle. Irene and I were feeling no pain when we joined his company at around midnight. I was so far gone I was indulging in my Embassy freebies. Many of the lads tried to smoke their allocation each day, so by Saturday night there was a lot of coughing going on, not least by one twitchy, asthmatic commentator. I was sucking and twirling my Hamlet like a total novice.

'Well, what a week I've had, Sidney, and what a brilliant week you've had,' Coleman gripped my shoulder. Praise from Caesar, I thought. Soon he was in deep discussion with Irene about her work at Yorkshire Television and the recent industrial action there. I was swirling in a boozy euphoria as the note of discord was struck.

'Well, the problem is that the men at the top don't know the people working for them,' said Irene, earnestly. 'Tony Preston hasn't made much effort since he arrived.'

Coleman frowned. 'That doesn't sound like my old friend Tony.'

I hastily leapt in with my Kissinger act and steered the conversation around to athletics – and she did it again.

'Athletics is my favourite sport on TV and I love your enthusiasm for it,' she said, trying to make amends. 'I mean you said what everyone thought when Hemery won the hurdles in Mexico. Who cares who's third? Pity it was John Sherwood.'

Coleman spluttered and began to turn purple. 'Nobody blamed me for that!' Even after ten years his mistake still obviously rankled. I steered Irene off to be chatted up outrageously by Cliff Lazarenko. She could say what she liked to him without sinking my commentating career.

Over the next few weeks it seemed nothing could stop the darts boom. Nick told me that we would be covering another week-long tournament in September, the Unipart World Team Championship from the Fiesta Club at Stockton. In addition, we would record in the same week a BBC invitation event called *Bullseye*, featuring the top players. He asked me to design a trophy for the event, which I did. It was in the style of a dartboard plus a single arrow and is now probably in some charity shop. The trophy had a chequered career. It was won twice by a rampant Jocky Wilson and was 'lost' at a holiday camp at Rye. Two of my pals, Mick Dempsey and Tom Docherty, both assistant producers, got so pissed with the players that they forgot they had locked the trophy in the camp safe. Two hours before play started they were running around panicking when a redcoat came up and told them where it was.

The most flamboyant aspect of the boom was the Marlboro Team of Champions. This was really the first time darts met up with show business. The team consisted of John Lowe, Scottish star Rab Smith, Alan Glazier, Leighton Rees and Tony Brown of Dover, the latter pair sporting extra-roomy red and white uniforms to contain their bellies. I went to watch them perform at a club in Leeds and was gob-smacked. First, they climbed out of a white Rolls-Royce Silver Cloud. Then the packed house rose to them as the strains of 'The Big Country' boomed out. They replied by showing a darts and drinking capacity of outrageous proportions. Leighton downed at least ten pints and several brandies and Tony Brown warmed up on a bottle of gin. Brown was a giant of a man, a ringer for Bluto, the character who made Popeye's life a misery and was always after Olive Oyl. Brown had almost made it as a county cricketer with Kent and was a phenomenal darter. He hurled the darts extra quickly, getting faster as the gin got a grip. A few years later he disappeared from the scene completely.

The stars beat a Yorkshire Select 6–1 and voted Ronnie Cockerham, a local lorry driver, man of the match for which he received a bottle of bubbly. It struck me that this was the key to the appeal of darts: an unknown could step up and hold his own or even beat the stars. There was nothing like it in football or cricket.

John Lowe told me that he was loving his new life. I had noted how level-headed he was and been impressed by the fact that he had insisted he would make a real career of darts after his world championship win 'rather than have a series of paid holidays'. Now, having given up his job as a master joiner, he was wide-eyed about the future. 'It looks as though I could make nearer £100,000 this year rather than my first estimate of £70,000,' he said, signing autographs.

I was eager to learn as much as I could about the game. So, with this in mind, a few days later I went to watch a John Lowe exhibition at East Ardsley, a mining village near Doncaster. The workingmen's club was packed to see fifteen local stars take on the world champion. I sat in the front row with Barry Twomlow, former *News of the World* champion and John's guru. For two hours I was completely spell-bound. Barry urged me to observe the 'perfect stance' of his protégé: 'The back foot is the rudder and should be locked. The front foot should be angled to the oche. That gives you the solid platform. The arm should come through smoothly with no jerking and the shoulder should not drop. Notice that John hardly ever blinks.' I watched the eyes and Barry was right. Once lined up for a shot John never blinked, and at one stage Optrex were considering using him in a commercial. It was this superb technique combined with the controlled dexterity involved in countless hours of precision joinery that accounted for the Lowe success. He was a craftsman with a will of iron. Years later he looked in a mirror, did not like what he saw and cut out lager and fatty foods. This application won him world championship titles in three separate decades. In terms of consistency, will power and dedication, only Phil Taylor has ever matched El Lobo.

In the spring of 1979, using his considerable clout within the BBC, Nick Hunter got me transferred on secondment from the documentary department to his sports team. The idea was to let me get experience as a sports production assistant with a view to a permanent position. My first outing was to the 1979 Embassy World Professional Snooker Championships in Sheffield. I found my first task no problem at all. At the world darts there had been free fags, but the snooker was in a different league, freebie-wise. Along with two other APs I spent the first day at the Crucible humping crates of booze into a spare dressing room. There was a precise plan to our work. First we piled high the champagne and the brandy – for use by the hard-working Beeb team on semis and finals nights – then we worked our way towards the door piling up wine, lager and beer, refreshment for the early days of the contest. All that was needed when we finished was Aladdin and the Forty Thieves.

Sadly, my next task, the one I was really there to master, found me seriously wanting. It is called logging and it demands patience and accuracy. It involved sitting for hours writing down the exact times that shots were played and a brief bare description of the action. So 'Brilliant double shot by Jimmy, wish I could play like that' and 'Superb use of left hand side by Davis after blob by opponent – must use!' were not much good to the people compiling highlights. So Nick sacked me from logging and gave me something right up my street. His star commentator was John Pulman, former world snooker champion and a gentleman of the old school, who had voice like Peter Allis strained through sandpaper but who was a tad over-fond of the whisky. 'I want you to be John's minder,' said Nick with a knowing wink. 'I want you to sit with him after work at night and make sure he stops drinking scotch at a reasonable hour. I know scotch is your tipple, so drink his when he goes to the loo, buy him singles when he thinks he's getting doubles, do anything. But when he starts slurring get him to bed. I don't care if you get arseholed every night.'

What a brief! It did not do my liver any favours but I did a good job. I got the great man to bed by one on most of the ten nights of the tournament. We chatted a lot about the art of commentary and he gave me a real boost, saying I should let my wit and sense of humour run free. Later, I let this advice go to my head a bit and got into hot water. And near the end of the week John came out with one of the greatest ad-lib lines I have ever heard.

I had escorted John to table-side for an evening match featuring the legendary Canadian Bill Werbeniuk. Bill was famous for consuming many pints of lager before and during games 'to steady his nerves'. John was not due to commentate until later and was half asleep as play began. At the table Bill was faced with a problem: he was considering a shot along the cushion that involved lifting his right leg on to the table. He slugged lager, tweaked his bow tie, loosened the bottom two buttons of his waistcoat – exposing a wodge of belly that any dart player would be proud of – and lifted his leg on to the rail. A ripping noise cut the silence of the Crucible and a pair of testicles that would have not been out of place in the *corrida* at Madrid spilled on to the green baize. Quick as a flash Pulman murmured: 'That's the first time in the history of the game we've had three pink balls on the table.' Pure verbal genius. I was inspired to match it at the earliest opportunity – at the Unipart World Team event.

Six months later my euphoria had disappeared and been replaced by dark depression. Despite hours in the Park Hotel in Pudsey practising the big shot-outs and poring over the *News of the World*, I knew that when the chips were down I would make mistakes. On the train to Stockton, Tony Green tried to give me a crash course in the main shots, but I just got more confused. I was a juddering wreck when I sat down to do my first match. Nick Hunter had told me that a senior London BBC executive said I should talk in proper sentences, and the result was that I talked over the darts. So Nick, nervous as ever on day one of a big event, screamed at me down the talkback: 'This is not fucking radio, Sidney, watch the bloody picture.' The whole crew – and especially Tony Green sitting alongside me – heard this and I went to pieces. I got several shots wrong and ended the recording practically monosyllabic. Tony did the next match and got every shot-out spot on. He was publicly congratulated by Nick. At the end of the night's play I went to my room and sulked. I even seriously considered packing up and going home.

The next morning at breakfast I allowed myself to be rallied a bit by Tony Green and Jack Price, the top referee/caller, who was bit of a snooker player. Later on that morning they were planning to go to the Malleable workingmen's club in Stockton for a few games and they persuaded me to join them. At the club I sat out the first match and watched Tony and Jack playing. Two local Middlesbrough boys in their early thirties were playing on an adjacent table and one of them with long greasy black hair and volcanic acne turned to greet Tony.

'Hey up, Greeny, still flogging them tatty flights out of the back of yer car?'

Tony did not mention that he was currently banned from driving. 'Hey up, Bull, will we be seeing you at the darts?'

Bull put his cue down with a bang. 'I'm not going and I'm not watching the box any more till you get rid of that stupid fucking Geordie.' I wanted to curl up and die. 'He's a pile of shite – he always gets the finishes wrong!' Bull was about to give chapter and verse, but Tony tactfully steered him out of my earshot. I left the club and got a taxi back to our hotel in Stockton High Street. I was crossing the lobby when more black clouds loomed. The receptionist gave me a message asking me to phone the local police! Surely fucking up the scores in a darts match is not a criminal offence, I thought bitterly. I made the call and was put through to a senior detective sergeant. He was polite, if somewhat menacing. A lady had rung them up saying she had listened to me the night before on the darts and reckoned I was the Yorkshire Ripper; she said I was definitely the voice on the tape sent to police taunting them over their efforts to catch him. The tape had been played on national television news that weekend.

Could I make myself available for interview the next day? I said the officer should meet me at the hotel at eleven.

How I ever managed to prepare myself for three hours of commentating that night, I'll never know. But I must say that the goldfish helped ...

It happened when I was halfway into my first match of the evening. My troubles were temporarily forgotten as I edged to within six inches of the monitor screen. I was so engrossed that I reached past my glass without looking and picked up the bell-shaped water jug and drank directly from it. Suddenly I was aware of movement in the jug. I tipped my eyes away from the screen to discover two goldfish swimming inches from my mouth. I thought I'd flipped completely. Snorts of laughter burst from Tony Green and Les, our floor manager, the man responsible for the wheeze.

'What the fuck is going on in that box?' screamed Nick.

'Sid has just tried to swallow two goldfish,' Les replied calmly.

'That's all right then,' said Nick.

I relaxed, forgot about mistakes and did a great job for the rest of the night. One more inch and I would have upstaged the famous *Sun* headline 'FREDDIE STARR ATE MY HAMSTER' with 'SID WADDELL DRANK MY GOLDFISH'.

I had a good drink with Nick, Tony, David Coleman and the lads that night but said nothing about the cops. Nick said we'd be doing a match live for *Sportsnight* the next night and I would be doing it. Tony looked a bit miffed but said nothing. I slept like a log and during a late breakfast had a dark premonition. Perhaps the police would give me a hard time. So I went in search of moral support. I asked BDO officials Ken Shallis and Bill Skipsey, both wearing ties and maroon blazers, to attend my interview as witnesses.

Just before eleven I was called to reception and greeted by two policemen. One was the detective sergeant I'd spoken to on the phone, the other was young and hungry-looking. We went into a conference room and Junior took prime position, opening a thick notebook and scowling at me. I excused myself for a minute, then returned with Ken and Bill.

'Who are these people?' asked the senior cop.

'Witnesses,' I replied.

Junior looked at Senior with a deep frown. Ken and Bill sat behind me. I felt like the kid in the famous painting being asked: 'When did you last see your father?'

Senior told me again quietly that a woman said my voice was the voice on the Ripper tape and that they were obliged to make enquiries. Then he handed over to Junior.

'Where do you live?'

'Pudsey in West Yorkshire.'

He then reeled off a list of dates and places in Yorkshire where the Ripper had attacked women. Where was I on these dates? I pulled out my pocket diary and began looking. Both coppers leant forward eagerly. I had in fact been in Headingley, central Leeds and Bradford on some of the nights in question. No surprise really because I lived, socialised and often worked in that area. Junior wrote down my replies eagerly, seeing promotion on the horizon. I turned to my witnesses and got a shock; my pals were looking at me a bit funny.

Junior's eyes flashed. 'Why do you keep such exact details of your movements?'

I gave a ponderous sigh. 'I work for the BBC making documentaries and I make notes of my travels so I can do my expenses.' Junior did not seem to buy this but there were satisfied grunts from behind me. He quizzed me about my work, social life and family for another fifteen minutes. Then he said, 'By the way, what kind of car do you drive?' Cue soft chuckles from witnesses and frowns from cops.

I paused a good ten seconds for maximum effect. 'I don't.'

'What do you mean?' asked Junior hollowly.

'I do not drive. I have had lessons but I'm crap. I have never taken a test. I go everywhere by bus, train or taxi.' I shrugged my shoulders. 'If you don't believe me, ask these two.'

Junior closed his notebook and flopped. Senior leaned forward with a pale apology for a grin. 'Why didn't you tell us at the start that you couldn't drive?'

'You didn't ask!'

Despite the fact that it was still not noon and that I was expected to be on top form for *Sportsnight*, I joined my witnesses in a pint of Strongarm best bitter. A few hours later I decided to take John Pulman's advice and enjoy myself to the hilt on *Sportsnight*. As I made my way to the commentary box I was accosted by a figure in a suit, with a long ponytail. Then I clocked the acne and recognised Bull from the Malleable. ''Ere, Sid, let me shake yer hand. I owe you an apology, mate. I was only having a bit of fun slagging yer off. I love yer patter. Let us buy yer a pint later.' I agreed and went to work.

For the next hour, live on BBC1, I had a ball. I used every bit of ad-lib verbiage I could lay my tongue to and Nick had several times to remind me that there was a darts match on. But I never missed a shot-out, and after the live transmission everybody seemed pleased. Tony was doing the last match of the night, so I went to the bar and had a pint. Suddenly Nick was at my shoulder looking peeved. 'You overdid the jokes tonight, Sidney,' he shook his head gravely. 'I don't mind Rod Stewart, Shakespeare, Milton, *Ivanhoe* and bit of the Old Testament now and then over a week, but you got them all into five minutes.' He strode off and my heart sank. What was I doing on this emotional roller coaster? One hour and three pints later I was still propping the club bar up, deep in the trough of despond. Then a hand fell on my shoulder and a large whisky was pressed into my grip. It was Nick. 'Forget previous bollocking. Controller Two has just been on the blower about Milton and Co. Says it's the best bit of sports commentary he's heard for yonks. Keep it up.'

Later that night there was an amazing scene in the bar of our hotel. Two-thirds of the Welsh team were so hammered that they were talking in tongues. Ceri Morgan, a bearded wild-eyed lad from Treorchy, who had the throwing style of a stick insect and put 'pub-crawling' as his hobby on his official biography – was conversing in what I assumed was Welsh with Rocky Jones. Rocky was a coal miner and very fond of a pint. They were propping each other up. Suddenly Leighton Rees, the Welsh captain, waltzed in with a lady darter wearing a maroon Crimplene trouser suit. Seeing his team paralytic, Leighton turned martinet. He waved his cigar at the lads and boomed: 'You are representing Wales tomorrow. No more drink. Early night!'

He pointed to the door and the boys scuttled off. Leighton turned to our BBC party and patted his lady friend on the rump. 'This is my early night.'

The portfolio of darts on the BBC was still expanding. January 1980 found the circus at the Royal Horticultural Hall in London for the British Open. Our commentary box was set on a gantry about fifty feet above the playing area. Below, dozens of boards were in play as the pairs competition reached its later stages. I had the headphones on and was standing by to record a quarter-final of the singles. There was no sign of Tony Green who was due to do the spotting. Nick asked for a voice level from Tony and I had to say he was not with me. In panic I went out on the gantry and looked down. There was Tony playing in the pairs with Nobby Clarke. I started yelling: 'Lose you buggers, lose,' and fortunately they did.

The second quarter-final of the singles produced literally a turn-up for the books. The BDO rules state categorically that once play moves from the floor to the stage 'no jeans-type trousers are allowed'. I was just describing the atmosphere as the two players walked out when what I took to be a fight broke out. I was mistaken. One of the players was wearing jeans; a marshal had spotted them and the culprit was dragged off stage to be re-trousered. Sadly, the new pants he had borrowed from a pal were miles too big and he had to play with his left hand holding them up. He lost.

Star of the day was undoubtedly Cliff Lazarenko, whose mighty physique was honed laying kerbstones but had fleshed out a bit since he turned professional dart player. Sixteen pints during an exhibition and then a double Chicken Madras at midnight do nothing for the waistline. Before the Open singles final, Cliff's opponent Ray Cornibert hammered away at the practice board. Big Laz wanted none of it. His eighteen stone was flopped in a collapsible chair that creaked every time Cliff took a swig of his pint. He reckoned it was about his tenth. You could not tell Cliff had had a drop as each player needed double top for the title. Ray missed and Cliff hit. He danced around the stage like a large gazelle.

Over the next twenty-five years Cliff's drinking would become the stuff of darting legend. Soon after his Open win, my *Indoor League* colleague John Meade tried to out-drink Cliff in a London hotel. Both men had already drunk several pints of lager when John challenged Cliff to go along the optics. There were sixteen in various shades from amber to blue and JB fell off his stool at number six. Cliff finished the lot then went back calmly to drinking pints. I once wrote in a programme that I'd never seen Cliff drunk. His wife Carol read it and put me straight: 'You've never seen Cliff drunk because we've usually put you to bed before he gets pissed.' Touché.

A couple of weeks later we were back at Jollees in Stoke for the 1980 Embassy World Professional Championship. I was glad to see from the *Times* preview that at last some people were getting the right message about darts. 'Just like snooker and chess, darts could have been invented for TV. In the small-screen's coverage of these indoor sports, the close-up comes into its own – the tense hand, the gleaming eye, the dampness on the brow, the aborted grin, the gnawed lip. This is man under pressure, without artifice.' Precisely. In the *Daily*

Mail, Paddy O'Neill dubbed me 'the only man I know who makes Eddie Waring sound posh.'

There was certainly plenty to wrap my Geordie tonsils around. John Lowe, the holder and number one seed was blitzed in the first round by Big Laz who came back from two sets down to win with a 117 finish. And in Bobby George, making his first appearance in the world championships, we had a commentator's dream. Bobby had only been playing darts for four years but had won the 1979 *News of the World* championship. He had been in the building trade and had nineteen-inch biceps, curly hair and a big grin. He was also a show-man of the first order: candelabra, cape and sequinned shirts, knocked up by his friend Lil of Barking. As Bobby battled through a class field he tested my every power of imagination: 'If Bobby walked into Las Vegas at one end, Liberace would walk out the other.' 'Bobby is giving his all … sweating like a swamp donkey.' This last reference I borrowed from a boyfriend of one of my daughters who had run a mile to be on time for a date. 'Bobby is done up like an electric purple liquorice allsort.' Everyone from the Beeb, and millions of television viewers, were praying that Bobby would make the final.

The only sad note was the fact that we had no Alan Evans. He was serving a year-long ban from all BDO events after allegedly assaulting an official and there were those who thought the draconian punish-ment was connected to his calling Olly Croft an idiot a year earlier.

Luckily, another Welshman – a bloke of no darting ability what-soever but very handy with a pint glass – enlivened the first couple of days of the tournament no end. His name was Tom Davies, he had a mop of curly blond hair and a trendily shabby white suit and he

At Ellington Primary school aged nine – I was top of the class at everything but Nature Study. I was teacher's pet and mummy's boy.

Proud captain of Morpeth Grammar School's finest at age 17. I had a hard job keeping the lads off the beer at away games in market towns.

Despite darts and debauchery I got a good degree in Modern History from St John's College, Cambridge, in summer 1962. Suit borrowed; gown hired.

Front cover picture of *TV Times* in 1973. Dave Lanning and I wined and dined the boss of the magazine, then went to Freddie Trueman's house in the Yorkshire Dales for the shoot. Fred had to have three pints of 'continuity'.

Hot action in *The Indoor League* at Leeds Irish Centre. Pubbers, tossers, winners and lossers crowd round the bar billiards. Behind the ref you can just see 'blind' Jean Smith, the ladies darts star.

Olly Croft did much for darts in the 70s and 80s, but his attempt to run the game his way was arguably the main cause of the big split.

Tony Green went from spotter to commentator to give me a break in the early days at the BBC.

We had a lot of fun at Middlesbrough around 1979 when my nerves were at their worst. I was about nine stone wet through with worry; not so Tony!

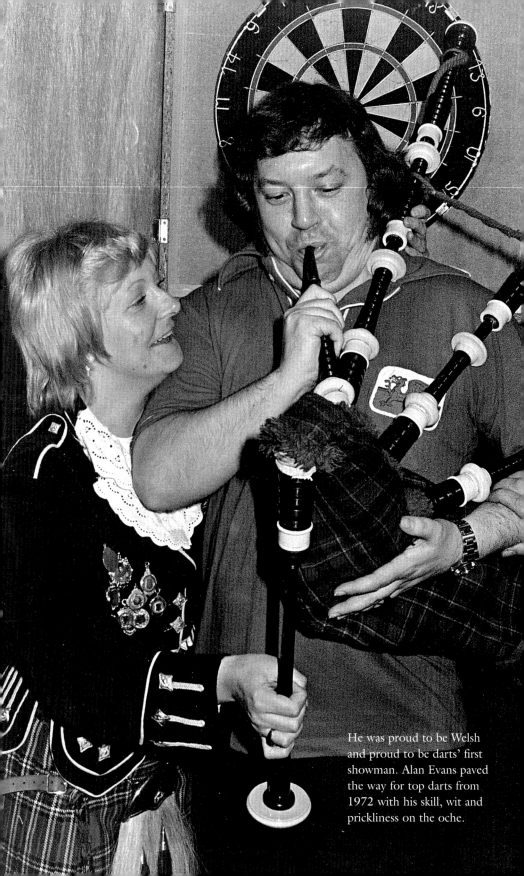

He was proud to be Welsh and proud to be darts' first showman. Alan Evans paved the way for top darts from 1972 with his skill, wit and prickliness on the oche.

There are not many pictures of the great Leighton Rees like this;
he is positively sylph-like. He is lifting one of many trophies, this
one from Eric Morecambe. Rees became a legend and the epitome
of the many-pint player.

Bobby George surrounded by plenty of what he likes best – bling.
Bobby never won a World Championship, but has since carved out
a media career by flashing his choppers and smiling.

Two real legends of our sport team up for a hot pairs competition. John Lowe is looking bulgy but would soon slim down, and Bob Anderson has that dashing Dartagnan look. Great players, great pals of mine.

El Lobo, John Lowe, kisses the Pentathlon trophy around 1980. And, being a master carpenter, he made arrows trophies in his spare time.

Cliff Lazarenko – a true gent of the sport, who is one of the greatest exhibition players ever. In thirty years of friendship and good crack I have never seen him drunk. Wife Carol reads Cath Cookson while Cliff hurls tungsten.

Who says Sidney cannot throw darts? Here I am in the early 80s with Brissy and the winners' cheques for the Fleet Street Pro-Am. He brainwashed me into hitting doubles.

Eric Bristow in his mercurial pomp. In the awful late-80s dartitis struck and the genius had to settle for five world championships rather than the ten he would have got otherwise.

turned up on the Monday afternoon. I was in the players' bar watching Lazarenko practise when a soft lilting valley voice bent my ear: 'I'm Tom Davies from the *Observer* and I'm thinking about doing my column about you and the boys.' Publicity-hound that I am, I bought him a pint and took him to the holy of holies, the band room at the back of the stage. Here, in the atmosphere of a smoky shebeen, the world's greats practised and got pissed under a giant poster of a busty nude. Jocky, fag on the go, was slamming in sixties. Rees was supping pints of lager. Dougie McCarthy was strumming on his ukelele. Tom's notebook was out in a flash and he began scribbling. When I introduced him to Leighton, he almost cried with Celtic pride. 'The *Observer*?' said Dougie. 'That's that religious paper all the Catholics read.' On this intellectual note I left.

Half an hour before midnight I retraced my steps. As I walked through the cellar, raucous singing echoed off the pyramids of metal casks. 'Bread of Heaven, feed me now and evermore …' Tom Davies, Rees and McCarthy had turned the band room into a Bethel chapel, give or take a few dozen pints of lager. 'I was either going to do my piece about the opening of Regine's night club in Kensington or the darts,' slurred the scribe. He didn't have to tell me his choice. Only a tough phone call from his editor two days later prised Tom away from the lads. And his 'Pendennis' piece on the darts was brilliant.

The week climaxed when we got the dream final: Bristow, the dark Prince of Dartness, and the extrovert glitter-clad Bobby George, stumbling for words to match the savage patter of his opponent who reckoned 'Bobby is a Mickey Mouse player.' The crowd was magic; half of them on their feet chanting for Eric and half for Bobby ten minutes before a dart was thrown. I tried my best to do verbal justice to the darting tableau: 'The atmosphere here is a cross between the Munich Beer festival and the Colosseum at Rome when the Christians were on the menu.'

Thankfully Bobby hit good form early doors and Eric did not dominate proceedings till the seventh set. I waxed mythological at one point when Eric snorted two nostrils full of fag smoke into the eyes of his opponent: 'Here's the Dragon ... and here's George.' In the end Brissy won by five sets to three to take his first world championship, gave Bobby a peck on the cheek and as ever was anything but gracious in victory. 'How do I rate Bobby? He'll make a good number two – some day.'

Once again our ratings topped eight million and the whole BBC team was delighted. The game had showed all its varied facets in two years on national telly: the lager-fuelled precision of Rees, the stone-faced grinding professionalism of Lowe, the arrogant Artful Dodger in the shape of Bristow. And what aspect had most tickled the public fancy? Of course, the ritual swilling of lager. Soon after the 1980 Embassy final the satirical BBC show *Not the Nine o'clock News* showed their 'Fat Belly versus Even Fatter Belly' sketch. In it Mel Smith and Griff Rhys Jones, wearing pillows stuffed down darts shirts, reeled about an oche hurling down pints of lager and large measures of shorts. The shiny Lycra shirts with super-flock lettering were exactly like those worn by Rees and Lazarenko. There was a mostachioed referee in evening dress, droning the shot-outs in bingo caller monotone: 'Fat Belly, you require treble vodka, double Drambuie.' 'Even Fatter Belly you require single pint of lager, treble rum and *double gin*.' To top it off they had Rowan Atkinson doing my screaming banshee Geordie voice: 'Fat Belly's gorritt … double whisky … nay bother!' I fell about laughing. They'd got the smoky lighting and the background clinking of pint glasses spot on, plus the glugging of lager, the squiffy damp-eyed concentration, even the occasional belch. It was satire of the quality of *That Was the Week that Was*. Sadly, Olly Croft and the BDO did not realise that we had touched a very human chord with our coverage. They thought the sketch was terrible for the image of the game. I was of the opposite opinion. I thought the boozing – and the fagging – counterpointed the skills of the players marvellously. It made them human, ordinary, familiar. Meanwhile, lurking in the wings was a laddie who would take the lowbrow, pot-bellied stereotype of the darter to new depths – John Thomas Wilson. And for a few manic weeks I tried, mainly in vain, to become Dr Wilson's Boswell.

4

Jocky Wilson Said

On a misty wet Tyneside morning a couple of days before Christmas 1995, Jocky Wilson, twice Embassy world darts champion and a household name to millions of people, turned his back on the game of darts for ever. He did it in circumstances that can only be described as bizarre, with a strong whiff of the tragi-comic.

The last few years had been hell for Jocky. He was suffering from diabetes, depression and a stomach ulcer. Still, he had flogged himself around pubs and clubs doing exhibitions to pay back over £27,000 that he owed the taxman. That debt was now down to £7,000. His exhibition darts had not been of the best, since he was totally off drink and supping only water when he played. In fact he had not touched alcohol since starring in a pairs tournament with Phil Taylor in October. Even then it had only been a couple of large brandies, taken after two narrow victories. There had been no binges on lager and vodka for many years – two or three pints of lager made him ill for days. Nor, sadly, had there been any real Jocky-style darts. It seemed that he needed the drink to bring out the brilliant darts.

So Jocky decide to pack it all in and take his family back to their roots. He collected about three hundred pounds that he was owed by his manager, Tommy Cox of Whitley Bay, but said nothing about his plans. He and his wife Malvina packed some suitcases and carrier bags and did a daylight flit from their house in Battle Hill, Wallsend, just a few miles from the centre of Newcastle. They went by taxi to the bus station and took a coach to Kirkcaldy on the Fife coast. They moved in with relatives till the council could find them a house.

And Jocky was really burning his boats. He was buying the house in Wallsend from the council on a mortgage but he did not tell them that he was leaving. Nor did he move out so much as a stick of furniture. He also left a car, which he was buying on the never-never, in the drive. He could not drive himself, but had a driver to take him to matches and exhibitions. The house and the car were repossessed and vandals made off with most of the house contents. Just how feckless, foolish and fed-up do you have to be to act in such a manner?

Just over four years after Jocky's flit I decided to try to find out. I was working in Dundee in April 2000 and as my train home approached Kirkcaldy I decided to jump off and try to find the man who once described himself to a newspaper as 'fat, boozy and toothless'. Only a couple of people had been to see Jocky in the intervening years. Tommy Cox had called at the Wilson council house in April 1997 and reported that Jocky did not look well; he had lost weight and the old spark had gone. He had no desire to mix at all with his old chums on the darts circuit. He only went out to walk his Jack Russell terrier and to attend the hospital. Phil Taylor told me a similar tale after he visited Jocky in late 1999. Jocky was now a recluse but had still urged Phil to 'beat them bastards I dinna like'. So maybe there was a touch of the old Jocky brio left. But both Phil and Tommy warned me that Jocky might tell me to bugger off.

I got in a taxi and asked to be taken to 15 Lauder Road. As we approached a street of dismal grey pebble-dashed semis, the driver turned round and asked me if I was 'that bloke off the darts'. I said I was and told him I was heading for Jocky's. He shook his head and pointed out of the window. I looked and was shocked to see that number 15 was all boarded up. 'Bit of bother,' said the driver. Seeing my crestfallen expression, the man decided to take pity on me. 'I'm no supposed to let on but aah ken where he stays now.' We drove past the Lister Bar, where Jocky and his dad Willie sang the night away after his world championship win in 1982. It hurt me to see Jocky's local boarded up too, and silent as the grave.

'It's that block there,' the driver pointed to a two-storey grey concrete box. 'It's one o' the wee flats where the put the old yins.'

I found the flat easily. It was on the first floor and had 'J. Wilson' etched on a small metal plate. I took it as a good omen. Jocky answered on my third knock. He opened the door a foot, recognised me and said 'Hello Sid' as though we had seen each other the day before. Once in, he shifted his fag to his left hand and shook my hand firmly. His voice was quiet, semi-apologetic like in his pomp – when he was sober. He seemed as bulky as ever, dressed in an old blue tracksuit and his face had none of the grog blossom that used to bloom there. He had the air of an old football coach, in his own private boot room.

As he made me a mug of tea, I scanned the premises. It did not take me long. There was a tiny kitchenette, a single bedroom and a lounge with two armchairs but no room for a settee. In the corner was a big television. When he handed me my tea and sat down, our knees touched. Then I realised that a bit of the old spark was still flickering. Above the fireplace was a giant colour photograph of Jocky, dewy-eyed, chin high, belly jutting proudly. He was holding the Embassy World Professional Darts trophy that he won in style in 1982.

When I asked him about the flit from Newcastle he had a good answer: 'I was out getting maybe £300 a night and it was for the tax man. My illnesses meant I had no energy. And I could not be Jocky Wilson on a dartboard without the drink. So I packed it in and came home. I have no regrets.'

It struck me as a reasonable strategy. Packing in darts at forty-five meant that Jocky at least was still alive to see his fiftieth birthday. His great rival Alan Evans, who put away oceans of cider to do his thing, died at the age of forty-nine from an alcohol-related illness.

We discussed the possibilities of a book and even a movie project but Jocky was super cautious. In 1997 he had declared himself bank-rupt and did not want any more problems with money. 'Mal and I can get by with what we get off the Social,' he said. I knew he meant it. But how many former world sports champions would be happy sitting in a senior citizen's council flat drawing the dole?

As I prepared to leave he flicked on Sky Sports. 'I still watch the lads on Sky. And I swear like fuck at the twats that used to wind me up.'

'Like who?' I asked.

He just grinned. 'Eric. Lowey. The ones I used to stuff.'

I looked from the smile on his face to the Embassy photo and saw the same sonsy look. I left him to his memories.

The drunken Scottish oaf who effed and blinded at me at Stoke in 1979 when he thought I was a shill for Tony Green, was not born with a silver spoon in his mouth. Evans' father stood his eight-year-old son on a box in his pub and encouraged him to play darts. Bristow's dad had taught Eric all the shot-outs by the time the lad was fourteen. Jocky told me that when he was ten, his dad Willie was sent to prison for receiving stolen goods. His mother could not manage to keep the home going on her own, so Jocky and his younger brother Tommy, spent most of the years from 1960 to 1965 at the St Margaret House orphanage in the village of Elie, a few miles north of Kirkcaldy. Jocky has always been unwilling to talk about those years, but I reckon his anti-social behaviour when drunk, his foul-mouthed rants at all and sundry, are connected to those years of feeling rejected. And this is not to deny the man's warmth and generosity. His errant dad Willie lived with the Wilsons and was looked after by them until he died.

As a boy Jocky was a bit of an athlete, believe it or not. He was a fair footballer and won the junior school pole vault; he did not develop the famous belly till he was in his twenties. After school he did some of the hardest, dirtiest jobs you could think of: spud peeler on a twelve-hour split shift, fish fin chopper in an open shed, coal miner, and labourer in a paint powder factory. These jobs put man muscle on the stocky frame and produced much fun for Jocky's pals.

'Whenever you seen Jocky he was covered in shite,' says Jimmy Skirving who later played with Jocky in the Fife county darts team.

And it was when 'covered in shite' in 1968 that Jocky met Malvina, who was to become his wife. On leave from the army, Jocky was working humping coal bags off a lorry when he met a shy lassie with dark curly hair who was born in Argentina, where she had lived until she was twelve. This fact was to produce enough aggravation later on to make the Wilsons decamp to England. Over the next three years John, Willie and Anne-Marie came along and Jocky had a tough time providing for them. He was often on the dole, sitting in the Lister Bar near his council flat chewing a pint and trying to make ten fags last the day.

Then Eureka: darts found wee Jocky. He was roped into the Lister team on a match night against the Auld House and humiliated. His opponent Colin Snowdon was a good player and he got the double to finish the game before Jocky got the double to start. A whitewash, or a 'Granny' as the Scots call it. Jocky went home, put up a board and practised day and night. He found he had a natural talent for the game, despite having to almost jump when throwing high on the board. He and his pal Willie Sime began hustling the pubs of Kirkcaldy for a few quid or a pint here and there. Soon he was throwing for the crack Fife team and in 1976 was capped by Scotland for the first time. He celebrated by beating Alan Glazier, one of England's top stars. With the Fife and Scottish teams he also learned to drink 'Magic Coke' – litres of Coke with half poured out and replaced by supermarket vodka. To see the Fife team ritually passing round the bottle and drinking deep was to be transported to the world of Eric the Red and his lads warming up for a spot of rape and pillage.

You think I'm kidding or being too fanciful? Well, consider this. In 1978 so hot did the atmosphere get at the England versus Scotland encounter at Perth in the Home International series, that the England team had to run the gauntlet of incensed Scottish fans and escape the venue in an unmarked lorry. A few years later in Edinburgh the local fans pelted Eric Bristow with full cans of McEwan's Export. Eric replied by hitting 60s at will, slurping the 'free' beer in between shots! With well-lubricated fans and players the auld enemies' match was always a tinderbox.

Though still on the dole, Jocky managed to hustle enough cash to get to the big tournaments. In 1978 he got to the semi-finals of the Butlin's Grand Masters and received a cheque for £500. Highly chuffed, he celebrated by waving the cheque around on a triumphal tour of the Lister and other local watering holes. He was not laughing for long. Either the folk at the Social had heard of his victory parade or had seen him playing on ITV; anyway they stopped his dole for a while. You could not call Jocky a model professional. A few months later Tommy Cox fixed him up with an exhibition match at the Talk of the Tyne in Gateshead. Jocky came down from Fife with two pals, played against the locals, got his £100, got plastered and lost the lot in a series of money matches. Tommy thought the lads had gone straight back to Kirkcaldy, but two days later Malvina phoned asking Tommy where Jocky was. He had to admit that he had no idea.

It was at this time that our unruly, feckless, boozy but brilliant hero got a most unlikely Fairy Godmother. Bobby George was as well organised as any dart player I have ever met. He had a great sponsorship deal with Courage, he bought and sold second-hand Rolls-Royces, he was always early for exhibitions with all the set packed in 'military' fashion in a special trailer. Bobby practised religiously, drank in moderation and if he wanted an extension to his house in Essex he built it himself, from damp course to dado rail. He had got pally with Jocky on the circuit and one night in the spring of 1979 he happened to be doing an exhibition near Kirkcaldy. The next afternoon Bobby asked round for Jocky and was directed to a grim tenement building. He banged on a few doors and eventually got lucky.

The door of the flat was opened an inch or two and Jocky's bleary, unshaven face appeared. He would not let Bobby in. He tried to push the door shut shouting: 'I dinna want you to see me like this, Bobby.' But Bobby is too big a lad to be denied his way by a laddie only 'five foot and a dimp' high. 'It was like Fagin's kitchen,' Bobby recalls. 'Drunken people, bottles everywhere, chucking wood on the fire – it could have been the furniture.' Bobby told Jocky that he was going to take him away from all this 'and make you a darts player.'

It was a hard and at times hilarious road, but it worked. Bobby put Jocky's career as a professional darter on a firm business basis. He loaned Jocky money for some natty playing shirts and Jocky began attending Bobby's exhibitions. After Bobby had played a dozen or so locals, Jocky would get up and play Bobby over several legs of 1001. He was quite brilliant but sometimes, out of respect for his mentor, Jocky would let Bobby win. Bobby drummed it into Jocky at these exhibitions that he did not need drink to play so should watch his intake at big events. Later Bobby took great pride in the achievements of 'Spike the Bulldog' or 'Gumsy', a nickname that Jocky never bridled at. At the end of the night Bobby would have a whip round for Jocky's wages, sometimes getting over £40.

Touring the country, and later the world, with John Thomas was an experience. In the summer of 1979 Bobby and Jocky were due to team up for a joint attack on the prize money available during the three-week annual professional darts season in the USA. Bobby and a few other British professionals were sitting on a plane at Heathrow awaiting take-off and Bobby was worried that there was no sign of Jocky. Suddenly Jocky flopped into the seat beside him and Bobby, relieved, told him to get the drinks in. Just after take-off Jocky paid out seven quid for four miniature vodkas and both men relaxed. Somewhere over Shannon Bobby got the round in, and soon Jocky got his round in again. Bobby sprung for round four then waved his empty glass at Jocky: 'Get 'em in John.' Jocky turned crimson with embarrassment and turned out his pockets. 'Ah cannae, I'm skint.' He had set off for three weeks in the USA with no cheque book, no credit cards and only £15 in cash!

To do Jocky justice, he applied himself totally to the hustle once they got across the Atlantic. He and Bobby did an exhibition in San Bernardino and were paid. Bobby was determined to drive off straight after the show so that they could register for a tournament in Las Vegas, a long drive away through the desert. But Jocky had got the taste for the local vodka and had been challenged by some locals to play for money. He was adamant that he was staying. So Bobby drove off and left him.

Two days later, Jocky showed up in Las Vegas, having hitch-hiked through the Nevada desert near Death Valley. 'He had come through cactus, rattlesnakes and cattle skulls,' recalls Bobby. 'He looked like Gabby Hayes, all sunburnt and covered in trail dust.'

Over the next two years Jocky was to set the darts world alight with some brilliant displays, but now and then his guard would drop and he would let himself down badly with the drink. And, stone cold sober, he nearly caused the death of his sugar daddy, Bobby George.

For me, the run of majestic form started in September 1980 at the Fiesta Club in Stockton. The venue was perfect: tiers of seats up to the gods, the fans' emotions funnelled down to the stage. For the past couple of years the locals there had seen the greats of world darts battling it out for big money and the BBC *Bullseye* invitation event had them all. Wildly popular with fans and well away with the drink, Jocky had a ball. In the team event the week before he had become the crowd favourite, fag on the go and pints of lager glugged down in three gulps: Andy Capp with a golden talent for tungsten. He had his own opinion of why the locals were behind him: 'There were no Geordies in the field and they say a Geordie is just a Jock with his heed kicked in, so they love me.'

I will never forget the atmosphere in the players' bar before the first match. The players had a refreshment kitty, augmented by the Lipthorpe brothers who owned the club, and the tables groaned with lager and spirits. Rees and Jocky were on brandy chasers, Tony Brown on gin and Lazarenko on anything wet. Just the ambience for the Fife Flyer to enjoy himself and entertain us all. Despite falling in the drums when he went to shake hands with one opponent, Jocky disposed of Tony Sontag, the holder, Tony Brown and Ceri Morgan. This set up a dream final, Jocky against world champion Eric Bristow.

The game was the best of eleven legs and you could not have had a bigger contrast in attitudes. Jocky jumped, postured and bounced round the stage, obviously pissed. Eric looked aloof, in a parallel universe, snorting fag smoke, oblivious to the jeers of the crowd. For once, I broke the unwritten commentators' code, I had a pint of Cameron's best bitter halfway through the match. I needed no thesaurus. 'Jocky on the oche looking cocky,' just rolled out and 'Bristow is looking as sick as a chip.' The match went to 5–5 in legs and the Fiesta was rocking. Eric wanted double 10 for the match and missed. Jocky went out from 75.

He had time for a pint and yet another large brandy before the presentation. It was to be made by John Ecclestone, a senior BBC executive and a stickler for protocol. I was standing behind him on stage and he whispered to me with a frown: 'I don't think nicknames are appropriate here. Do you know Jocky's real name?'

I winced, waited a moment and said: 'John Thomas Wilson.'

Pregnant pause. 'Right – I'll call him Jocky.'

It did not take long for Eric to get sweet revenge. At the Butlin's Grand Masters the following year, a week-long event, Jocky cruised to the semi-finals. By then he had signed a management deal with the Ron Clover organisation but nobody was on hand to guard the star from his own demons. One of Jocky's pals described how he came out for the match against Bristow. 'He normally bounced on to the stage, but here he trudged out, trying pathetically to run on the spot. It was obvious he had been up most of the night on the booze.' He was humiliated, losing five-nil in sets to Bristow. But that still did not stop the bookies making him favourite to win the Unipart British Professional championships back at Stockton in October 1981.

I don't think that the Jekyll and Hyde dichotomy in Jocky's character has ever been better illustrated than it was that week. Jocky and some of the Scots had traipsed the streets of Teesside in vain the year before trying to get traditional mince, tatties and neeps (swede). The people who ran the Crest Hotel where the players, officials and BBC team were staying heard of this and put them specially on the menu for Jocky. Not that he really needed feeding up; in little more than a year he had gone from twelve stone to sixteen. 'Gumsy' told me that even without a tooth in his head he could eat fillet steak, 'but I have a wee bit of trouble with walnuts.'

Jocky and Bobby were sharing a room and they both avoided socialising on the Saturday night before the event started. They did not attend the 'Brandy and Bacon Butties' party laid on by Terry O'Dea and the other Aussies, ostensibly an act of friendship but in effect a scheme designed to scupper the chances of opponents. Nor did they attend the premier of some porn movies put on by Richie Gardner's manager in a private lounge. I took one look into the latter, spotted that there were a couple of 'Boro Boots', ladies of the night, looking for punters and left quickly.

Sunday was the first day of play and Jocky and Bobby both won their first round matches. Jocky beat fellow Scot Angus Ross 3–1 in sets and Bobby, looking flushed and sweating profusely, struggled to beat Ireland's Bill Mateer. Back at the hotel that night Bobby was worse. He had severe stomach pains, was white as a sheet and was sweating and retching. Jocky called in a doctor who gave Bobby some pills. By now it was about ten o'clock, Bobby was still groaning and Jocky could get no sleep so, naturally, he went to the bar. It was a good job for Bobby that Jocky's socialising was minimal by his standards. In the bar Jocky got word that he had been elected BDO Personality of the Year, but resisted the temptation to celebrate. Instead, after a few pints of lager he had a brainwave: what Bobby needed was a large brandy. Back in the room Bobby said his stomach hurt too much to take the drink, so Jocky downed it and went to sleep.

At around seven next morning, Jocky was awakened by Bobby's groans. His sheets were soaked in sweat and he begged Jocky to get him to hospital. Jocky sought the assistance of Olly Croft and Andrea Hanson, a one-time nurse who was the girl friend of Alan Glazier. These two rapidly organised an ambulance and Bobby was operated on for a ruptured spleen in the next couple of hours. The surgeon told Andrea and Olly that if Bobby had been brought in five minutes later, it would have been touch and go. And when he was told of Jocky's brandy brainwave he shuddered; it could well have been fatal.

Back at the Fiesta there was a lighter atmosphere in the commentary box. Julie Welch, a football-loving journalist who had real respect for darts, had come to do a piece about the lads and me, and somehow that made me relax. So much so that I really made the most of an hilarious incident in the match between Alan Evans, back from his year-long ban, and his fellow Welshman Byron Wozencraft. Byron was built like a basketball player and hurled his 35-gram bombers with great force. Often he had to tug them out of the board like a dentist pulling a reluctant molar. Result: during one tug the surround fell forward and completely blocked the 60 bed. Quick as a flash Evans hurled three darts *underarm* at the bull. 'It could only happen in darts, the tyre's tipped and blocked the 20,' I chortled. I was cut short by Nick Hunter's sharp words: 'This is no laughing matter, Sidney, this is a major darts championship.' No laughing matter? The crowd thought it was, the players thought it was, even referee Jack Price could not call for laughing. Soon I myself was the cause of more laughter. On a later game, I began fiddling with the on/off commentary button. Then the big scores came flying in and I went into verbal orbit: 'Top of the tree with leaves on … terrific tungsten tossing … a Fiesta feast that Hemingway would have savoured …'

I was stopped by a dry sarcastic voice: 'Is there by any chance going to be any commentary on this?' It was director Mike Adley. I had switched myself off. Julie Welch heard about my gaffe and at the end of the match was talking to Tony Green about it. 'The viewers have been ringing up in their hundreds,' said Tony. 'They say it's the finest bit of commentary he's ever done.'

The tournament really came alight on the Wednesday night, when Alan Evans took on Eric Bristow. Evans was always a great favourite with the Teesside crowd and they gave him a standing welcome, while Eric was jeered at for most of the game. Evans dominated the tactics of the match, pulling his darts out slowly and mooching down the oche. He never looked at Bristow; he just played the crowd. Eric could find no rhythm at all and Alan won 3–2. He danced like a drunken Apache round the stage, glad to be back in the limelight.

Now you would think that with a semi-final place against his great rival Evans coming up, John Thomas would have prepared quietly and in moderation. Not a bit of it. He drank far too much the night before the match and began slagging people off. In particular he gave an obscene drunken mouthful to Olly Croft's wife, Lorna. Great behaviour by the BDO's Personality of the Year. Next morning he crawled on his hands and knees into breakfast with a bunch of flowers for Lorna and made a literally grovelling apology. It did not cut much ice.

On the oche however there was no stopping him. Subdued, no doubt by Bobby's illness and his own drunken outburst, Jocky tore into Alan Evans. He lost the first set but then fired in two 11-darters and a 14. He won 5–2 and the pair's handshakes at the end showed genuine respect. Then he and Lowe got to 5–5 in sets in the final and Jocky won the deciding set. He was the first ever British Professional Champion, his proudest moment in darts to date. And it was Dr Jekyll Jocky who, polite as a choirboy, gave an emotional but dignified interview to Peter Purves. He presaged every answer with the phrase 'With respect ...' That is certainly what he had gained from all the players. Dave Whitcombe said that Jocky was the greatest player he had ever seen.

And it was nice to end that dramatic week on happy note. On the morning after the final Jocky, Mike Adley, director of our TV coverage, and I went to see Bobby in the hospital. A hard-faced staff nurse told us we would have to be brief, and we must not make the patient laugh. Bobby looked quite chirpy considering all the drips and the dozens of stitches in his abdomen. He congratulated Jocky on his win and wanted all the gossip. I told him that we had done a vox pop asking the players 'How do you beat Bristow?'

'I said "Hide the bastard's fags",' said Jocky. Bobby laughed and grimaced with pain at the same time. Hard Face stopped outside the door and glared in at the merriment.

Then Adley chipped in. 'Brissy heard what we were asking and suggested we bring the cameras up here and interview you. You reply: "Bristow. Bloody Bristow. All I wanted was double 12 and look what he did to me!" '

Bobby's face turned purple. He clutched at his stitched-up guts as he tried not to laugh. His tubes and drip-feeds almost knotted. Hard Face gave us the bum's rush. We forgot to give the patient his grapes.

Jocky's roller coaster career ricocheted on. He beat Tony Brown 13–0 in a £2,000 challenge match. At the World Cup in New Zealand the sole fell off his only pair of shoes and he bought a pair of white plimsolls to play in, insisting they were the only things suitable. More seriously, he 'had words' with some Scottish officials during the event. He was fined £250 by the Scottish Darts Association and, after another outburst at an international match, he was given a two-year suspended sentence. Now this might seem very lenient after what happened to Alan Evans, but the Scots selectors were not daft. In his previous thirteen matches for Scotland Jocky had only lost twice. He regularly did 12-darters and was the man the crowds, of whatever nationality, wanted to see.

What Ron Clover, Jocky's manager, and Jocky's family did not want to see was Jocky in the bar with the other players. As Eric Bristow said years later: 'One pint was plenty for Jocky, but twenty pints were not enough.' When he got with Brissy, Laz and the boys in a bar he was like a cow in a field of juicy clover; he did not know when to stop. So it came about that Jocky and his brother Tommy spent Hogmanay 1981 sitting in a London hotel room, rather than boozing it up and first-footing till dawn. They slowly chewed a can or two of lager while they watched the *White Heather Club*, all senti- mental singing and Highland flinging. Jocky rang Malvina at midnight and the boys went to bed. Reason: the first round of the British Open at the Rainbow Suite, Kensington High Street, started at nine sharp the next morning and Jocky was favourite to win.

We were covering the British Open for *Grandstand* and I was at the venue at half past eight. It amazed me to see dozens of players downing pints at that time, then forming orderly queues at the prac- tice boards to take their turn, like so many schoolkids waiting for dinner. I was gently soaking up the ambience, but not the booze, when I was suddenly made aware of how my commentary polarised opinion.

I bumped into two Lancastrian lads I knew and began to chat. Two women approached us talking animatedly. 'This is the missus,' said one of the blokes with a half-apologetic grin. I stuck out my hand in greeting and was met by a horror-stricken shriek. The woman put her hands over her eyes, turned round and began stamping her feet. 'Get him away from me,' she screeched. 'I can't bear to look at him. His voice on telly sends me up the wall.' The rest of the party shrugged and I moved on. I was shaking with emotion.

Over the past few months I'd had a pretty negative press. In the *Guardian* Matthew Engel had so much contempt for me that he refused to use my surname: 'They have a new ethnic-sounding commentator called Sid, who read history at Cambridge, where they taught him to say things like "Stoke Newington's answer to Attila the Hun"'. And there was worse in a letter to the *Radio Times*: 'The appalling commentary, with its excruciating clichés, degrades both the sport and the otherwise professional coverage.' Another letter to the BBC, from Surrey and on embossed note paper, said I spoke 'banal drivel' and was probably suffering from 'cacoethes loquendi' (verbal diarrhoea). The pinnacle came in the buffet at Sheffield railway station when I was asking for a pie and a pint and a bloke shouted to his mate: 'Hey, it's that fucking idiot off the darts.' In my bones I knew all this meant that I was making a big impact, and sometimes I went OTT or did deliberate mistakes, e.g. 'Alfred' instead of 'Albert' Einstein. But it did mean my nerves were always jangled when I went on air.

At the time, I did not know of the Wilson camp's 'isolation and moderation' campaign to keep Jock on the straight and narrow. But I do recall how bright-eyed and bouncy he was as he cut through the field. He made it relatively easily to the last sixteen, then he blitzed John Lowe. In the semi-final he beat Londoner Colin Baker 2–1 to set up a final against Eric Bristow. Brissy was looking for his third British Open title, having won in 1978 and 1981. In the final set, with Eric needing 48 to win, Jocky needed 46 for the title. Now most players would have been psyched out by the arrogant Bristow presence, the cocky gestures to the crowd and the sarcastic verbals. But not John Thomas; throughout his career he respected Eric, but never too much. Jocky planted double 18 and danced. Bristow blew a resigned cloud of fag smoke.

I joined Jocky and his manager Ron Clover in the bar, expecting a Wilson celebratory vodkathon. No way. Jocky had a large vodka and a pint of lager – and that was it. Ron Clover told me that the policy of isolating Jocky from the other players would continue in Stoke in eight days' time at the World Championship. I wished them both luck. It was a very fine line they were treading: Jocky could only do his thing with at least three pints warm-up, three pints during the game and the odd nip of vodka. Enough to send most folk seeking their bed, but often just an aperitif to Jocky. The problem was persuading Jocky to turn monastic every night for what would be eight nights if he was to become world champ. The plan worked, except for one almighty glitch.

The 1982 Embassy was one of the most dramatic darts events ever. It took me about five hours to get from Pudsey to Stoke by train because of blizzards. The whole country was frozen. When I got to our hotel in Newcastle-under-Lyme there were reports that some of the Welsh players were snowbound and would not be able to play. Mind you, the snow was a blessing to some. When I went for a walk round the hotel car park, I came across an amazing sight. Tim Brown and Terry O'Dea, two of Oz's finest, were digging a cave in a five-foot snow drift and putting cardboard boxes inside. Reason? 'The tinnies are from Swan lager, our sponsors, and there are no fridges in the rooms. We can't drink warm lager, mate,' Terry explained. The only problem was that when the lads wanted a beer ten hours later they couldn't drink it – the tinnies were frozen solid. So they thawed them out on the radiators in the bar. Eventually they supped their Swans – warm.

I was in anything but a cool mood on day one of the tournament. At breakfast Nick Hunter told my to my surprise that we were going on *Grandstand* live at one o'clock with Bristow, the reigning champion, against Steve Brennan of Northern Ireland. I panicked completely. I went to my room and threw up. Flicking through the shot-out charts, I was convinced I'd make a mess and get the sack. I got to the commentary box half an hour before show time and sat dry-heaving, watching enviously through the window as a suave relaxed David Coleman chatted to the fans. With five minutes to go I felt wretched. Olly Croft had a freebie cigar on the go and Greeny was blowing out Marlboro smoke. I asked them to pack it in for the sake of my dodgy tubes and they agreed reluctantly. Suddenly, Nick announced that Bobby George was coming in to share commentary. My head whirled and my mouth was like old kindling. A hot greasy smell assailed me and Bobby's voice rasped: "Ere, Sidney mate, have a bite of this. Calm you down.' A giant burger with all the trimmings, oozing ketchup, was stuck under my nose. I began to retch as Frank Bough said: 'Your commentators at Stoke are Bobby George and Sid Waddell ...'

The next ten seconds seemed to last an hour. The crowd bayed as the players did practice darts, I retched convulsively and our floor manager Harry Coventry held a tiny tin ashtray up to my mouth in case I puked. Olly, Tony and Bobby had hysterics. My opening words were punctuated by odd off-mike retches: 'Welcome to Jollees ... aargh ... the Crafty Cockney poised like a preying mantis ... aaargh ... Brennan is no mug ...' Then I was off and flying and the ashtray remained empty.

Suppose I say it myself, the commentary was among the best I have ever done. My nervy tone and the strained staccato delivery totally matched the drama that unfolded. Eric wilted under the mantle of being the favourite, just like he had in 1978, and the clean-cut Brennan won. Nick Hunter praised me down the talkback for my 'control'.

With Bristow out, the bookies made Jocky hot favourite to become world champion. Looking chipper and every inch 'Spike the Bulldog', Jocky beat Rab Smith easily to set up a cracker against Alan Evans. Just like Evans versus Bristow in 1979, this match had the potential to be explosive and hence great box office. Evans, as usual, had bussed in dozens of boozy, raucous fans and as the players warmed up they gave Jocky plenty of stick. Lashed up with drink he would have given Alan and the fans verbals, but ice-cold sober, Jocky held himself aloof from the taunts – for a wee while anyway.

Although I did not mention it in commentary, I knew Evans would try to upset Jocky. Alan was aware that Jocky was on a two-year suspended sentence that would take effect if he did not keep his nose clean. I was not wrong. Evans started the slow-down tactics straight away, sneering at Jocky as he dawdled down the oche. Jocky simply shook his head and pretended to disapprove; he said nothing. Then Evans complained that Jocky was blowing smoke at him and at the board as a screen over the 60. Jocky pantomimed blowing smoke at the crowd. Then Evans really did light Jocky's fuse. He said to the referee that Jocky was clicking his big brass lighter when Evans was throwing. Jocky gave Alan a mouthful. Evans gestured to his own jaw and said 'Do that again and I'll break your fucking jaw.' I could clearly lip-read the words and people at the front began abusing Evans. The ref spoke to both players and Evans glowered. Jocky was obviously on the verge of tears.

In the end Jocky stumbled over the winning line 2–2 in sets. There were no handshakes at the end. Jocky ran off the stage in tears screaming 'I'm no cheat' to the press people. He sought refuge in the band room, began drinking recklessly and refused to give any interviews. Nothing that Ron Clover or anybody else could say or do would stop Jocky, and his bender was the main topic of conversation at our hotel the next day. At about eleven I was having a coffee with Bobby George in the lounge when a man with a greying mullet, a posh Crombie coat and a notebook entered. Somebody identified him as William Marshall, a feature writer for the *Daily Mirror*. The general opinion was that if he was in town he was after a 'booze and bellies' exposé of darts. 'I hope to hell he doesn't bump into Jocky,' said Bobby.

Bump into! Marshall actually had fixed an *appointment* with Jocky. After a few minutes Jocky, unshaven, tousle-headed and carrying a large Bloody Mary for breakfast, joined the journalist and began to talk. Bobby leapt up and walked past Jocky, gesturing that he should shut up and clear off. It did not work; Jocky animatedly rambled on about not being a cheat and Marshall scribbled furiously. I tried a similar tack, indicating in gestures that Jocky should leave. He shook his head and as he did a blood vessel burst in the white of his right eye, flooding round the pupil. I winced, knowing what kind of article would follow. Marshall scribbled faster.

For some reason the nerves kicked in badly with me before Jocky's semi-final against Stefan Lord of Sweden. Nick Hunter had been on at me again about talking over the darts, so I had a wheeze to get over the problem. I went to a pub in mid-afternoon, loaded up the jukebox with 'Jumping Jack Flash' – six plays on the trot – and began playing pool on my own. I tried to imagine that I was Jagger on vocals and the band was the darts. Mad? The locals certainly thought it was, and gave me very funny looks, especially when they heard me hissing 'Double 10 … in like a whippet …' But it calmed me down and filled in an hour that would have been spent worrying.

I was ice cool a few hours later as I watched Jocky practising in the band room. It was the norm those days to keep players in separate practice areas, so Stefan was on a board at the other end of the club. Jocky was on fire. Ten minutes before the game was due to start, he fired in a 9-darter. 'Fuck,' he said. 'If I'd have waited ten minutes and done it on the stage I'd have won fifty thousand quid.' He nearly did it again in his demolition of Stefan, with back-to-back 180s. When Stefan tried to slow the match down Jocky pouted and wagged his finger at him like a school marm. The crowd loved it.

The Marshall article appeared on the Saturday morning before Jocky met John Lowe in the final. It slagged Jocky and it mentioned the bloodshot eye, and it slagged the audience: 'people dressed for a Yukon gold rush – shaggy men accompanied by timorous women.' Jocky refused to read it and nobody was of a mind to tell him the gist. In the final the wee man was inspired. He raced into a 3–1 lead, and despite Lowe rallying to 3–3, Jocky upped the ante. He had finishes of 116 and 141 and won 5–3. He started to cry and I nearly did the same, almost choking on the words: 'They'll be singing and Highland flinging in Kirkcaldy tonight.'

Ron Clover waited till the third lager and vodka chaser to drop his bombshell. Jocky and his family were now homeless! Four days earlier the Wilson council flat had been evacuated because of flooding in the flat above. Water had seeped down and there were fears about the electrical supply, so Malvina and the three kids had moved out to stay with friends. Each night Malvina had put on wellies and gone back to the flat to take Jocky's calls. She had not said a word about the flooding.

The next few weeks were a triumphal parade for the new world champion. A gala night was held at the Lister Bar and Jocky was feted with drinks, cakes and a ship's bell! This was a present from the landlady to her most famous customer and, after starring on the karaoke, Jocky and his dad rang it through the sleeping streets on their way home in the wee hours. The Scottish tabloids pictured Jocky dressed as a cowboy, a magician and even a pantomime fairy. ITV stumped up £2,000 to get Jocky a custom-made pair of false teeth from a specialist in Wimpole Street. The new choppers were great so far as eating was concerned, but Jocky complained that they made him boak (retch) when he drank. So the teeth were largely ceremonial: brandished after a narrow victory or occasionally flying into the audience when Jocky abused an opponent or cursed a bad shot.

And then the fun really started for me: I signed with a sports publisher to become Jocky's Boswell for a few weeks and write the real story of his life. It turned out to be a cross between the movie *Shallow Grave* and life at the But and Ben with the Broons.

My trip with Jocky started in June 1982 at the pleasant Wiltshire village of Pewsey, near Marlborough. Jocky was due to play an exhibition at the local sports centre that night against sixteen local stars, and I joined him at about six that evening at the pub where he was staying. He was with his amanuensis Sandy Mortimer, a slim, dry-humoured Kirkcaldy lad, who drove, butlered and joked with Jocky on the road. Jocky looked very smart in a blazer, white shirt and tie. But he was noticeably thirsty; in just over an hour he downed two pints of lager shandy and two pints without lemonade. He threw a few practice darts. At seven we left for the venue.

As the crowd filled up Jocky, Sandy and I were entertained by the organisers in a posh upstairs lounge. Sandy and I sipped pints of lager, while Jocky downed a pint every ten minutes. Then the telly was switched on and we watched the start of Scotland versus Brazil in the World Cup. Within ten minutes the Scots were ahead and Jocky postponed the start of the exhibition and began chasing his pints with vodka and Coke. It was nearly eight o'clock when Jocky took the stage to rapturous applause, which reached crescendo in game two when Jocky hit a brilliant 25-dart leg of 1001. Jocky acknowledged the applause by grabbing the mike and promising to come back soon and do an exhibition for no fee, adding that it would be hard to forget a place like Pewsey 'because it sounds like pussy!' Sandy looked at me with a frown; he knew the signs and Jocky was definitely on the alcoholic cusp. We had no time to debate the issue because Jocky was angrily waving his empty glass at Sandy.

Over the next two hours I was stunned by the little man's performance. Gradually the lager stopped flowing and less and less Coke diluted the pure vodka. By the time he lost the last match – to a woman – Jocky had drunk over a bottle of vodka but had beaten all the other challengers and he had even planted a 24-dart 1,001. And there was more booze to come. Sandy, Jocky and I went back to the lounge and were fed and watered. I stuck to pints, Sandy to lemonade, but Jocky had several more Magic Cokes. At about midnight Jocky's mood became surly to the locals and he stroppily suggested that Sandy should not have been drinking earlier. There was bit of swearing between the two, but it seemed merely par for the course. We were all in bed by one.

Next morning the three of us were on the road at 6.30 for the drive to Leicester where Jocky was due to play for Fife in the British Knockout Cup. The plan was to stop for breakfast after about an hour. Having had five or six pints myself the night before, I was rehydrating myself by taking slugs from a Lucozade bottle full of water. Jocky was sitting in the front beside Sandy puffing on a fag.

'Is that gin or voddy?' he asked, pointing to my bottle. I could see by his expression that it was no joke.

'It's water. Your body needs it after a night on the pop,' I said.

'I never drink English water,' said Jocky solemnly. 'My granny said the English put poison in the water.'

Again I realised he was not kidding. 'So how do you clean your teeth?' There was a long moment. Daft question, I thought, Jocky has none.

'When I did have teeth I cleaned them with Fanta!' said Jocky.

'Aye, he did that,' said Sandy solemnly.

We completed the journey more or less in silence.

It would have been much better if, after consuming well over forty units of alcohol the night before, Jocky had stuck to Fanta when we got to the darts. Fat chance. After registering at eleven o'clock,

Jocky had a few pints of lager before the first match at 3 p.m. Fife played Suffolk and won, then after shots of Magic Coke, they took on London. That's when Jocky, topped-up from the night before, lost the plot. He was playing Ray Cornibert and suddenly began using foul language to the lady official doing the scoring. He accused her of urging Ray on to beat him. It was obvious to all observers that Jocky was pissed.

The outburst cost him dearly. He was given a three-month ban by the BDO that on appeal was reduced to nine weeks. But it still meant that he could not defend his Unipart British Professional title at Stockton in October.

Despite this setback, Jocky was in good spirits when I joined him at his home in Kirkcaldy two weeks after the Leicester debacle. The new Wilson family bungalow was smart on the outside, though the inside left a lot to be desired. The kitchen was full of crusted dirty dishes and the lino was mucky and only one room, the lounge, had been decorated. I was shown into a large back room with bare walls that looked like an Aladdin's cave for alcoholics. Half the room was piled to the ceiling with crates of Strongbow cider and 100 Pipers whisky, courtesy of Jocky's sponsors. He pointed at the hoard as he pulled out a table for me to work at. 'Have a wee drink if you want, I never touch it.' It was the god's honest truth: in his own home, John Thomas Wilson never touched a drop of booze. Once he got with the darts lads, he would drink anything. But by his own fire, tea and Fanta sufficed.

Whatever her shortcomings with the mop and the Hoover, Malvina was a dab hand at cooking. At 3.30 that Saturday I returned from chatting to Jocky's pals in town to encounter a wonderful smell in the Wilson kitchen. Malvina, in a tatty pinny and with her black curly hair sticking to her head, was slaving over a hot pan. 'I'm deein' mince and tatties for them twa, do you want a plate?' I nodded and went into the back room. Jocky followed me in and presented me with a six-pack of cider and a bottle of whisky 'just to wash yer dinner doon.' Malvina gave me a large plate of mince, tatties and neeps and it was magnificent. I ate every bite and did a bit of work on the newspaper cuttings, but not the booze. Just after half past four I went into the lounge to ask Jocky a question. Frank Bough was murmuring purposefully on *Grandstand* as Jocky and his dad snored blissfully in their armchairs.

Then I caught sight of their plates on the mantelpiece. Willie's was licked clean but Jocky's had a big blob of mince left, topped by his £2,000 false teeth! It made me retch just as Malvina came in.

'That bloody man,' she hissed. 'It's disgusting.' I was about to agree but she went on. 'That man never finishes a meal!'

Over the next few months the roller coaster continued. Jocky beat Bristow and Lowe in £2,000 challenge matches. Despite his suspended ban by Scotland, he captained the team against England, beating Lazarenko 3–0 in 18, 16 and 18 darts. He even appeared on *Top of the Pops* in the autumn of 1982. The pop group Dexy's Midnight Runners were high in the charts with 'Jackie Wilson Said' and a researcher made one of telly's biggest ever blunders. To the consternation of millions of both darts and pop fans, Jocky's toothless grin beamed out from a screen as the band played their hit. But it was not all glory and laughs. Jocky had a big row with Sandy at an exhibition at a golf club a couple of miles north of Kirkcaldy, with drink as usual playing a big part. Sandy went home, leaving the car in the car park. At the end of the night, Jocky, well gone, managed to get the car into gear and to the top of a hill, planning to freewheel home! He had never had a single driving lesson, never mind a test. Thankfully he ran slowly off the road and into a ditch and neither he nor the car was damaged.

Apart from commentating on his matches, I did not come into direct contact with Jocky again until the middle of 1985, and once again the circumstances were bizarre to say the least. Jocky claimed that he had been drunk when he signed his contract with Ron Clover and that therefore he was entitled to sign with a new manager. So I was summoned to the High Court in London as a witness for Jocky in the legal case that ensued. I remember sitting in the Wig and Pen pub vaguely wary of the optimism exuding from Jocky and his manager-to-be Mel Coombes as the pints went down before we went over to the court.

I had been told to take a copy of the book I'd ghosted for Jocky with me. The judge asked me to go to the page where the contract was mentioned and to read out what Jocky had told me about his state when he signed it. I began reading, and was about to put into Jocky's own words a bit about 'having had a few', thinking I'd liven proceedings up a bit, when the judge ordered me to stop. He wanted to know if Jocky said he'd signed the contract. 'I was coming to that, m'lud, it's the punchline.' I was told in no uncertain terms that I was not in the dock to crack jokes. So I lamely said that Jocky had told me that he signed it.

After that, things went from bad to worse. Jocky's claim that he was drunk when he signed was almost laughed at and in the end he lost the case. His total bill, with costs, was upward of £70,000.

Jocky arranged to pay this massive amount off in instalments. He had had a stomach ulcer since he was in his teens, but had drunk heavily nonetheless. He now vowed to Mel Coombes that he would limit his drinking and spent a week at a health farm to start his new regime. He took on a massive workload of exhibitions at home and abroad. But, most significantly for the future, he moved from Kirkcaldy to Wallsend on Tyneside. Mel Coombes located a bungalow in Hadrian's Park and the Wilsons moved into it, sight unseen. The move made sense in many ways: Jocky's travel to exhibitions, mainly south of the border, would be easier, and there would be no more hate mail and worse coming through the letter box addressed to Malvina. Also, Jocky knew many Geordie darters and, thanks to Tommy Cox, a local darts official and manager of a string of players, he joined the Northumberland County darts team.

Things did not work out between Jocky and Mel Coombes and in 1988 Tommy Cox took over as Jocky's manager. Being an ex-player, Tommy was able to keep his eye on his charge by practising with him, and he re-introduced the Ron Clover policy of keeping Jocky away from the lads at big week-long tournaments. But exhibitions and all-day Open events were at times a nightmare. On Jocky's first night in Tommy's stable he turned up at an exhibition in Darlington the worse for drink. He proceeded to get drunker and ended up shouting obscenities at his new sponsors. They refused to pay his fee for the evening. On a trip to the USA, Jocky joined Tommy in the hotel bar at Loughlin, Nevada, after a hairy flight in a biplane from Los Angeles. He said he would have a drink or two and was still in the bar with Cliff Lazarenko when Tommy came down for breakfast eleven hours later. That was the reason Jocky won so few Opens; he would start drinking at ten o'clock in the morning, reach the last sixteen and be paralytic.

So how did he manage to curb his demons and win his second Embassy World Professional Championship in 1989?

For starters, Tommy booked himself and Jocky into a separate hotel to the other players. Tommy and Jocky practised together and Tommy remembers how Jocky constantly needed reassurance about his ability. 'He seemed to be needing affection, love even,' said Tommy. And Jocky got it in spades from a strange source. During the week of the world championship, Tommy and Jocky went to see Watford play Newcastle United in a cup replay and eight thousand Geordie fans began singing 'There's only one Jocky Wilson.'

The boost worked. I was watching Jocky practise for the final against Eric Bristow and he was bouncing on the oche, eager to get at the Crafty Cockney. I could scarcely believe it when Jocky shot to a five-nil in sets lead. I was so excited on commentary I reused a line from 1982: 'Jocky Wilson – all the psychology of a claymore.' The tension became unbearable as Brissy struck back, but then the relics of dartitis hit Eric, and Jocky won 6–4. I was nearly in tears as I announced the winner: 'So John Thomas Wilson, once of Kirkcaldy, now resident in Newcastle upon Tyne, becomes world champion once again.' Jocky himself was sober, gracious and even witty in his triumph. 'No, years ago I didn't think twice about becoming a darts professional – I was unemployed at the time.'

Sadly, even with Tommy's vigilance, the old Jocky demons occasionally did their destructive dance. Jocky was often baited when playing and with drink taken, he often overreacted. In Sweden in 1990 there was a fight after Jocky accused a supporter of his opponent Russell Stewart of kicking him while he threw. A year later, baiting at an exhibition in Scotland caused Jocky to dive into the audience with fists flailing – and he connected with somebody's granny. The tabloids had a field day. Then in 1992 Jocky's health got worse and he was diagnosed with diabetes. In 1993, after losing in the world championship he gave me an obscene mouthful in public, merely because I had not tipped him to win the title. Tommy had been delayed in the USA and Jocky had 'prepared' till late in the bar with the lads. Next, total disaster. He had just finished paying off the £70,000 from the court case when he was hit with a tax bill for £27,000. This was the last straw. From then on he was out most nights earning £300 and giving it all to the tax man.

Although Jocky soldiered on in top darts till October 1995 – by which time he had paid off £20,000 of the back tax – my last vivid impression of him was at Blackpool that August. He played in the World Matchplay tournament at the Winter Gardens, and he took the place by storm. In the crowd of 2,000 were about 700 Scots on their annual holidays. They wore tammies, face paint and many waved the saltire flag. Jocky walked on to the Gaelic rock band Runrig's version of 'Ye Take the High Road' and he was besieged. The song only lasts three minutes, but Sky played it nearly three whole times while Jocky kissed babies and cuddled matrons as he nudged and scrummed the fifty yards to the stage. The director Martin Turner screamed down talkback: 'Fuck the match, let's just keep doing the walk-on.' He had a point. But Jocky was not on stage for nostalgia. He blitzed the world ranked number one Rod Harrington, 8–4. It was his last great darting exhibition.

5

Cue Alexander of Macedonia

If Jocky Wilson hooked the crowd with the vulnerability of the extrovert boozer, Eric Bristow brought to the oche the arrogance of a darting patrician. He looked and acted as if born to the darting purple: flowing locks, prominent nose, total self-belief and the tongue of a Cockney viper. It's no surprise that when the producers of *Ant & Dec's Saturday Night Takeaway* and *Celebrity Weakest Link* want a racy voice from the world of arrows, they send for Eric. It is all the more amazing, since the last time Eric cut the mustard in a big tournament was in late December 1996 when he pushed Phil Taylor all the way in the World Championship semi-final.

I personally would like to thank Eric's parents, George and Pam, for bringing a sporting phenomenon into the world, buying him a dartboard for his eleventh birthday and giving me a superb subject for my exotic verbals. In Eric's case these peaked with the phrase: 'When Alexander of Macedonia was thirty-three he cried salt tears because there were no more worlds to conquer. Bristow's only twenty-seven.' I did not prepare a single word of that line. It simply flew out of my history-steeped imagination as I endeavoured to do justice to Eric's fantastic darting achievement. In five years he had won the world darts championship four times. The fourth came in January 1985 when he hammered his arch rival John Lowe 6–2 in sets in front of a screaming crowd at Jollees, where they treated the Crafty Cockney as a local. Eric held his head proud, fag smoke snorting from his flared nostrils, a look of almost contempt for his drained opponent, who had lost the psychological battle early in the game.

In November 2002 the *Observer Sports Monthly* quoted my Alexander line and set a picture of Eric next to a picture of the Great and, stone me, the two could have been twins, right down to the conk and the thrusting chin.

Eric was bred for darting glory. His dad George was a fair pub player, but probably more important was the fact that George excelled at crib, dominoes and darts and could reckon up as fast as a mathematician. By the time Eric was fourteen he had learned all the shot combinations so never had to stop his rhythm to do the sums. For my money, he is the greatest 'counter' our sport has ever seen. As a boy, Eric was cocky, sharp-tongued, super-confident and a bit of a tearaway. He admits to having had a few run-ins with the police and indulging in the odd bit of shoplifting. A well-meaning policeman set him straight, saying: 'You can be an old lag, or make a lot of money playing darts.' Eric listened.

He went to Hackney Downs Grammar School till he was fifteen, then left to train as a furniture salesman. By then he was seriously into darts and kept his parents awake at night practising in his bedroom. By this time Eric could give George a 200 start in a game of 1001 – and beat him. George responded by taking his very tall son down the Arundel Arms pub and getting him into the darts team, where he immediately became lead-off man. As Tony Brown said in 1981: 'I wish George had taken Eric to Sunday school and not down the pub all those years ago, then we might've got a sniff at the trophies.' He became a member of the crack London County team when he was seventeen and played for England at eighteen.

After a couple of perfunctory meetings, I first got to talk to Eric at an exhibition at Barnsley in the summer of 1978. I found him polite and hospitable. He ordered his driver and best mate, Eddie Rayson, to get me a pint of bitter and chatted happily about his family and his ambitions. Then he got up on stage and, sipping at the odd pint of lager, hammered the best fourteen players South Yorkshire had to offer. Eric was single at the time and a very pretty local girl was sitting with Eddie and me. She was, I gathered, Eric's girlfriend for the night. Only trouble was, she seemed to be buying Eddie's chat-up line wholesale. Now Eddie was a very handsome lad with big dark eyes, and he was in pole position while Eric was up on the stage working, and he had the car outside...

I detected a bit of friction in the camp when I left at the half-time interval. And I was not surprised to hear that there had been a fight between Eric and Eddie. The row began in a restaurant and Eric punched Eddie, who replied by smacking Eric in the face with a candelabra. This caused the dissolution of their arrangement.

I have already described the way Eric put Bobby George in his place at the 1980 Embassy, when Eric became world champion for the first time. But it was a year later that the Crafty Cockney – named after a bar in Beverly Hills – legend really took off. Eric dropped only one set before the final against John Lowe. In round one he beat

Terry O'Dea 2–0; in round two he put out Dave Whitcombe 2–0 and in the quarter-final, Nicky Virachkul 4–0. Of his performance in the semi-final, where he beat Cliff Lazarenko 4–1, I said: 'If Emily Pankhurst had been able to chuck darts like that there'd have been no need to tie herself to the railings.'

Even though Eric was an honorary Stokie by now, for the final the crowd was very much for John Lowe. When John went 2–0 up in sets, playing with the consistency of a thoroughbred, I thought it was all over. But I did not reckon on the determination of Bristow. If any other player in the world had been in such a hole against Lowe he would have been sunk. But Eric always seemed to have the hex on Lobo, winking at the crowd when they booed him and stepping in arrogantly to pick off leg after leg. He eventually won 5–3 and was immensely gracious in victory, pointing out that he and John were England team colleagues and the best two players in the world.

A few months later I joined Eric on the road, and was not surprised to find his lifestyle had changed a bit from copping spare birds in Barnsley. Our first stop was a betting shop in Kensington High Street at 11 a.m. Despite being there to open the premises with Jonjo O'Neill, Eric had not bothered to shave and nobody seemed to mind. As a few punters – firemen, pub regulars and a couple of bankers – practised to try to win fifty quid for beating the Crafty Cockney, champagne was offered. Eric declined and took tiny sips from one single can of Long Life as he whipped the challengers.

At about five that afternoon we had tea at a Bayswater hotel and were joined by Eric's girlfriend, Maureen Flowers. She was then the best woman darts player in the world and the pair had set up home together in the village of Tean, near Stoke. Maureen acted as Eric's driver, ferrying him around as many as six exhibitions a week for which his nightly fee was £300. He explained his popularity thus: 'I don't need to play the bad guy any more. I don't do what I used to do, shout "If you all hate Bristow clap your hands!" then take their best players apart. They accept me now as the best: World Champion twice, World Master twice. See what I mean?'

I saw exactly what he meant three hours later. Three hundred and fifty people – including blazered old gents, young mums and about forty kids – gave him a standing ovation as he entered Lindford Workingmen's Club in Hampshire. For no apparent reason Eric was invited to an impromptu wine tasting, his second of the day, declined a glass of plonk and settled for an undistinguished pint of lager. He then beat the fourteen local challengers easily, despite a fire at the hamburger stall that blew black smoke all over the oche during the last match, and which Eric jokily described as 'sabotage'. All evening, Maureen had been doing a steady trade selling Eric Bristow dinner plates and Eric gave one to the winner of the raffle. On the microphone he winked and pulled faces as hecklers called out the names of his rivals Jocky Wilson and Alan Evans.

I had noticed that all evening he had had no more than three pints of lager. When I raised the topic of drink and darts, he gave me his philosophy: 'A few pints will relax you, but shorts and darts don't mix.' Over the next twenty-five years he stuck to this dictum. He would have a couple of pints of lager before, during and after a match. But he would never go near the whisky or the vodka.

133

Nor did I when, a few weeks later, I paired up with Eric at the 1981 Fleet Street Pro-Am Championships. I had been at a boozy BBC sports lunch and had about four pints of lager. Nobody told me that I was expected to actually play in the event so I went along happy to spectate. Next thing I knew, my name was in a hat and I pulled Eric as my partner. Ever a winner, he reminded me that this was serious; even though he was making around £2,000 a week, he was determined we'd have the trophy and the first prize of £100 each.

Sensing his mood, I switched to shandy and we took on our first opponents, Cliff Lazarenko and a journalist. At first I did not do too badly, averaging around fifty. But then I just could not get the dart accurately in the sixty area. Eric thumped in a big score, leaving me double 16. I squinted at the target, twisted my body round and leaned forward. Suddenly Brissy grabbed my tense shoulders and hissed in my ear: 'Sidney, you are a bag of bloody nerves. Relax and just go for the bloody thing.' I did, landing my first dart just inside the 16 wire. Again the hands gripped my shoulders and the voice rasped: 'Go for it but don't bust it.' I landed the two darts on the wire of double 8. 'Lovely,' said my coach and he won the game for us first dart.

Suddenly we were in the final and taking on Dave Whitcombe and a very handy, but very nervous, bearded bloke from the *Morning Star*. Again Eric scored brilliantly and soon left me double 16 again, this time for the title. My mouth was dry and my arm made of jelly. Then I felt a strong hand on my right shoulder. 'Don't bloody bust it, leave me a shot,' icy calm but totally commanding. I did. I put two darts outside the wire and one just inside. We wanted double eight to win. Eric planted it with a flourish. 'If I was you Sidney, I'd stick to commentating,' he said. On reflection, I had been given an early condensed version of what Bristow did for Phil Taylor years later. He spotted your weaknesses and cajoled and bullied you to overcome them. Inside the arrogant maestro was a latent Aristotle, eager to pass on his knowledge, just like the great philosopher himself had done with little Alexander in guiding him on the path to greatness.

A week later I got a mighty shock. I went to Middlesbrough for the British Professional championship having proudly put my £100 cheque from winning the Pro-Am in the bank. News of my successful partnership with Eric had got round and a couple of the lads congratulated me. Then Tony Green approached me with a long face. I asked him what was up.

'I was sorry to hear about your cheque, mate. Irene must be upset.' He shook his head and looked at the ground.

'What do you mean?' I gasped.

'Watneys and MY Darts have stopped your cheque – and Eric's,' Tony said gravely. 'They say the draw was fiddled so you got paired together. You could be charged with bringing the game into disrepute.'

Disrepute? As if I hadn't enough on my plate: asthmatic tubes, dodgy on the shot-outs, being slagged in *Darts World*. I was a trembling wreck as I used the phone in the hotel lobby to call home. I was going to get Irene to apologise to our bank.

'Hey up Sidney, spent the winnings yet?'

With the pips going in my ear and making a scramble for coins in my pocket, I turned to see a grinning Bristow. I blurted out: 'Cheque's been stopped, Tony says. Sponsors say we fiddled ...'

Eric snorted in derision. 'Bollocks. Greeny's pulling your leg. You know what a wind-up merchant he is.'

The pips stopped. There was no need to call home. Tony Green, who once had printed a special edition of a North London newspaper with a headline saying 'LOCAL MAN DESIGNS VERTICAL LANDING AIRPORT', describing how jumbo jets would swap wings for rotors in mid-flight and land in downtown Muswell Hill, had struck again. I really had to lighten up when in the company of these wide boys.

My next encounter with the Bristow clan was nowhere near as jolly. It occurred in January 1983 at the Embassy World Darts Championship at Jollees, in a week that could be classed as the most dramatic ever in the history of the game.

I got to Stoke in poor health, both mentally and physically. Once again, I had been trying to learn the shot-outs and once again I had failed. During my first commentary stint I developed gout in my right knee, which blew up like a balloon when, later, I jumped up with excitement and banged my leg on the commentary-box door. The door fell off a hinge and my howls of pain upset the players on stage. There were strong complaints. Next day my knee was so swollen that I could scarcely walk; nor could I put my normal trousers on. So I was loaned a light blue extra-large tracksuit with 'Jollees Stage Crew' emblazoned on the back and half-carried into the club past the queue of jeering fans. But there was an upside to the proceedings. I was not expecting to hear Nick Hunter's posh tones over talkback because he'd gone out at noon for his annual boozy lunch with snooker star Ray Reardon. This usually involved the best food and wines available at the multi-starred Poacher's Cottage restaurant, and usually lasted six or seven hours. Nick worked like a Trojan to get the coverage going and this was his sabbatical day. Or it was supposed to be.

'Who's on commentary, mmmm?' This, mumbled slowly as if by an invalid, two minutes before 'Game on'. Surely it's not Nick after a seven-hour lunch, I thought. He's not going to direct a darts match. He did. And you could not spot the joins. Mind you, he said not a single word to me about finishing sentences or talking over the darts. All I heard for an hour were breathy grunts of intense concentration. Then a gruff farewell as he sloped off to the Embassy hospitality lounge for a livener with Ray, who had challenged him to go in the scanner and show the young whippersnappers how to direct.

On the oche real drama was unfolding minute by minute. Ever fearful of the early rounds with their short format, Eric Bristow, the favourite, was living on the edge. Peter Masson of Scotland missed a dart at a double to put him out. Then Dave Lee, a blond giant with hinges tattooed inside his elbows, gave Eric a hard time. Eric struggled against Dave Whitcombe, who I described as 'Kent's answer to Dracula' since he spent all day in bed and only came out at night, and only narrowly won their quarter-final 4–3. So he was not best pleased to be sitting at home before his semi-final to see me pop up on telly and predict that he would not win his third world title. I foresaw a win for Jocky Wilson next day in the other semi against Keith Deller, aged twenty-two and a 66–1 outsider. I also gave my view that Jocky would go on to beat Eric in the final: 'Because the only man in this tournament that Eric Bristow is scared of is Jocky Wilson. In fact I reckon that in the middle of the night Eric gets out of kip and checks in the wardrobe and under the bed for the Jocky monster.' Me and my big Geordie mouth …

The reception committee waiting for me in the practice room at Jollees the next night would have put the wind up the Kray twins. Still in my stage crew tracksuit, I was greeted by a snort of fag smoke from Eric and a single word putdown: 'Dickhead!' But the real venom came from Pam, Eric's mum. She was dressed up to the nines in a shiny black outfit straight out of *Chicago*, ready to sit at ringside and support her boy. But first there was the business of the gobby Geordie non-believer to attend to. She glared at me, gritted her teeth and spat out her credo: 'MY – ERIC – IS – SCARED – OF – NO – MAN.' Each barb was emphasised by sharp taps on my chest with her handbag.

As it happens I was bag-smacked but not gobsmacked. I swiftly rustled up a pretty witty riposte: 'Jocky is not a man, he's a beast.' But I decided, as the Cockneys say, to leave it out. I swallowed the line, shrugged and went off to commentate on a Jocky win. Only it wasn't.

Keith Deller had come to the world championships as a qualifier. He was completely unknown to the general public at the start of the week. Insiders knew that he had quite a darting pedigree. Keith had learned the game from his mother: legend has it that she cooked chips with one hand and threw arrows at a board hung on the kitchen door with the other in their Ipswich home. He was a member of the crack London County side, had won the Los Angeles Open in 1982 and had just been selected for the England fifteen-man team. At Jollees he didn't half show his class. Drinking only milk away from the oche and water during his matches, he had taken some notable scalps before his semi with Jocky. Before coming up against John Lowe in the quarters he had put out the number seven seed Nicky Virachkul and the experienced Les Capewell. Lowe led Keith by 3–2 in sets, but the Tractor Boy did not panic. Face paler than the milk that was his social tipple, I called him a 'slumming angel' amongst the tattooed lager drinkers. He was almost in tears when he beat Lowe 4–3.

Then he went one better, putting out the reigning champion Jocky Wilson. But surely over eleven legs against Bristow, who would be playing in front of a 'home' crowd, the magic run of this whey-faced stripling who was attracting millions to our coverage, would hit the buffers? Wouldn't it?

I have to admit that my preparation for the Bristow/Deller final was not exactly ideal, thanks in part to Ray Reardon. I unwound as usual after the two semi-final matches with a couple of pints of bitter, having got changed from my tracksuit and put on smarter clothes. Then I was dragooned into a BBC pool team, skippered by Ray, which was taking on a BDO select. Suppose I say it myself, I played pretty well and did some nifty long potting. 'Played before, boyo,' purred Ray and I told him of my apprenticeship losing my pocket money to hustlers in Docherty's billiard hall in Ashington. He began to do a Sid-style commentary in a comic Geordie voice – 'and it's the whippet from Geordieland burnin' up the blue baize' – and I let it go to my head. I am highly allergic to alcohol after a certain amount, and I had three more pints of beer, making five in all. But the thing that did for me was that I 'smoked', or more correctly chewed, two of the buckshee Embassy panatellas. It was a totally idiotic move for an asthmatic who had been working in a smoky nightclub for a week. When

I woke up the next morning my gout was gone but I had a headache and was coughing and wheezing – great preparation for the world darts final. I cursed inwardly as I sat in a corner of the Embassy hospitality room an hour before kick-off. All around me posh-suited folk chatted and drank the free bubbly, while I hunched over a bitter lemon in a short-sleeved shirt and, for no reason I can remember, Newcastle United wrist bands.

Still, once I got into the commentary box, the sheer drama of what was unfolding banished my nerves and I forgot all about my sadly abused tubes. I was due to do the second half of the final, with Tony Green doing the first five sets. I sat behind him and could not believe what I was witnessing. Keith sailed into a 2–0 in sets lead, and the Bristow fans were stunned. Eric's eyes were glazed and his usual gladiatorial poise was replaced by the hunch of a wounded giraffe looking up at a tree bare of leaves.

Suddenly it was my turn and the intensity of the drama made me icy calm, in mind if not lip. Deller pushed the score to 5–3. He needed just one more set to beat Brissy and become world champion. Keith kept up the high-scoring, chalk from his barrels clotting the flock round the sixty bed. 'The red bit looks like it's been hit by a blizzard,' I yelled. 'Deller has all the firepower of Baby Face Nelson.' I later got a letter accusing me of making up the name of the famous American gangster! 'Deller – all the open-eyed innocence of Luke Skywalker.' And then the drama became unbelievable. 'Brissy looks as peevish as a peckish pterodactyl' – think beaked nose, goggly eyes, arms flapping like broken windmills. The score was two legs each in set nine and Deller just wanted a double for the title. He had seven attempts and missed the lot! Brissy pegged back to 5–4, then 5–5. Surely the class and the experience of the Crafty Cockney would dominate proceedings now? They didn't. In the heat of the fray, Eric Bristow, genius of the sport, the most instinctive finisher ever, committed one of the biggest blunders in the history of the game.

At 2–1 to Keith in the eleventh set, Eric, with one dart in his hand, needed 50 to save the match. Keith needed 138 to win the title. Deller's shot was hard, but Brissy should have gone for the bull. He did not. He threw a single 18 to leave double 16 next time. He gambled on Keith missing. Keith stepped up calmly and hit 60, treble 18, double 12. He danced round the stage as Eric slumped, looking up to the gods of darts for a reason. 'Deller's MP has been on from Ipswich, probably to give him the freedom of the city. If he was my lad I'd *give* him Ipswich,' was my summing up.

To say that the incident still rankles with Eric is to put it mildly. Every time a player wants 138 during our Sky coverage, Eric's voice pleads from the spotter position: 'Don't mention bloody Deller and bloody 1983, Sidney.' I try not to, honest.

Over the next twelve months Eric did not brood or let the grass grow under his feet. If anything, he was cockier than ever. He played Jocky Wilson at Livingston in West Lothian, in a challenge match and goaded the crowd so much that a punter threw a can of McEwan's export at him. It missed Eric and crashed into the surround. Quick as a flash Eric grabbed the mike and said: 'You're just like Jocky, pal – can't hit the fucking target.' He took on Keith Deller in two replays of their world final classic and honours were even. Then the pair fought out a brilliant final of the British Matchplay championship and Eric just squeaked it. He seemed to have mellowed, saying Keith was 'a great player'. Mind you, Bobby George still got branded a 'Mickey Mouse' player whenever his name cropped up!

Eric came to the 1984 Embassy as world ranked number one by a street: he had fifty-four points to Jocky's thirty-nine, and Dave Whitcombe's thirty. This time there was no self-doubt, no outsider to grab his glory, no first-round jitters and no daft decisions. Brissy sailed through the field, 'little finger poised, fit to grace any garden party', as I felt obliged to put it. He crushed Dave Whitcombe 7–1 in sets to become world champion for the third time. During the 'exhibition', at which Dave was a virtual spectator, I tried to sum up the Bristow performance: 'Bristow reasons; Bristow quickens; aaaaah Bristow!' And maybe my enthusiasm was getting through to the doubters; the *Sunday Times* said of the world championships that only Jocky and Eric 'could raise darts to the level of championship sport.' Nancy Banks-Smith, writing in the *Guardian*, thought I was doing a grand job: 'Sid Waddell's commentaries are the black puddings of sports reporting, hot and bursting with blood and guts.' She also liked my analysis of the mental side of the sport: 'I don't know if Freud and Jung would agree with me, but you can overpsyche sometimes for a darts match.' I was now getting confident that my own sense of humour, sometimes dry, sometimes slapstick, was helping folk appreciate the skills and character of the players.

In the run-up to the 1985 Embassy, Eric had continued to rewrite the darts history book. By the time he took the stage at Jollees as favourite, this was his list of major achievements: *News of the World*

Champion twice; British Open Champion and Embassy World Champion three times; World Master four times. I once got off a train at Bradford station and went into the bar for a quickie. It was Saturday afternoon and a big darts event had been on ITV. I asked a lad at the bar who had won.

'Who *always* wins, bloody Bristow, of course!' came the reply. You'd have thought I'd asked him if the sun had risen in the east that day.

Eric's preparation, he told me, had been perfect. 'Me and Maureen live in a house alongside a church and graveyard. So the next-door neighbours are no trouble. I'll not hang about down Jollees with the lads, I'll be back here after every match trying to get some sleep. I'll listen to the church clock strike the wee hours and maybe nod off as the birdies start to sing. But some of my rivals will still be tossing and turning, believe you me.'

But it was Eric who was tossing and turning in his first-round match against the qualifier Kenny Summers. First-round nerves again got to Eric, and Kenny only needed double 16 in leg three of the second set to put him out 2–0. Then class kicked in and Eric won the next six legs to take the match. Just before the match I looked in the programme for something to say about the little-known Summers and read that he was a 'shop proprietor'. I asked a group of officials if they knew what kind of shop. I was told that it was a bookshop. So I told the viewers solemnly: 'Kenny proves that not all darts players are Philistines, he runs a bookshop in Peterborough.' After the match I was passing a table where Cliff Lazarenko was holding court and he called me over. 'You gave us a right laugh there about Kenny's bookshop; he sells porn!' And sure enough, not long after, the shop was raided and Kenny sent to prison for a spell.

The Cockney continued in cruise control for the rest of the week, before beating John Lowe 6–2 in the final. It was his fourth Embassy victory and I told the viewers that I could see him winning the title ten times. I also gave the opinion that 'If Eric Bristow was at Cape Canaveral he'd take off before the rocket.' Nobody had the merest clue that a very dark star was about to enter the Bristow orbit and it was set on a collision course.

There were no signs of any mental or physical glitches in the Bristow progress through 1985 to a third world championship on the trot. He won the MFI World Matchplay and the World Cup singles in a golden autumn and seemed nailed on for the Embassy. The venue would be very different from his 'home pitch' at Jollees in Stoke. Darts was moving its showpiece event to Frimley Green in the stock-broker belt of Surrey. And what a splendid gaff we walked into: the Lakeside Country Club, otherwise known as Bob Potter's Palace. Bob, a former dance band drummer, had built up arguably the best club in Britain. Tom Jones, Jim Davidson and other stars packed the joint, while Mrs Thatcher herself said it was one of her favourite places for Tory party jollies.

When I got to Frimley Green and saw the draw, I was completely gobsmacked. First round: Alan Evans versus Eric Bristow. Who is writing this script? I asked myself, Roald Dahl? Ring Lardner? Woody Allen? The Crafty Cockney against the Prince of Dartness was bound to be a belter. It wasn't. After an early burst of pure Celtic fire, Alan had shot his bolt and Eric and his fans breathed easier. The score-line was 3–1. After the match I had a couple of beers with a mellow Evans. He had enjoyed the match, he said and was revelling in his new appointment as Welsh team captain. Needle between him and Eric? I asked. 'Only for the cameras, Sidney, nothing personal,' he winked. I did not believe a word. Then one of Alan's hangers-on, a big guy with scars and tattoos and a Manchester accent, asked if I wanted to step outside. This was in no way a threat – he simply said he wanted to show me a sawn-off shotgun he kept in his trunk. I shook my head, supped up and sloped off.

I ended up having a nightcap in the Embassy hospitality suite, usually the star dressing room, with Nick Hunter and Peter Dyke, the flamboyant dynamo behind the sponsor's efforts. Suddenly in walked Bob Potter himself, eager to find out what Nick thought about the venue after day one. Nick praised everything, with one important exception. 'The only thing I can criticise, Bob, is the lighting.' He winked at Peter and me: 'It would be better for us if it were more powerful.' Bob frowned and shot out of the room.

Next morning Nick and I walked into the club when a beaming Bob approached us. I noticed that he was not his usual suave, well-groomed self. He was unshaven, dusty-faced and wearing tatty overalls. 'Come and see the lights now,' he said to Nick. 'Me and a couple of the lads have been up most of the night and we've changed all the bulbs.' They had been up ladders replacing well over 1,000 bulbs in the chandeliers with more powerful ones. 'Be with you in a tick, said Nick. Bob left. 'Spoof?' I asked. 'Spoof,' Nick replied. 'What a bloke!'

The week was dominated by Eric Bristow's regal procession to his third Embassy on the trot. Eric said before a dart was thrown that he would meet Dave Whitcombe in the final and beat him six–nil. He did precisely that and got this accolade from John Sadler in the *Sun*: 'Bristow's win was achieved with an acceptance and confidence bordering on contempt. The Crafty Cockney is a phenomenon. Quite simply, the most dominating and invincible figure in British sport.' During my commentaries that week I had been as bold as to broaden that concept considerably. I said that Eric was fit to be ranked with world sporting greats like Carl Lewis, John McEnroe and Viv Richards. I also waxed topical on the semi-final, when Eric took on Alan Glazier. Eric's doubling was spot on and I reached for a current political allusion. The telly news had just shown Michael Heseltine sweeping out of 10 Downing Street, gold locks streaming like battle flags, having resigned over the Westland helicopter affair. 'Brissy is going out quicker than the Secretary of State for Trade and Industry,' I yelled. Nick Hunter liked it so much that he stopped calling me Ayatollah and started calling me Hezza instead.

Eric was in superb form when interviewed after the match. 'I was just starting to warm up when it was all over. Sorry for Dave? Yeah, of course, I'll feel sorry for Dave when I'm downing my last large brandy to celebrate.' Then he said something that in hindsight could have been recklessly tempting fate. 'The further you go in any sport, you wonder how long it can last. *But I think I can still dominate this game when I'm forty.*' In fact, he was twenty-eight, and by the time he was thirty, due to dartitis, he had stopped dominating the game. Eric reached the Embassy finals of 1987, 1989 and 1990, but never won another world championship.

Despite Eric's achievements, it was sometimes difficult to

convince some people to take the sport seriously. Just hours before Eric won his third title, I was carefully making the case for darts to a highly sceptical John Inverdale on sports radio. He was insisting that, with all the beer flowing about, darts players could not be as fit as, for example, jockeys. 'Don't be daft,' I said. 'The jockeys don't have to be fit – it's the horses that do the galloping and jumping.' And John was at it again on *A Question of Sport* in 2004. I was on a roll, getting half a dozen right answers, much to the delight of my skipper Ally McCoist. 'It's not fair,' bleated Invers. 'He's getting all the questions on pub sports, not proper sports.' So, how long have baseball, indoor bowls and rugby league been played in boozers? I wouldn't care, but John was on my team!

Being the champion of darts in the media can be dangerous. Before the 1986 Embassy world championship I went on the radio show *Start the Week*, hosted by Henry Kelly. After I had made the case for darts, Henry asked me if women's darts was as good as men's. I said that women's darts was 'like watching paint dry', even at the top level. I ventured the suggestion that having breasts was a disadvantage in getting the right stance. This angered Jeanette Winterson, the novelist, who was another guest on the show so much that she screeched: 'Why don't they cut their tits off then?' Henry swiftly moved to discussing photographing celebrities with David Bailey before Jeanette hit me.

There is no doubt in my mind that dartitis robbed Eric Bristow of five more world darts championship titles. Dartitis is like the 'yips' that happens in golf: the player cannot co-ordinate mind and muscle to make the right shot. The worst case I have ever seen was in 1984 when Rab Fotheringham, an experienced Scottish international, toed the oche against England in Edinburgh. It was embarrassing to watch. Rab just could not release the dart at the right time. In the end he just straightened his arm hopefully and let gravity take its course.

The viewing millions never saw Brissy so badly affected. In fact, after the onset of dartitis in the autumn of 1986, Eric got to the Embassy finals of 1987, 1989 and 1990 and won the World Cup singles. I don't think he ever got rid of the condition completely, and he himself admits that for the rest of his career it was always at the back of his mind: 'I'd be standing in a pub practising on my own and it would strike. I couldn't let go of the bloody dart. I was gutted. There were floods of tears. I thought the only world I had known since I was eleven was gone.'

I did not know about the problem when I went to the Crafty Cockney club in the Burslem area of Stoke in early December 1986. Eric had overseen the conversion of a miners' institute into a darts palace, and had been its star attraction since it opened in the middle of 1985. I wanted to talk about his drop in form; since winning the North American and Australian Opens in August he had had a very lean time at top tournaments. Was he worried? 'Nah. I've just done a showbiz pairs for telly and I was with Frank Carson. John Lowe was with Lord Charles. Great casting! Me with a comic and Lobo with a wooden dummy.'

Our interview about the upcoming Embassy world championship was conducted over a game of snooker and Eric was awaiting the arrival of a coachload of darters. He would play several games against them, just like he did every night. It struck me that Brissy had a lot on his plate. I was even more convinced of this when he said that he had so many exhibitions lined up he was only getting three nights off per month. 'My agent Dick Allix put my fee up to between £800 and £1,000 a night to try to cut the work down, but I'm more in demand than ever.' Dick Allix confirms that the workload was a major factor in Eric's nightmare with the dartitis, which got worse.

Eric's practice sessions were stymied by it and he struggled in tournaments. It got so bad that he did not want to go to any of the hundred exhibition dates arranged with Mitchells & Butler brewery. When told of Eric's problem, Malcolm Powell, the company's director of PR, said: 'If Bristow can't let go of his darts, we'll just stick a chair on stage and have him talk for an hour.' It never got to that, but if it had, Eric would have knocked them in the aisles; he was always a good bet for charisma and cracking wise. He even tried hypnotherapy, but it was to no avail. He said to Allix: 'I thought myself into this and I'll think myself out.' Another factor was that in early 1988 Eric split up with Maureen Flowers, his partner of several years. Happily, there were patches of the old Bristow magic in the gloom. In July 1988 he went to Tokyo and blitzed a top field to take the World Darts Grand Prix and a first prize of one million yen – £42,500.

Something else that I think is relevant is captured in the phrase that Dave Lanning once used. 'Taylor is a mugger; Bristow was a burglar.' This is a key concept in the discussion of Eric's unique talent and how the dartitis crippled it. Taylor's three-dart average in world championships is around 102, and opponents know they have to match this. Eric's best-ever Embassy average was 95, which he achieved in 1984. It was never his heavy scoring that beat opponents; it was the element of 'burglary'. He *instinctively* stepped in when given an opportunity. He never had to pause to count. Most players, with the exception of Jocky and Alan Evans, let themselves be psyched out by him. But that was before the dartitis struck. And though it was past its worst when Eric narrowly lost to Jocky Wilson in the 1989 Embassy final, it lurks to this day.

It is well known that Eric became a mentor and sponsor of Phil Taylor, but what is possibly not so widely known is that the partnership was forged when Phil helped Brissy struggle with the dartitis. In June 1985 Phil and his wife Yvonne had one of their rare nights out. They chose the Crafty Cockney club because it was close to their home and the prices were reasonable for their tight budget. Phil watched, unimpressed, as Eric gave an exhibition on stage. He told Yvonne that he did not like Eric's big-headed attitude and apparent lack of respect for his opponents. 'I could beat him,' he told her. At first she thought he was kidding, but nevertheless bought Phil a set of darts for his birthday.

In a matter of months Phil became a member of the crack Huntsman pub team and by autumn 1987 was in the Staffordshire county side alongside Eric. The pair began practising hard together and there is no doubt that these sessions helped Eric fight dartitis. Early in 1988 Eric suggested that Phil pack in work making ceramic toilet-chain and beer-pump handles and try life as a professional darter. He was willing to put up thousands of pounds to back Phil's efforts on the basis: 'Pay me back if you win anything.' I personally do not think Eric ever hoped to make a single penny out of the arrangement. I reckon it was partly gratitude for the help in combating dartitis and partly a bit of 'insurance' – to groom a protégé to reach the heights that he himself might be denied. Me – an incurable romantic?

'Winning is the best medicine known to man' was the motto Eric had lived by and he wanted to drum the message into Phil. The methods he used certainly lacked psychological subtlety and were at times positively humiliating. When Phil won his first big title, the 1988 Canadian Open, Eric was waiting at the bottom of the stage to collect the $5,000 cheque from him. When Phil made a rare appearance in the bar to buy a Coke before a county match, Eric looked up from a crib game and said: ''Ere, you shouldn't be in bars enjoying yourself. You owe me money, so get practising.' If Phil rang Eric from a tournament and said he'd played well but got knocked out, Eric would sneer and tell him only to ring when he won.

The dartitis had affected Brissy's throwing arm, but not his tongue. At an international match in Scotland around this time, he and Jocky Wilson were the opposing captains. Each was supposed to make a short speech after the draw, which was held in the closing stages of a very boozy dinner. Now, I had been in Eric and Jocky's company and observed that both were taking the drink very carefully. Not so two of the VIPs on the top table. Both Olly Croft of the BDO and the chairman of the sponsors had been well into the whisky before the speeches were due. It showed. There were mumblings and mistakes from both parties that did not go unnoticed by the lads. Bristow did not waste the opportunity, nor any words. 'Well, here's a turn-up for the books,' he indicated the two VIPs. 'Remember how many times us players have been bollocked for being pissed at the dinner? Well, just take a look at the bosses.' It brought the house down, with both teams cheering Eric on.

Nor was Eric stuck for a rejoinder when some MPs criticised his MBE award in 1989. One said: 'All you have to do is have a big fat beer gut and you get a gong.' Eric's reply: 'Every time you listen to a broadcast from the House of Commons, the MPs sound like a bunch of schoolboys. The furthest they walk is to the bar.'

I have mentioned the romance of darts, and I was not kidding. What kind of writer other than a Barbara Cartland or Rudyard Kipling could have come up with this plot? The scene is the world darts final and the contestants are the sorcerer and his apprentice. In one corner Eric Bristow, five times world champion, who seems to have cast off the thrall of dartitis and is ranked world number one. In the other corner his protégé Phil Taylor, unknown outside the Potteries, who the bookies make a 100–1 shot for the title.

I commentated on the first half of the 1990 Embassy world darts final and gave the viewers the full story. 'These two have practised together for weeks now, over marathon distances. Eric has a beer and a fag on the go down the pub and Phil wears carpet slippers and drinks black tea.' I also coined the phrase 'the Crafty Potter' for Taylor. He told me later that he preferred it to 'Eric's sidekick', as some of the other players had sneeringly dubbed him. They did not call him that for long; for two sets Eric was in the hunt, then he was blitzed. Phil took the match six–one in sets with a 97.5 average, and he was only just starting; the 100+ averages were yet to come. Eric hardly spoke to Phil for six months afterwards, but George, Eric's dad, had advice for his son that possibly really rankled: 'Never, never teach somebody to take your job.'

My favourite Eric Bristow story concerns a run-in he had with the police over a plastic snowman around Christmas 1994. Eric had been voted Scallywag of the Month by *Loaded* magazine and they sent me to interview him about the incident. Apparently the cops near Eric's home in Staffordshire had him and some boozing pals under surveillance, expecting high jinks over the festive season. They were not wrong. Eric takes up the story: 'So we're in this pub, four of us, and we know the landlord. Now he's got this five-foot plastic snowman out in the car park and he's a bit worried, what with all the vandalism, that it might get damaged or nicked. So we've had a few beers and we volunteer to go outside and bring it in for him. It's a right laugh, four grown men dancing around with this snowman.

'Next thing you know a police car comes up, stops and I put the snowman on top of it saying, "Take him home, he's drunk." The police are not amused. They said their car has been scratched. "Send us a bill and we'll pay it tomorrow," I say, rubbing at the mark. Next thing you know there's thirteen bloody cars there, twenty-seven police, dogs, the lot. You'd have thought I was Mike bloody Tyson.'

Result: a £1,300 fine. Sometimes, when you lead with your lip …

I must admit that I and many others thought that Eric would now only appear in the headlines as a Jack the Lad, sarcastic elder statesman of the darts circus or a voluble pundit. We were all wrong. On Friday, 3 January, 1997 Eric's demon darts put him back in the sporting limelight big time. BRISTOW GRAVY TRAIN ROLLS AGAIN screamed the message across two pages of the *Daily Express*.

The article reported Eric's progress to the quarter-finals of the WDC World Darts Championship and mentioned the storm that his renaissance had caused in the Sky commentary box.

Dave Lanning and I took up the fairy story the next night, when Eric took on Alan Warriner. The winner would go on to play Phil Taylor in the semi-final. Dave told the viewers that we were all privileged to be seeing the old Eric: 'It takes your breath away to see the resuscitation of a legend.' I concurred and dared to dream the impossible dream, 'They made Dick Whittington lord mayor of London, maybe Eric is on some secret list up in the sky...'

The dream continued as Eric beat Alan.

I still could scarcely believe that I was about to commentate on a Bristow/Taylor semi when I woke up at the Palms Hotel in Grays the next morning. I was cleaning my teeth and trembling at the prospect like a nervous whippet when my phone rang. It was Harry the Dog, alias Harry Findlay, a professional gambler who I worked with on Sky. Years before Harry had won £80,000 when Arsenal won the double, but had lost about £30,000 when Gina Gee failed to win the Eurovision Song Contest.

''Ere, Sidney, old Brissy ain't got a prayer against Phil, has he?'

I stopped brushing for a thoughtful second.

'Tell me Eric's got no chance – please.' Harry was pleading.

'Well, the way he's playing, he could possibly beat the Power,' I almost whispered.

A giant squeaky groan fizzled down the airwaves. 'I stand to lose eighteen grand if Taylor does not win the final,' said Harry.

'In that case, Harry, my only advice is to have a stiff drink, hide behind the settee and watch the match with your hands over your eyes.'

He did not answer.

In going on thirty years of commentating I don't think I've ever been in an atmosphere quite like the one generated by the Bristow/Taylor clash. Ten minutes before Eric was announced, three-quarters of the crowd, many of whom were in nappies when Eric was Mr Darts, were on their feet and singing 'Walking in a Bristow Wonderland'. Then he appeared to 'London Calling' and they raised their arms and their glasses to him as if he were a Caesar, come to the Circus Tavern to accept homage. When he reached the stage his cheeks were smeared with lipstick from female fans. 'Eric looks as though he has been mugged by an Avon lady,' I yelled. Taylor ran a similar gamut. Despite being at the centre of a flying wedge of bouncers, his carefully styled hair was a Worzel Gummidge by the time he got on stage. It was obvious the crowd was 90 per cent for Brissy; the arrogant brat they all loved to hate in his heyday was now the scarred veteran, an object of affection as well as veneration.

The match caught fire at the end of the eighth set. Eric was 4–3 down in sets but was playing very coolly. He had a mean look in his eyes. But Taylor looked poised to win when he got to 2–1 in legs. Eric looked at the floor as Taylor went for double four for the match. He missed. Eric wanted 141 with three darts to save the match. 'Eric does not look like a man in the form to get this three-darter,' I screeched. But he did. And the crowd went wild as he made it 4–4 in sets. 'Stay behind that settee, Harry,' I said, 'Old Brissy's on a roll.' The crowd were now wild, singing 'There's only one Eric

Bristow'. The players were in a cauldron of pure darting hysteria so we had a five-minute break before the ninth set, which had to be won by two clear legs.

Taylor looked angry at the start of the set. He said later that when he high-fived Eric after Eric's 141 escape shot, Eric's hand came in 'like a Tyson cross' and had really hurt him. He did not mean that Eric had meant it to hurt, but his reaction was: 'Right you bastard, you are going to get it now.' But in the event, Phil did not need the aggro. Eric began rushing his darts and going off balance. At 4–3 down in legs, Eric had two darts at double 8 to save the match. He failed and Taylor won on double 2.

The crowd chanted 'Bristow, Bristow' as the players shook hands. Our cameras cut to a profile of the proud warrior, tears welling in his eyes, framed by straggly garlands of tarnished Christmas tinsel. 'Yet more of the cruel poetry of the game,' I said softly. Years later, Phil Taylor agreed. He said that if Eric had beaten him that night he would probably have got his name on the world trophy at least one more time.

That match against Taylor was Eric's last realistic stab at reviving the old glory days. But he never gave up hope. In the first week of December 2004 Alan Fraser of the *Daily Mail* rang me up and asked for my thoughts on Eric turning up at the New Walton workingmen's club in Hull to try to qualify for the 2005 Ladbrokes.com World Championship. There were eight places up for grabs and 163 hopefuls. He had failed to win through.

I was tempted to speak of Hemingway's leopard and why he was cooling his heels in the snows of Kilimanjaro. I settled for much more mundane prosody: 'Brissy is like an old cowboy with his beans and saddle sores on his bum. He just loves being out on the range.'

I think the analogy is illuminating. The movies are full of old cowboys and grizzled gunslingers reluctant to give up the thrills of life on the frontier. I predict that Eric, who turned fifty this year, will be still trying to qualify for the world championship or the Windy City Open when he is seventy. Because, to liquidise yet another great western cliché: 'A man's gotta go where a man's gotta throw.'

6

Singing Pirate of Lakeside

By the time we moved the Embassy world darts circus to Lakeside I had just about completed my apprenticeship as a commentator. But I had also been grafting hard at another role: a mixture of ringmaster, court jester and workingmen's club concert secretary. 'Right you lot, if you don't behave I'll cancel the bingo and bring that comedian back on.'

You'll not be surprised to learn that in this field I was a natural. Ever since I was a little lad larking around the back lanes of a Geordie pit village, I have had a strong, but very skewed, Thespian streak. In 1944 I used to make people laugh with my Winston Churchill impressions. I would pretend to smoke a clothes-peg cigar and growl about 'more tanks and more ships'. At grammar school in the 1950s I was always made a spear carrier in school plays because I would never do lines straight; I'd ad-lib for laughs. At Cambridge University Rag Week in 1960 I played a camp goalie in a mixed-sex soccer team and went down a bomb. I even got invites to tea and crumpet from a couple of gays.

The peak came in 1964 when a pal of mine called Charles E Hall and I went on the boards as 'The Steaming Hot Gravyboatmen'. We did pubs, clubs and even *Tonight* on BBC national television. We were meant to be a satirical version of Simon and Garfunkel but there were two big problems: Charles could only play two chords on his guitar, and I am tone deaf. We packed up after we were booed off and almost lynched at the South Bank Sporting Club in Middlesbrough.

When I joined up with the darts lads I could never overcome my compulsion to make people laugh. I think wanting to be liked is a very working-class thing and it can run deep. I always feel the need to be popular, especially amongst strangers, because it covers up a mass of insecurities. Will I get the scores wrong? Will my accent go down badly with the viewers? Will the darts players object if I take the piss occasionally with lines like 'Cliff's idea of exercise is a firm press on a soda siphon' or 'Jocky Wilson – what an athlete'? You would never get away with cracks like this on air about Roy Keane or Andy Flintoff, but darts is different. Darts commentators socialise with the players. For thirty years I have sung rugby songs and karaoke, played darts, dominoes, pool, even spoon fighting over late-night rounds of drinks with just about everybody in the game. And there has always been an unspoken *quid pro quo*: 'You can take the piss out of us, Sidney, if now and then you make a fool of yourself.'

Because the first few Embassy world championships were so intense, the 'cabaret' element of top darts seemed to crystallise at the Unipart British Professional championships on Teesside in the years from 1982 to 1988. Once or twice players qualified for this event, jumped in the car with a couple of mates and came along for a jolly. I remember Rocky Jones, built like a prop forward and with the thirst of a coalface worker, coming into the workingmen's club next to the venue, the Redcar Bowl, obviously well refreshed by a few pints on the journey up from the pits of South Wales. He swiftly downed a couple of pints of Strongarm before shooting off to play his first-round match. Our BBC team and some BDO officials were made members of the club for a week each year. One year the club football team even recruited ex-Tranmere professional Ray Stubbs, now presenter of *Grandstand*, as a midfield dynamo. Ray played so well that they did not want him to leave.

But the main cause of the annual outbreak of histrionics and other extrovert behaviour was the sponsor's pre-semi-final bash, which kicked off at noon on the Friday and which kind of melted into the evening's play. Tony Green and I had made a pact a couple of years earlier that, come what may, we would not get the sack for boozing at the wrong time. But what do you do, when, all suited and tied up at noon, you are offered free drink and cigars for the next six hours? Well, over the years I did my best to sip the water while all around me drank the wine, and the beer and the brandy. It was made easier by the fact that a little party piece was expected from a few select Beeb people and BDO lads, and I often had been up all night working on mine. I felt that alcohol might jade my performance.

So it was at the 1982 event that I found myself outside an open window of the banqueting suite at about 3.30 awaiting my cue. I was dressed in a blue tammy, T-shirt, kilt and had a toilet roll around my hips as a sporran. I was toting a bottle of Bacardi. The point was that Jocky Wilson, the holder, had been banned from the tournament, but was now turning up – disguised as a Geordie.

The MC shouted: 'So please put you hands together for John Thomas Wilson ...' I climbed in through the window shouting meaningless Celtic drivel and declaimed a poem I'd written proclaiming Jocky's innocence. It was cheered to the rafters by the bibulous throng. But more to the point, it was a benchmark. Yet more exotic 'cabaret' was expected from me at future tournaments. Why could I not simply give a witty speech like Tony Green or sing 'Danny Boy' like Tony Gubba? Part of the answer is that I am tone deaf and that I am truly hopeless at making after-dinner speeches. Pantomime, with its broad brushstrokes, has always appealed. And my Jocky Wilson impression was only the start.

While I was researching the book on Jocky, Bobby George had become a good pal of mine. We had in common that we were both patter merchants, the kind of lads who could never resist a wisecrack in school. Bobby coined the phrase '180s for show – doubles for dough' and I used it frequently. He was always tickled when I used lines about him like 'Bobby's done up like an electric purple liquorice allsort.' And, knowingly or otherwise, he sometimes talked complete bollocks. He once pulled me up about suggesting to a newspaper that darts players were thick. 'I'll have you know,' he said pompously, 'that one of my relatives has five GECs!'

During the 1982 Unipart Bobby came to me with tidings from my own relatives. He had recently been doing exhibitions in the Ashington area and had had his ear bent. He joined me and my stepson Nicholas at breakfast in our Middlesbrough hotel and let rip: 'You are a disgrace Sidney, a disgrace to your family.' He was frowning, but knowing Bobby, I was waiting for a joke and a giggle. But he continued in serious vein: 'I have just done a week in your neck of the woods and some of your cousins came up and said you never visit them, or your mum and dad. Too big for your boots they reckon.'

It wasn't true. Irene and the kids and I had spent New Year up in Lynemouth with my parents. Still, it hurt. 'So?' I said defensively.

'So, meet me in the car park in ten minutes and I'll whizz the pair of you over there in my white Roller,' said Bobby.

It was not exactly a state-of-the-art Rolls-Royce; its canvas roof sagged a bit, but its brightwork was shiny and its seats were plushly comfy. I sat in the front next to Bobby and Nicholas sat snug in the back. All the way to the Tyne Tunnel, Bobby had us fascinated by his stories about his money-making ventures. The Roller was second-hand and one of a fleet that Bobby rented out for weddings and film shoots. Nick and I soon realised that we were travelling with a very sharp operator. As we swished through East Northumberland, I recalled the one and only time Bobby's razor-sharp antenna did not spot genuine trouble.

A few months earlier at the Embassy world championships, two men walked into the reception of our hotel and asked for Bobby George. I happened to be in the area and got a bit worried; the men were big, sombre-suited and wore extremely severe expressions. I put them down for police. 'Can I help?' I asked. They asked if I knew Bobby and I said I did. Then they asked me to ring his room and ask him down 'to answer a few questions'. I went in a booth, rang Bobby and told him flatly that two blokes wanted to see him – adding, 'I reckon they're fuzz.' I should have known what to expect.

I was sitting with the two men in the crowded bar area when Bobby breezed in five minutes later. He was glowing with bonhomie and smelled of aftershave as he stretched his be-ringed right hand out in greeting. The men looked askance at the umpteen carats on display and exchanged tight glances. 'What's this all about then, lads?' asked Bobby. I was frantically gesturing, with my thumbs up, that the cops were kosher.

'Mr George, a lady has rung in saying that she believes some of your jewellery was stolen from her house.' The policeman's tone was firm and foreboding. He went on, 'Can you give us any proof that the rings belong to you?' Bobby looked quizzical, then he beamed: 'This one is definitely mine. I've got the paperwork at home.' He began twiddling at the bigger rings. 'But as for these others, as you've copped me fair and square, I'll come clean. I nicked this one from a house in Barking and this one from Dagenham ...' He was halfway through a long list of 'offences' when he realised that the 'blokes' were not amused. One of them reached inside his jacket and flipped open a warrant card. Bobby turned as bright as one of his sequins. 'But Sid ... I thought ... spoof ...'

Maybe my recounting this yarn put ideas into Bobby's head, because as we came past the chimneys of Lynemouth colliery, Bobby stopped the car and ordered me to get out and get in the back. He told Nicholas and I to slide down on to the floor. 'I'm gonna surprise your dad,' he said. He stopped the Roller outside the terraced cottage at 102 Dalton Avenue, strode past my dad's leek trench and banged his rock-clad fist on the door.

The door opened and my dad, also named Bob, peered out. Nick and I could hear the exchange through the open window.

'Mr Waddell, I'm from the police. We are anxious to trace the whereabouts of one Sidney Waddell, a con man who is going around claiming to be a darts commentator …'

'Police?' said my dad. 'In a leather jacket and a car the length of the street? Howway in and stop working yersell, Bobby.'

The next twenty minutes were pure comedy. Over mugs of tea and bacon sandwiches, provided by Martha, my mum, the two Bobs set the world to rights, talking about about darts, football, whippets and politics. Bob spoke in guttural Geordie, punctuated by 'ye knaas', and Bobby in racy Estuary English, with the odd 'fuck' for emphasis. Occasionally they swapped a vigorous nod and a 'Yes, Bob.' But they might as well have each been chatting to a Russian.

As we climbed back into the Roller, laden with Martha's home-made sausage rolls and fruit cake – because no wayfarer leaves a Geordie home empty-handed – Bobby laughed. 'Great man yer dad, Sid. Didn't understand a word he said, but what a lovely fellow.'

The following summer I repaid the favour by having Bobby and top referee Martin Fitzmaurice as my house-guests in Pudsey. The occasion was a testimonial cricket match for Colin Johnson, of Pudsey St Lawrence and Yorkshire, and Bobby had agreed to stage a darts exhibition after the game. The pair were due at my house at about two o'clock on the Sunday, and I started getting worried at about half-past three. Mobile phones were not de rigueur in those days, so all I could do was fret and imagine breakdowns on the long drive up from Essex. Then all was well; Bobby's car pulled up outside my house and he and Martin came in – famished. There had been horren-dous traffic and the journey had taken them six hours. Now, Bobby is a big lad and, in those days, Martin was even bigger, so what could I do? Answer: carve up two chickens that were intended as Sunday dinner for Irene and our five kids, who were at the park. I nibbled some bread and a sliver of slimy meat as the Essex lads set to like Friar Tuck and Little John breaking a week-long fast. Soon there was nothing left but a pile of well-gnawed chicken bones. We were due to leave and show our faces at the cricket, so I scrawled a note for Irene. 'Sorry about the kids' dinner – there's some cheese in the fridge.' I was not popular when the family joined me later at the match.

Although he was often the life and soul of the party at the Unipart event on Teesside, Bobby was never much of a boozer, so he sometimes missed out on late-night fun – like the spoonfighting.

I did not particularly like drinking with the Beeb lot after play was finished for the night; the finer points of video editing or office politics at the telly centre left me cold. I much preferred to have a few jars with the players, particularly Peter Locke and Ceri Morgan. One of their favourite after-hours watering holes was the Saltscar pub in Redcar. This is where I was introduced to spoonfighting.

It was about midnight and I was feeling no pain when landlord Trevor Fowler pulled the curtains and set up more ale. Apart from Peter and Ceri, there were a couple of other darters there for the lock-in and a dozen or so locals. Somebody chucked more coal on the fire and a couple of beery voices rose in ragged song, only to be hushed by the mighty arm of Peter Locke, raised gladiatorially. 'I reckon it's time for a spoonfight, Wales against the rest,' he growled. The bearded Morgan, rumoured to have acquired boozy ways to spite religious parents, agreed. I was surprised how quickly Trevor took up the challenge, nominating two local lads apparently at random. 'You can be the referee, Sid,' said Trevor. I protested ignorance but was handed a large soup spoon and told to get on with it.

Subtle the game was not. The Welshmen, as challengers, both knelt on the floor with their heads bowed and their eyes shut. One of the two Saltscar team members, a burly bloke in overalls, placed the soup spoon between his teeth and began to whack Locke on the head. I was ordered to count the blows. When I got to ten I was shocked to see that the second local kid, skinny and spotty-faced, had in his hand a large ladle. He began thumping it rhythmically on Locke's head. Trevor motioned that I keep counting. I did – to six, when Locke yelled 'Enough.' He remained kneeling with his eyes closed while Ceri got the same treatment. He lasted for only seven spoons and three ladles. Both the Welshmen agreed that a total of twenty-six was unbeatable. Trevor winked at me and some of the locals lads giggled.

Locke began the second half with the spoon in his teeth, aiming it at the spotty kid. After ten heavy taps he cued in Ceri with the ladle. By now Ceri was a bit erratic, but he still landed a few sold crunches, and a few more, and a few more. When he got to seventeen he was red-faced and sweating but Spotty's face was as beatific as if he was having a scalp massage. I stopped the contest and declared a victory for the Salty. Spotty opened his eyes and made inroads on his pint. He didn't even rub his head.

'He's been coming in here for two years and he's never been beat,' said Trevor. 'Says he doesn't feel a thing.'

Peter talked about nothing else on the way back to our hotel in a taxi, but I never did get Ceri's opinion. He was so overcome by the defeat that he slept the night on a bench in the Salty's bar.

Now, I feel it appropriate to give an honest blow-by-blow account of my own biggest night of darting shame. It happened on Teesside at the 1988 Unipart event and it was pure hubris: I went from hero to zero in less than twenty-four hours.

In the previous few months the national press had started writing me up as some kind of genius manqué. At the 1988 Embassy the *Daily Star* dubbed me 'Silly Sid, the well-known English grammar strangler' after I described Bob Anderson's defeat of John Lowe: 'The Limestone Cowboy rode into town and left Lowe in Dry Gulch Creek.' And that October week at Redcar I really went to town. I was praised for my one-liners from Monday onwards and I let my hair and my guard down on Thursday night. I woke up at about eleven after a skinful of Newcastle Brown, had a shave and got smart for the pre-semi-final lunch. I did not have breakfast, but drank several tomato juices before sitting down to lunch. All round my pals were getting stuck into wine and lager, courtesy of the sponsors. Surely a couple of glasses of Chablis would not put me off my stroke …

By the time I made my traditional satirical speech at around four o'clock, I'd had four glasses of wine and was in top form. I got a lot of laughs and so, instead of going back to my room to chill before commentating, I joined the merry throng in the bar and had a couple more glasses of wine. As usual, we were not going out live till the final, and I sat down to record the first semi at about 7.15. I felt as though I had a thick elastic band round my head; I could not concentrate properly. Ten minutes into the match I was collared by producer Keith Phillips and gently eased out of my chair: 'Sid, you're slurring. Come into the scanner and listen.' There was more concern in his voice than anger. Tony edged past me and took over the commentary. I did not follow Keith to the scanner; I didn't need to. I knew I was drunk.

I raced out of the Coatham Bowl, past the kiddies' paddling pool and on to the prom. I was swearing at the top of my voice, flinging curses at my own sheer stupidity out over the pounding North Sea. Sixty-odd miles further north my mum and dad and my brother Derrick would soon be tuning in to the darts, waiting proudly to listen to me. When your voice, personality and enthusiasm are due to go out to millions of fans you are in a responsible and highly privileged position. And I was guilty of gross abuse. I was certain I would be sacked once and for all from the job I loved. Through scalding tears I looked along the prom at blurry lights twinkling from merry pubs.

In for a penny ... In the first one I set about a double whisky and halfway through it I was joined by some young lads.

'What you doing in here Sid? You should be doon the Bowl.'

I explained that I'd got pissed and been given the heave-ho. I was expecting the sack. There were cries of horror. 'They cannot sack you, Sid. Darts wouldn't be the same without you.'

The reaction produced a warm flicker of hope that lasted till halfway down the next double whisky. I moved on to other pubs, had more to drink and got more boozy votes of confidence. I finally came to a rocky roost in the Saltscar. Trevor Fowler knew I was not there for a quick spoonfight. He persuaded me to leave the spirits alone and drink a slow pint shandy. 'Don't make things any worse,' was his advice. 'Get in a taxi and get yersell to bed.'

That's what I did – eventually. Back at the hotel I made one last crazy farewell gesture. I entered the bar, which was heaving with Beeb people and darters, trying to ignore the nods and winks. In splendid woozy isolation I downed a pint of Newcastle Brown, wheeled and lurched to bed. Spasmodic applause sped my departure.

My phone rang at eight next morning. It was Keith Phillips. Sack time, I reckoned.

'Have you got it out of your system, then?'

I dribbled out an apology.

'You're doing all the final live tonight, so get your act together. OK?' said Keith.

'OK!'

I got out of bed and mixed an Alka-Seltzer. As it fizzled I made a resolution: 'You will never let booze cramp your style ever again.' I never needed another life lesson like that night in Redcar. I sealed the deal with a slurp of the belly powder. It tasted like Roederer Cristal.

Sadly, the 1988 Unipart British Professional event on Teesside was the last, and the whole focus of top darts, sports and social, shifted to the Lakeside Country Club at Frimley Green in Surrey.

I have already described how Eric Bristow won his third Embassy title on the trot there in 1986, and he was again favourite to win in 1987. Most pundits thought that John Lowe would run Eric close, but I did not agree. In fact, in the programme for the event I tipped

Bobby George to beat John in the first round. How wrong can you be? My prediction was a mile out, and it started the tradition of 'Sid the Black Spot': if I tip a player to win, he might as well pack his bag.

If Eric Bristow had not been around, the mid-1980s would have been known as the John Lowe Era. He even achieved a feat that I never thought we would see on TV – he hit the magic 9-darter. And, sod it, I was not the commentator!

I got the bad news in a boozer in Bradford. It was around five o'clock on a Saturday in May 1984 and I had just spent all day at my day job for the BBC in Manchester, working on a kids' entertainment show. Hot off the train, I dived into the buffet for a swifty.

'You've missed the 9-dart. Your mate Dave Lanning has just called it on ITV.' My informant was a regular, unshaven, dirty jeans, tattoos, wind-up merchant.

'Bollocks,' I said.

He shuffled along the bar. He called over the barman. 'Tell him.'

'He's not kidding. MFI World Matchplay at Slough. Playing against Keith Deller. Finished on treble 18, double 18. A hundred thousand quid.'

My veins filled with ice. It had to be true. For six years we'd been praying for a nine-dart at an event covered by the BBC, and now we'd been upstaged. It was worse. When I got home and looked at the tape I marvelled at how cool Dave's voice was as the last dart went in. Lowe's eighth dart was in the treble 18 at an angle, and the double 18 bed was blocked to view. But Dave had seen Lowe's reaction and now gushed calmly: 'John Lowe wins one hundred thousand pounds.' The sangfroid was all the more amazing when I learned a few days later that Dave had won £12,000 on a bet saying that the 9-dart would be done that season.

What I did not know before the 1987 Embassy was just how badly Eric had the dartitis and just how self-disciplined John Lowe was. The night before the tournament started I had a drink with John at our hotel at Bracknell, a few miles down the road from Lakeside. I was about to order two pints of lager when John stopped me. 'Make mine a gin – with a lot of orange.' Now, John was never a big drinker, but he had been known to enjoy a few pints of the amber nectar until the early hours. I asked him what was up.

'I had a look in the mirror a few months back and did not like what I saw,' he said. 'My belly was bulging and I weighed about sixteen stones. I reckoned it was no way for the "Ambassador of Darts" to look on TV. So I've cut out lager, I'm watching what I eat and I'm down to just over thirteen stone.'

It certainly paid off. John slashed through the field. In the semi-final he annihilated Jocky Wilson 5–0 in sets. Then he and Bristow diced out a brilliant final and John won 6–4. I remember sitting in the lobby of our hotel having a few beers with the fans when the newly crowned champ came in with the trophy. He was cheered to the echo and responded by buying ten magnums of champagne and personally dishing them out round the room. I was mildly surprised, because odd players had suggested that Lobo was a bit of a skinflint. Mind you, he had just won £14,000. We both raised a glass of bubbly. John drank deep. 'What about the fitness regime?' I enquired.

'Back on it tomorrow,' he replied.

The Lakeside Era began in earnest in January 1988. For the first two years most of the players and the BBC team had stayed and socialised at a hotel in Bracknell. But in year three we set up our full camp in the Lakeside International Hotel, a kind of week-long boy scout jamboree with beer, only a matter of yards from the Embassy oche. As self-appointed bard of the dartboard, here is how I set the tone in the programme:

Bobbe the Potter doth run a smashing gaffe,
Full of jolly giants who throw and quaffe.

Bob Potter had really taken to the darts fraternity; after all we did generate excellent business in sales of beer and sausage and chips. But Bob did not stop at fitting out his club for the darters and over a thousand fans per night. He also ensured that the après-arrows entertainment went with a swing. We were given our own large private lounge and our own band! An organist, drummer and female singer were ordered to be on duty till as late as the darts company wished. More than that, Bob appointed me master of the nightly revels in a solemn moving ceremony. First, he gave me a book about his building of Lakeside. Next, he gave me a silk tie with a logo. Finally, he hung round my neck a Bobby George-style glitter chain complete with the club's kingfisher medallion. I felt as proud as a rookie Freemason on his first night down the Lodge. But I had no idea what I was taking on, because year by year the role was to become ever more demanding.

The 'cabaret' was not exactly sophisticated. After play finished some of the BBC team, some BDO officials and the star players of the night would go to the star dressing room and enjoy Embassy's hospitality. Peter Dyke, head of World Promotions and PR guru to the whole tournament, would lash out champagne and entertain us all with impressions of Tommy Cooper and Marlon Brando's Godfather. Peter himself had designed the new darts stage set in blushing pink. He was chuffed to hear me describe it on air as looking 'like a ladies' boudoir' – in fact I was thinking 'knocking shop'. Just after midnight we would wander round the lake to the hotel and my 'night job' would start.

This was a typical bill of fare. To an audience of about a hundred – officials, players, hangers-on, some of them in carpet slippers and some older women in dressing gowns – Sid welcomed the crowd to Potter's palace with his boisterous version of 'Your Cheatin' Heart' or Fats Domino's 'Ain't That a Shame'. Then I introduced Marie Hawkins, wife of BDO chairman Sam, who brought a touch of Vera Lynn to proceedings with 'The White Cliffs of Dover'. I then brought up the boss of Merseyside darts, Jimmy McGovern, who led the assembly in a selection of Scouse favourites. Also, that first week, I persuaded other impromptu acts to perform. Ron Gubba of the Beeb belted out a moving version of 'Jerusalem'. Tony Green left the card school long enough to do Ray Charles impressions and Bob Anderson, much fancied to do well on the oche, brought the house down with his Worzel Gummidge impressions. About two in the morning I sent them all to their beds and bought the band a nightcap.

This performance as court jester had a two-fold object. It relaxed me and kept my mind off my asthma and my shortcomings on the scores. More important, it developed a friendly bond between the players, officials and the BBC team. Sometimes the BDO thought the 'professionals' of the BBC pushed them around a bit, so the cabaret took the edge off things. Olly Croft always said that the BDO were a 'family' and I did my best to keep that ethos alive.

Star of the Embassy of 1988 turned out to be Bob Anderson. Bob had given up a top job in the civil service to become 'The Limestone Cowboy' – my nickname for him because of his West Country background and frilled cowboy shirts – and he gave me plenty to get my imagination going that week. 'Anderson, eyes like a barracuda, appetite like a shark.' 'Bob came on like the Laughing Cavalier, now he looks like Lee Van Cleef on a bad night.' 'The hands of Anderson weaving their own fairy tale.' I have to own up here that the last line was not my own; I stole it from Tony Green. There was a last minute change of roster, so I found myself sitting with the microphone as Bob got throwing. By chance I looked down and saw some scribblings by Tony on an old betting slip. 'Hans of Anderson …' it said. Not bad! So I asked the director to give me some close-ups of Bob's throwing hand and used the line. Tony was not best pleased. In fact he gave me some pretty Grimm looks.

The Anderson versus Lowe world final was one of the best ever. Bob has always had one of the cleanest controlled throws in the game: he stabs the darts in rather than floats them and uses a lot of finger-spin on release. He showed little respect for John Lowe's reputation. He beat John 6–4 in sets and it should have been the start of his era. But what we did not know then was that lurking in the wings were Dennis Priestley and Phil Taylor.

The 1988 Embassy was also notable for the staging of the Haywards Pickles Youth championships, which we recorded. In the field were two fifteen-year-olds who went on to make big names for themselves, Wayne Mardle and Andy Jenkins. Sadly, some of the young lads were led astray by older darters and got drunk before the tournament – not that you could tell by the standard of play next day. And there was another plus. After the Unipart tournament on Teesside we always got a courtesy tool box full of spark plugs and spanners. At the Haywards Pickles event I opened my hotel room door next morning and fell over a hamper of pickled onions, beetroot and gherkins.

As if being the lead commentator on the Embassy world darts and being the social/concert secretary was not enough on my manic plate, in 1990 I added piracy to the list. Several guests wanted to join me at the Lakeside for the last three nights of the event, so I had to work a bit of a flanker on my mate Bob Potter. I booked one extra room in the name of my son Daniel, which he would share with his mate Jason. My other three guests – my brother Derrick and Richie and Lee Stafford, old pals from Lynemouth – would rub shoulders with the stars, booze and carouse till late then kip on my floor, or in my bath, as necessary. Before you ring the Serious Fraud Squad, look at it this way: most rooms were let out as doubles, so having an extra person in a room was the norm. Nor was having three snoring Geordies on my floor cheating Bob out of income, considering how much the lads spent on beer and spirits downstairs.

But I must admit that the bacon sandwich scam was a bit naughty. Each morning Daniel and I would have a cooked breakfast during which we would make bacon butties on the sly, secrete them about our persons and take them upstairs to the lads. We even borrowed the sauce bottles.

The system worked a treat, but having guests during normal sleeping hours did not help with a special extra task I had that year. After the boozy lunch on the Friday there was going to be a special *This is Your Life* for Keith Phillips, a good friend who had been a key producer at all our darts events since 1978. Keith was leaving the Beeb and I had been designated as impresario of his farewell do. So, sparrow fart and duck belch of that dawn found me sitting on my bed in a fug of beer fumes, writing speeches for a cod Wing Commander from Keith's RAF days and a cod Faith Brown, buxom Scottish entertainer, from his time in Light Entertainment. Thanks to lashings of goodwill and much lager, it went down a bomb.

One year later, in January 1991, Lakeside staged its first darting fairy tale, comparable to the Deller victory over Brissy in 1983, and I began one of my firmest friendships in darts. Dennis Priestley comes from a very similar background to my own. The Priestleys hail from Mexborough, in the heart of what was the South Yorkshire coalfield, and Dennis's dad worked down Manvers Main colliery for many years. The family also ran a small coal-selling business that Dennis took over and developed. He was very much a hands-on boss, humping the bags of nutty slack ten hours a day. But that didn't stop Dennis tickling tungsten well enough to represent Yorkshire and England. Still, when he arrived at Lakeside he was 100–1 to win the title.

Being a miner's son and an adopted Yorkie, it was natural that Dennis and I would get on together. Before I started my nightly stints as court jester, I had a few beers with him and we discussed people we knew, like the legendary Yorkshire darter Brian

Langworth. 'Langy is a reet case,' said Dennis. 'He talks to his darts, kisses his darts, then has a bevvy and loses the bloody things.' He also told me before play started that week how he would love to go fully professional at darts. Then he shot off upstairs to watch tapes of *Neighbours*, saying: 'I can't let this darts job spoil my viewing.'

The rest of that week is darting legend. In the last eight Dennis trailed to Phil Taylor, the holder, by 3–1 in sets but pegged back unflappably to 3–3. Then Dennis applied pressure and went to 2–1 in legs in the deciding set. He took the match with a 161 shot-out, the highest of the championship. It was the biggest win of his career and better was to come. Dennis became Embassy world champion by annihilating Eric Bristow 6–0 in the final. Ever an apostle of moderation, Dennis had a few bottles of brown ale with his pals from Mexborough and went off for a slap-up feed. He told me he was definitely turning professional.

My own last-night celebrations were excessive. I took my usual place in the lounge with our band, belted out a song and was happy to be swamped by would-be acts. There were singers galore, so I put my feet up with Daniel, Derrick and some other friends and let my hair down. About one o'clock I was hurled back into the firing line. A bloke had asked if his two little lads could do a turn – sit on his knee and sing the Rolf Harris hit 'Two Little Boys'. I introduced the act and for about a minute the boys sang lustily along with the band. Then they clammed up, totally overcome by stage fright. Almost in tears, their dad led them from the stage. The band leader looked at me and I waved my hands for something upbeat. They started to play 'The Stripper' and I began a pretend strip. But before I knew it, two

BDO lads grabbed me and took off all my clothes but my undies. The crowd cheered and jeered and Derrick and Daniel hid behind a chesterfield settee.

'He's my bloody brother,' shouted Derrick.

'He's my bloody father,' shouted Daniel.

It's sometimes tough when you've got show business and session lager and Johnny Walker in your veins.

My commentating performance, however, did make headlines in the *Sun* a couple of days later. They printed a dozen of my best ever lines over the years and proclaimed this the best: 'The fans now, with their eyes pierced on the dartboard.' This was a line I had used in 1984 at Jollees and had been designed to get me into *Private Eye*'s 'Colemanballs' – and it did appear. But soon after, my pal Mike Wood who presents historical documentaries, told the *Eye* lot at a lunch that I was having them on, and they ignored me for several years.

I was glad, in view of my swiping his Hans of Anderson line, that the *Sun* included a couple of Tony Green's classics. A few years earlier at the British Open we had recorded a match between two top women that had been very poor. At one stage, with the girls' scores averaging about thirty, the director took a shot of one of the player's feet. She was standing about a foot behind the mark. 'Audrey's now standing well behind the oche. She obviously likes that extra few inches,' said Tony. Surprisingly, when it went out on *Grandstand* nobody said a dicky bird. They also quoted Tony's reaction to some bad throwing by a player called Randy Bache: 'Randy's going to be glad to get this leg over.' I don't think either was a deliberate attempt at smut, but with English the language it is, double entendres will happen.

There was also a chance of getting into trouble with one of the names in the Embassy line-up for 1992. How do you say Oyvind Aasland of Norway without it sounding rude? But I thank God that the great Japanese star Akuro Fukusowa never made it through to the Lakeside finals.

Now to the very serious question of the crisis that was facing the sport at this time. Since Deller's fairy tale win over Brissy in 1983, watched by 8.3 million people on television, things had gone downhill. And the nadir had been reached in 1990. In the two years from 1988 to 1990 the number of televised events dropped from fourteen to two. These are some that we lost: MFI World Matchplay and Pairs, Unipart British Professional, Butlin's Grand Masters, Dry Blackthorn Masters, Autumn Gold Masters, British Open and the World Masters. The upshot was that there was a drought of funds in the professional game and Embassy world champions like Phil Taylor and Dennis Priestley were nobodies to the man in the street. Dennis made about £50,000 in the twelve months after his win at Lakeside; if he had won six years earlier the figure would have been over £100,000.

There is no doubt that the decline was partly due to policy changes at the BBC and ITV. The Beeb said they were cutting back on 'minority' sports like darts, bowls and rugby league. ITV boss Greg Dyke was much more blunt. He axed darts from the schedules because its large audiences were from the lower income groups.

But there was a strong feeling that a large portion of the blame had to be laid at the door of the British Darts Organisation. I was amongst those who thought the BDO had rested on their laurels and let the game stagnate. In response, sixteen top players – John Lowe,

Eric Bristow, Cliff Lazarenko, Phil Taylor, Keith Deller, Jamie Harvey, Bob Anderson, Dennis Priestley, Rod Harrington, Kevin Spiolek, Alan Warriner, Jocky Wilson, Peter Evison, Richie Gardner, Mike Gregory and Chris Johns – players' agents and companies involved in darts formed the World Darts Council to resuscitate the game and its fortunes. It was inevitable that there would be friction with the BDO, who saw itself as running the entire game from grass roots up. But this is how Dick Allix, agent to Eric Bristow and others and a leading light in the WDC, saw the situation in a letter to *Darts World*: 'If the BDO wants to accept the accolades of success, it must accept the responsibility for failure.'

I was in total agreement and, unusually for a bloke who tends to look on the bright side, I was very pessimistic in the days running up to the 1992 Embassy. I told Alan Fraser of the *Daily Mail*: 'I think the game has had its day as a TV sport. I do not see any light at all in the gloom.' But desperate times produce desperate measures. Dick Allix and the WDC committee decided on a bold publicity stunt to boost interest in the world championship. They said they would put up the money for me to stand as a Member of Parliament. I had to choose a constituency – Morpeth? My adopted home town of Pudsey? For some reason, Dartford came into my head. Little did I know that I would be spending every New Year in that town, staying at the Hilton Hotel, during the future glory years at the Circus Tavern. So I posed for the national press in my garden with my head looking through the screen of a telly. It got lots of column inches, but we had to wait a couple of years before Sky Sports came along to save the game.

By early 1992 I was an adopted member of the Mexborough Mafia, Dennis Priestley's group of family and pals. I had done a short film with Dennis at his local, in the snooker hall and shared some of his missus Jenny's famous stew. I had socialised widely and been treated royally. So I felt it fitting to take Dennis, Mick Critchlow and Alan Critchlow out for a fancy meal before play at Lakeside started.

I had heard good reports of an upmarket Italian restaurant in Frimley Green so I booked us in. We got there about eight, with murmurs of 'We want none of that spaghetti muck' and 'We'll strangle yer if there's no rump steak.' We sat down, ordered lager and wine and the lads were delighted that prime steak was a feature of the menu. They even agreed to have some exotic sauce dolloped on it. The meal went fine, with everybody scoffing me for the messy way I set about my spaghetti bolognese.

By dessert time, most of the Mafia were what in Yorkshire is called 'fresh', i.e. merry, and I found out just how little political correctness had infiltrated into South Yorkshire.

'I reckon it's time to spot the Luigi,' said Mick Critchlow, a dark twinkle in his eye.

Dennis and Alan agreed. I had a cold shudder. 'What is spot the Luigi?' I whispered.

Dennis explained. 'We play it when we go to Italian places in Donny. We all put a fiver on the table and try to guess which waiter is called Luigi. Winner takes the kitty.'

'But what if there's not a Luigi?' again in a whisper.

'There's always a Luigi,' said Mick.

We all put our money on the table and pointed at different

waiters. Our own waiter, nominated by Dennis, noticed the money and asked what we were up to. Dennis very politely explained the rules and I feared the worst when our waiter frowned deeply.

'I am not Luigi, I am Renzo,' he said solemnly. Then he pointed round to Carlo, Mario and Luca. Still frowning, he walked off and talked to the other waiters. There was a frantic pointing to the kitchen. Off went Renzo. I was terrified. Cue racially insulted angry giants with meat cleavers from the back.

I was wrong. Renzo led out a little bloke with a potato peeler in his hand. Both were beaming. 'This is Luigi!' shouted Renzo in triumph.

'Void game,' said Dennis.

Both Renzo and little Luigi were fascinated to know what we northerners were doing in town. We explained about the darts and they were gobsmacked to learn that Dennis was the world champ. Soon the kitchen was emptied and everybody was shaking Dennis's hand and getting his autograph. With my hands trembling in sheer relief I gave Renzo a £10 tip and we left. And there was a sad ending to the story. The Italian lads lumped large on Dennis to win the title and of course he lost to Alan Warriner in round two.

That piece of cabaret was a fitting start to a momentous week.

An early visitor from the national press was old William Marshall of the *Daily Mirror*, the man who had slagged off darts in general and Jocky in particular at Jollees in 1982. Now he excelled himself by rubbishing not only darts players but also the Lakeside club. In passing, he had a swipe at the 'gorilla-like' bouncers. Then, incredibly, later in the week he waltzed back into the players' bar in his fancy Crombie coat and began sipping red wine. Word got round and fell on the ears of the bouncers. As Willy left the club later, two of the bouncers escorted him to the edge of the lake. They lifted him gently and sat him in the shallow end, just downriver from the Mississippi paddle steamer. It's one thing to insult the boys with beer bellies, but leave the heavies out of it.

My histrionic and scriptwriting talents were again called on, and this time it was an epic. The BBC/BDO 'turn' this year was to be a religious pantomime for production assistant Jacqueline Hobbs who was leaving sport for the religious department. So I burnt my midnight candle all week writing a work for twelve characters, including a bishop and two mother superiors. On top of this, all of Thursday was spent touring theatrical costumiers with Bob Potter selecting wardrobe. To give Bob his due, he paid for all the costumes and bought me a superb Chinese lunch. During this I had pangs of guilt about having my family and friends dossing in Bob's rooms, so I resolved to give the lads fifty quid to put over the bar.

And, oh yes! We had Phil Taylor versus Mike Gregory in one of the greatest ever darts finals.

I was not happy about my part in proceedings. Keith McKenzie was now our boss and he said he thought it was messy for me to start and end the Embassy final. He reckoned that my taking the microphone from Tony as the climax approached was not neat. So I was told I would do the first half of the final and Tony would finish. Quite bluntly, I thought Tony's prosaic style would lose the atmosphere, but I said nowt.

As it happened, the drama that developed from 5–5 in sets needed no commentator to gild the lily.

At 3–2 in legs in set 11 Gregory needed 61 for the title. He hit treble 15 to leave double 8. Then he snatched the next two darts. Taylor stepped in to draw level at 3–3. At 5–4 in legs in his favour, Gregory again looked a winner. With Taylor on 215, Mike wanted 80 for the title. He hit two single 20s and then missed tops. *He'd missed three doubles, any one of which would have won him the Embassy.* The tension was showing more on Mike than Phil. He missed with three shot at tops. Taylor levelled the set at 5–5. The six missed doubles to take the title preyed on Mike's mind, but Taylor was ice-cold. He did a 13-darter to become champion.

What happened next can be compared to the assassination of the Archduke Franz Ferdinand at Sarajevo. In 1914, war clouds had been looming all over Europe, waiting to burst. In January 1992 a mighty storm was brewing in darts and the BDO lit the blue touch paper. It all centred around a simple little videotape.

A couple of weeks after the sensational Embassy final I got a phone call from Tony Green. He said the BBC and the BDO were thinking of issuing a video of the Taylor/Gregory classic. My voice would of course be on it. How did £250 sound as a fee? I said fine and looked forward to getting a copy in a matter of weeks. Three days later a copy of the video clattered through my letterbox. The words fait accompli came to mind. There were some other matches on the tape, but half of it was the match between Phil and Mike.

Then a can of worms was opened. Not only had neither of the players nor their representatives been consulted about the project, but they were not offered a penny piece! The BDO argued that the players had signed over all their rights and so weren't entitled to payment or notice.

Nothing symbolised the oppressive attitude of the BDO and its leader Olly Croft more graphically than this episode. It set the tone for five years of strife that culminated in legal action. Although I knew I had to play my cards carefully as a BBC man, my sympathies from the outset were with the sixteen players and the WDC. It was a straight fight between democracy and autocracy, and there could be only one winner.

Three months later, there was another crisis, and this one was much nearer home. I was made redundant from my job as assistant producer at the BBC in Manchester. Since 1976 I had worked on documentaries, sports programmes, *The Russell Harty Show* and children's shows as a film director and occasional reporter. I was always given time off to do the darts. I got the news in April 1992 and was down in the dumps for a few days. My wife Irene was a tower of strength, insisting that I would do very well as a freelance. I was not so sure, but then Lady Luck stepped in. While still working out my notice at the Beeb, I bumped into Ian Squires, a very bright TV executive who was boss of Zenith North TV in Newcastle. He took me for a beer and suggested I think about fronting a series called *Waddell's World* that his company would make for Tyne Tees Television. He did not know that I was about to be a freelance. When I told him and mentioned that the WDC were looking for television exposure, his eyes lit up.

Within a few weeks a meeting was arranged in Newcastle with Ian and me, WDC representatives and the bosses of Vaux Brewery. The upshot was the Samson Darts Classic that would feature the top WDC players and would be recorded in Newcastle in April 1993. I was going to be busy: I was to be the producer, presenter and commentator. Dick Allix even asked if I'd like to play in the qualifiers. I had nailed my colours firmly alongside the Jolly Roger on the mast of the good ship WDC. For this I was to pay a price.

After the videotape episode relations between the BDO and the WDC went downhill rapidly. Just as had already happened in tennis and athletics, the players realised their own market value and wanted a big say in running their sport. They suggested to the BDO that the WDC promote about four tournaments a year, with the BDO running them. This was dismissed out of hand. The BDO acted as though professional players like Eric Bristow and Jocky Wilson did not have contracts with their agents. Often at the Embassy world championship presentations I would end up in a corner with Dick Allix and Tommy Cox, who represented Eric and Jocky respectively, and listen to their tales of BDO arrogance and intransigence.

In October 1992 I attended another new plank in the WDC platform, the recording of the Lada UK Masters in Norwich by Anglia TV, and the commentators were John Gwynne and Dave Lanning. There were rumours that the players there – the 'rebel' sixteen – would be banned by the BDO, but the spirit in the WDC camp was high. Old stagers like Lazarenko talked of democracy and player power, and there was also talk that the sixteen would boycott the 1993 Embassy world championship.

So you can well imagine the wary steps I trod when I got to Lakeside for the tournament; I felt like Henry Kissinger testing the water on a flying visit to North Korea. There was one plus: the boycott idea had been dropped and some WDC players were to take part – under protest. They were Dennis Priestley, Jocky Wilson, Eric Bristow, Bob Anderson, Alan Warriner, Rod Harrington, Mike Gregory, Jamie Harvey, John Lowe, Chris Johns, Kevin Spiolek and Phil Taylor.

Still, there was bother from day one. As Eric Bristow and Jocky Wilson were practising for their matches, they were ordered to take the WDC badges off their playing shirts. Eric was all for walking out, but Tommy Cox, the only WDC official present told him to hang fire. Tommy discussed the situation with BBC, BDO and Embassy officials and was told the badges must go. Tommy was furious. He told the players to play without the badges but made it clear that the WDC would never be treated like that again.

I continued my nightly role as Lakeside concert secretary but found myself getting some funny looks from the BDO old guard. Word of the proposed Samson tournament in Newcastle had got around. Late on the Tuesday night, Olly Croft and his wife Lorna took me aside as the music played round us. Olly, as usual, was blunt and to the point. Why was I upsetting the BDO 'family' and dealing with these 'unofficial people'? I did not go into semantics or argue the case for player power and democracy. I merely stated that in the past year I had gone freelance and had a duty to my family to make money. If this meant becoming involved with the WDC and their tournaments then so be it. They said they were very disappointed and we left it there.

It was at this point that I really did in fact become Kissinger.

The WDC had put out a press release confirming that the sixteen players had aligned with them and that they were introducing a new ranking system. They also listed confirmed future events, including the Samson Darts Classic. But the main point was a much broader and highly contentious issue. The WDC said it wanted eventually to run *all* professional tournaments including the world championship. There would be a boycott of the 1994 Embassy if the WDC were not given control. Our executive producer Keith McKenzie said there was only one person who knew both sides of the case and could give a balanced overview – me. So the headline would be: CONCERT SECRETARY BECOMES SECRETARY OF STATE.

At two o'clock on the Thursday I put on my best suit and sat on the Lakeside terrace with Dougie Donnelly and recorded my take on the dispute. I said in essence that I thought generally that the BDO should be more democratic and take more notice of the genuine concerns of the professional players. I said that I thought the WDC were an excellent organisation and were doing well at finding new sponsors. I ended by saying that I thought the WDC were being far too 'greedy' in wanting to run everything including the world championship. They were running where they should have been walking.

The interview was shown just before five o'clock that evening on the end of our BBC2 highlights show. A few minutes later I walked into the reception of the Lakeside International hotel and was applauded by several BDO officials. I was told I had been very fair.

I walked round the lake to the club feeling good. On entering, I got a shock. A WDC posse was in reception and Tommy Cox, face red with rage, peeled off from them and began yelling at me. 'What kind of man are you? Doing deals with us one minute and then calling us greedy buggers the next?' I did not grace him with a reply. I shrugged and walked on.

Dick Allix followed me. 'Does this change anything about where we stand on the Samson deal?'

'Not at all,' I said quietly. 'But don't tell Tommy till tomorrow. Let him stew.'

Dick winked assent.

Now that I had little matters like the internecine dispute and the latter stages of the world finals in hand, I could turn my fertile brain to more serious business. Earlier that day my brother Derrick had rung me from Geordieland to confirm that he would be arriving on Thursday evening with a party of five. Although I had booked another room at Potter's hotel for my sons Daniel and Nicholas, I was worried about having so many dossers. So I'd had a brainwave; I would arrange for the Geordie Six to park their transit in the car park of the boozer on Frimley Green. The landlord was happy for the lads to use his outside toilets during the night and during the day they would eat and drink at his pub. As for personal hygiene, the lads could use my hotel bathroom, in shifts.

I got to the pub about six to find Derrick and the lads had just arrived. I gave them their BDO courtesy passes, resisted the urge to have a pint and joined in the crack.

The plan worked well. The next couple of nights the Geordies partied at 'Sid's cabaret', drinking with John Lowe and Dennis Priestley, and went back to their transit at about two.

I had a lunchtime lemonade with the lads before Saturday's final and unwittingly became privy to just how personal the dispute had become. The bar we were in was partitioned off from a small lounge and suddenly I heard familiar voices raised in strife. I peeked round and saw Olly and Lorna Croft deep in conversation with Rod Harrington. Rod had been one of the seeds in the competition and was a key figure in the dispute. He had spoken very convincingly of why the sixteen WDC players had to leave the BDO and go it alone. It was obvious that he was not selling the idea to the Crofts. Lorna was weeping and Olly was red-faced. No doubt Rod was being accused of letting down the 'family'. 'We are determined,' said Rod. 'It will be hard, but we are breaking away.'

Sadly for Olly another key figure in the dispute won a lacklustre final. John Lowe defeated Alan Warriner 6–3 in sets to take his third Embassy title in three separate decades. Since 1987 John had been chairman of the World Professional Darts Players Association and had been arguing the 'rebels' case to the BDO in vain for years. When asked about the talk of the banning of WDC players, John said: 'If there are bans the BDO will be shooting themselves in the foot.'

It wasn't long before the dispute became a shooting war and I, being bang in the middle, purchased a tin hat.

7

Bright Sky Ahead

In the opening weeks of 1993 the fissure running through the world of darts suddenly became a canyon. First the sixteen 'rebels' issued a statement saying 'we recognise the WDC as the *only* governing body empowered to commit our participation in any darts tournaments worldwide.' The BDO reply was draconian; the sixteen were suspended from all matches under their jurisdiction, from pub to international level. The grounds given were that the sixteen 'rebels' were 'bringing the game into disrepute'. This was a pretty bizarre explanation since half the people on the list had recently been included in the BDO England squad, so were presumably the cream of the crop. The truth was that Olly Croft and his organisation wanted a complete monopoly on the game and would say anything to justify their stance.

This was borne out when a seven-man WDC delegation went to Finchley in April, ostensibly to meet and discuss matters with the full BDO council. All that happened was that they were verbally abused from all quarters. A Lancashire representative said the WDC people should be 'binned'. A Yorkshire bloke said he would not like to live in the same street as the WDC group. And, when the WDC people got a word in, the BDO chairman said: 'They are telling porkies, boys.' It's hardly Hansard, is it? These insults were an indication that the suspensions would become a full-scale ban. After the WDC group left, the BDO council passed three resolutions. They would ban anyone associating with the activities of the WDC, anyone playing in WDC events, and even anybody who attended exhibitions by the sixteen players. This proclamation could have effectively stopped the sixteen players earning a living from darts. That is why a long and bitter battle eventually went to the High Court. It was not about pride, loyalty or even money; it was about being denied the right to ply one's trade. It was about feeding yourself and your family.

What a contrast with the friendly let's-get-buzzing atmosphere on Tyneside a few days later when the WDC sixteen joined local qualifiers to play in the 'Sid Waddell Show' – the Samson Darts Classic. I directed a few short films with the players and they pitched in with gusto. John Lowe drove his flashy sports car to Newcastle Marina – next door to a tatty scrapyard – and priced up the yachts. Peter Evison and Rod Harrington trained with Sunderland FC and impressed veteran player Mick Harford. But my favourite item was when I made Dennis Priestley and Chris Johns do a bit of real graft for a change.

As a boy I had often gone 'sea-coaling' with my dad at Lyne Sands, a beach near our village where wild spring tides washed up tons of coal. Gathering it was easy; you got a horse and cart backed up to the waves, leapt in the sea and shovelled till your fingers bled. This was the task I had in mind for my darting pals. They got kitted out at my mum's house in Lynemouth in my dad's old moleskin pants from the pit and two sets of waders. I've got to admit Dennis and Chris worked their trolleys off and even impressed the locals who did the job for a living. Afterwards they did a real job on my mum's broth and stotty cakes before heading back to the darts.

Back at Tyne Tees studios, Bob Anderson won a cracking final against Phil Taylor and a vocal, well-refreshed Geordie crowd applauded the players at every throw. The sponsors signed up to re-stage the tournament in a year's time. The Anglia event had gone well, but the Samson did give the WDC lads the firm conviction that the future was bright.

I was deeply unsure about my own darting future. I knew that my involvement with the WDC had many people at the BDO marking my card. But many of the 'rebels' were my friends and I was convinced that the WDC were pointing the way ahead for the professional game. I knew that the next Embassy, due to start in January 1994, would be anything but a cosy ride for me. If the BDO was a family, I had done something nasty in the nest. I was also aware that Al Capone did many vile deeds in the name of 'family'.

I did however get a laugh a few days before Christmas. The WDC had arranged with Sky Sports to have their own rival world darts championship the week before the Embassy. To publicise it, John Lowe and Jocky Wilson picketed Lakeside with placards saying the *real* world championship would be held at the Circus Tavern in Purfleet. The stunt got a lot of media coverage and got folks in my Pudsey local talking. I was dubious. Surely Sky, coming in cold, could not cover seven days of live darts with anything like the production values of the Beeb? How wrong can you be …

*

I had a great Christmas in 1993 at home in Pudsey with Irene and the kids. The Tetley's Bitter and odd Wild Turkey went down a treat and so did the turkey, trimmings and plum pud. I also got all the shirts, sweaters and books I wanted. I was due to report for commentary duty with the BBC at the Embassy World Championships early in January. My worst fears had been justified at the Embassy qualifiers in Fulham, where I had been treated like a pariah by BDO officials. There were gibes about my joining 'that lot' and two of the Crimplene-clad ladies on the registration desk had even refused to give me the list of runners and riders. So I was sure to be Mr Popularity at Frimley Green. Also, I had the feeling that a field that boasted Bobby George as its star attraction would be eclipsed by the rival WDC world championship.

Not surprisingly, given my penchant for playing darts and pool, my 'burning bush' moment happened in a public house.

I did not have Sky, so on day one of the WDC tournament I trekked through blinding snow to the Railway Arms in Pudsey. I had arranged to meet my pal Stuart Briggs there and shortly before one o'clock we settled in front of a roaring fire with pints of Tetley's to watch the action. Just before he switched on the telly, landlord John Oxley, a darts fanatic, asked me if I'd prefer to be with the lads at the Circus. 'No,' I replied. 'Sky have never done darts before so they'll probably cock it up.' I was dead right – for all of five minutes.

As the brash music and garish title sequence started I had a hollow feeling in my gut; I was half-hoping the coverage would be crap and half-wishing I was there with John Gwynne, Dave Lanning and my pals Dennis Priestley, Jocky Wilson, and the rest. Suddenly they cut live to the Circus Tavern and the screen was filled with clouds of white fumes as the bloke on the dry ice machine went tectonic. Coughing and spluttering and wearing an electric maroon jacket that was a ringer for those worn by Wallace Arnold coach drivers, Jeff Stelling came groping towards camera with two ghostly figures coughing and clawing at the fug behind him. John, Stuart and I fell about with laughter.

'Welcome to day one of the first ever WDC World Darts Championship,' Jeff gasped. 'First up we have a cracking match between two household names – Dennis Priestley and Jocky BROWN ...'

John Oxley stopped laughing and pointed at the screen. 'Prize cock-up right off Sidney – that bloke thinks he's *you*!'

But five minutes later – as Jocky Wilson and Dennis Priestley played classic darts – Stu, John and I stopped laughing. The rock music that punctuated the action, the clouds of dry ice, a beery-cheery holiday crowd, scantily clad Page Three girls, with a shiny black 2000cc motorbike chucked in for good measure – it all added up to vivid, in-yer-chops, vulgar, totally compelling telly. It made our BBC coverage look pastel pale and very old fashioned. I was as sick as the proverbial parrot. I had seen the future for darts, but I was locked into the boring past.

As it happened, I managed to get through the first four days of the Embassy tournament without getting excommunicated, handbagged or chucked into the lake. Each night after my commentating stint I had a couple of swift halves and shot back to my room in Bob Potter's hotel. I sat on the bed looking forward to the high jinks that would start on Thursday when my brother Derrick led a posse of Lynemouth lads into town, and Nicholas and Daniel showed up with a couple of thirsty friends. I had booked a room in Daniel's name, and in that room and my own, we would, as usual, illicitly billet about a dozen revellers.

It was impossible, however, to avoid another grilling by Olly Croft, the man whose dictatorial policy as secretary of the BDO had fomented the whole dispute with the World Darts Council players, and his wife Lorna. These two again accused me of treason against 'our family of darts'. I felt it was the sort of thing the Capones would have said to a stroppy junior member of the gang. I played the economic card. Here I was, a poor freelance broadcaster and journalist, with five hungry mouths to feed. If promoting, presenting, producing and commentating on events featuring the 'rebels' earned me a crust, then so be it. It did not wash. Lorna was near tears and Olly sent me no more Christmas cards or plastic diaries.

On the Thursday night, however, I was cocooned from the BDO hostility by family and friends. At the after darts soirée, for once I did not compere the sing-song. Instead I sat between Richie Stafford, looking louche in a white Gatsby floppy cap, and Derrick in a Newcastle United away top. This pair, and four other Lynemouth lads, had arrived just before seven and been given ringside seats by a bouncer who recognised them. They were indeed privileged, because there was a rule that football tops were banned from Lakeside. I had left passes at the Kingfisher pub, but had been amazed to see two Toon tops in the Lynemouth posse. I thought the lads would have been forced to change into 'proper' clothes.

My lads Nicholas and Daniel and a couple of pals were also in the company. We drank and sang till just before 2 a.m., when Richie's chest started acting up and he retired to my room. Then Nicholas came up to me looking worried. His pal Dave was missing and when last seen had been mumbling about walking round the lake. So I went to look for him. After half an hour wading through reeds and mud in my best loafers, I gave up.

When I got back to my room, it was like the first day on the Somme. Two bodies were snoring under blankets on the floor and Richie was spread all over the double bed, bashing his chest and wheezing like an old tractor. Laughing at the sheer madness of it all – where was the *star commentator* going to kip? – I sat down on a chair and tried to doze off. Then my door was hurled open and a naked Dave was hurled in, followed by his clothes. Tony Green's distinctive voice roared at me: 'If you bring these drunken young sods here you should look after them.' Dave had not gone walkabout in the woods; he had staggered down the corridor and, mistaking Tony's room for mine, went in, got undressed and got into bed.

Tony's tetchiness did not surprise me. My relationship with him had been cooling off for the past couple of years. I think he really resented the fact that I was billed in the TV listings as the number one commentator and got the bulk of the newspaper publicity. He thought that as an ex-player of county standard he should be the number one, and never lost an opportunity to tell folks that I could not count. For my part, I had one serious bone of contention. Under Nick Hunter and Keith Phillips I always did the start and end of the Embassy final. But from about 1992 when Keith McKenzie took over as boss, he thought it 'neater' that Tony should take over at halfway and go through to the end. I never said anything about it. But I felt strongly that Tony's limitations of vocabulary, imagination and intonation did not help convey the drama of the darts action – a view I still hold.

Even though it was to be my last Embassy, the semi-final between Bobby George and Magnus Caris gave me a feast to get my literary teeth into. The match started with sheer comedy and rose to greatness, as a crippled Bobby somehow hung on to win. As Magnus shambled onstage, the BDO official record man played 'Money, Money, Money' by Abba. It was greeted with derisive hoots. I ran out of the commentary box and asked why he had chosen that song. The answer: 'Well, he's Swedish, and that's the only Swedish tune we got.'

It was ever thus with the BDO. I remember a few years earlier a player swearing on camera and lip-readers complaining. 'If that happens again we'll dock the swearer a leg,' said Olly Croft. 'Is that official?' asked Nick Hunter. 'It bloody is now,' said Olly.

Bobby walked on to 'Land of Hope and Glory' and the punters went ape. Curled like Long John Silver after a night on the rum, he sweated and slugged back from 4–2 down. It was later revealed that his back was in fact broken, and it was only very strong tendons developed in the building trade that were keeping him going. Then, suddenly, with excitement at fever pitch, our director took a picture of a bloke piling bangers on top of chips and a bread roll. So I yelped: 'We couldn't have more excitement if Elvis walked in and asked for a chip sandwich.' Performance? Just try to stop me when the action's hot and my adrenalin is coursing.

Mind you, there was sometimes poetic justice. Take my last Embassy final. On the Saturday night Bobby George, his back getting worse by the hour, played the twenty-seven-year-old Canadian John Part. The darts, and the commentary, were completely one-dimensional. There was no real match to get cranked up about; Bobby was never in the hunt. Onstage Part beat Bobby hollow by six sets to nil, and in the box The Geordie Lip did four bland sets before letting in Tony Green for two. It was a whimper of a final rather than a bang. I had no idea at the time, but it was to be the end of my seventeen-year career with the BBC darts team and the end of my uneasy relationship with Olly Croft and his pals.

My move to Sky Sports in June 1994 did not come out of the blue. I had been working closely with Tommy Cox and Dick Allix of the World Darts Council on the second Samson Classic in the spring and both had said that Sky were very keen to have me on board. I was invited down to Isleworth to talk to Roger Moody, one of their top executives. At Leeds City station I bought a new lads' magazine called *Loaded* and inside was what I took to be an omen. In between the bums and tits was a league table of sports commentators and I was very high on it. In fact, I was number three in the Premier Division, behind Stuart Hall and David Coleman. What's more, John Motson and Murray Walker were relegated to the First Division.

A ten-minute chat with Roger Moody and the deal was done. I would join Dave Lanning and John Gwynne in Blackpool at the end of July for the World Matchplay tournament. The next day my brother Derrick rang from Lynemouth and read out the front page story in the Newcastle *Journal*, a posh paper that normally features rugger buggers, farmers and aristos. It was in headlines one-inch high and read 'BULLSEYE – SID'S ON SKY'.

It was good to see a miner's son getting acclaimed in a paper read by all the nobs and all the real folks in Northumberland.

I was pleased to see that the Sky 'blitz 'em with glitz' philosophy had cranked up a notch higher in Blackpool than at the Circus Tavern. I walked into the Winter Gardens and gasped: it was Lenin's Tomb, the Milan Opera House and a Springsteen concert all rolled into one. The rococo pillars and cupid-carved roof were dappled in rainbow colours, ready and waiting for a holiday crowd of 2,500 people. Producers Martin Turner and Rory Hopkins were as enthusiastic as any of the commentary team. 'You have to *design* a big raucous event like this for television,' said Turner. 'It's no good letting it dribble on to the air like the BBC do at Frimley Green.' He also reminded me that about sixty hours of television, in fact every dart thrown, would go out live 'so don't take your foot off that pedal in the commentary box. Hit them bloody viewers and hold them.' It's been my motto ever since.

Sad to say the only thing not 'designed' in the whole production was the commentary box. It was in a tiny prefab hut on the roof and only reachable by fighting through seagulls and pigeons on a narrow gantry. Still, it did not cramp the style of John, Dave or me. I had at first been highly dubious about doing dual, as opposed to solo, commentary. At the Beeb Tony Green and I had never done it in tandem. But my fears about messy overlaps disappeared on day one.

The new Sky team dovetailed immediately; John whacking in relevant statistics and Dave and I recycling *Indoor League* gags. And the whole act had to be conducted at shouting pitch because of the maelstrom of action down on the floor of the arena. The only time we could stop to draw breath was during the players' walk-ons.

We were flying by the seat of our pants and we loved it. And at times the excitement almost overwhelmed us. At one stage Dave was commentating with John and I was brewing up when Dave motioned to me that he had to go to the toilet. Before I could replace him at the microphone John pulled out a little brown medicine bottle and began to *gargle*. At this I began to laugh, so the commentary went like this: 'Ha-ha, AAAAArgh, Ha-ha ...' There are some things you cannot do live on television.

In the old days at the Beeb Nick Hunter had bollocked me for giving a 'performance'. With Sky you got roasted if you did *not* perform. It suited me just fine. What is more, even though we worked live for up to eight hours a day, I had none of the horrendous nerves and vomiting that I did with the BBC. Reason? Part of it was definitely being given a free rein, but another factor was that if my dodgy tubes brought on a cough or a spit I could switch myself off and let my partner fill in.

The week of the 1995 WDC World Championship at the Circus Tavern, Purfleet, was a resounding success. Despite the defection of Chris Johns and Mike Gregory from the original sixteen, the 'rebels' were on a roll. Apart from the glitz we had a classic match between John Lowe and the eventual champion Phil Taylor in which for twelve consecutive legs neither player needed more than sixteen darts to finish. But I have to record that Martin Turner and Rory Hopkins did take the gimmickry a step – I should really say a 'trot' – too far. On the Tuesday night Jerry Umberger of America was due to face Bob Anderson, 'The Limestone Cowboy'. Ten minutes before he was due on the oche Bob was at the bar at the southern end of the Circus Tavern having a jar. Suddenly, through the doors at the north end came Boz, an ancient Essex showjumping horse, saddled and bridled, ready to be led on stage by Bob to the tune of 'Cotton-Eyed Joe'. Cue rapid swallow of drink and blind panicky rush into the car park by Bob. The producers had not checked out the stunt with Bob, who, as he explained later, is terrified of horses. 'I've never been on one in my life and I was once attacked by a wild pony out on a West Country moor. It tried to kick and bite me.' I didn't dare say that senile spavined Boz would probably have cosied up to the Cowboy hoping for a sugar lump.

But that one blip did not spoil the party. Under a headline reading 'WADDELL RIDES INTO TOWN WITH NEW POSSE', the *Independent* hailed the new brighter style of darts. The piece contained this opinion: 'The WDC's "180" has been completed by the arrival of a name more important even than Bristow or Wilson. Sid Waddell, the voice of darts on the BBC since 1977, has signed up with Sky and suddenly a dish seems worth the money.' I had found the dream home for my zany breathy style.

And there was no doubt professional darts had found its new glitzy home, a place where Arthur Daley meets *Gone with the Wind*.

The hotel where we stayed was like a little piece of California set down just off the Southend Arterial Road. It was called the Palms and had a plastic palm tree swaying outside in the sleet blowing from the marshes. But inside the reception was hot. One of the players, a Geordie Lothario, scored with a local who had drifted over from the disco before he had time to check in. Later, she whisked him off to her dad's love shack near Billericay.

Now, back to the check-outs. The Circus Tavern looks like a truck-stop that turns into a niterie. It looks a bit like a warehouse and it hosts strippers, dodgy comics and stag nights. If it was in Alabama you would call it redneck heaven. The owner, Paul Aaron Stone, is a gent and so is his manager, Peter Roue, and the bouncers are the cuddliest in the world. The Pukka pies are good and the session lager is cheap and potable. When I spieled my first match there it was a pure delight; crowd heaving, players sweating, my adrenalin streaming. It was Jocky versus John Lowe and at the end I was drenched and dizzy with excitement. I have since done 180s and nine-darters elsewhere but take it from me, my volcanic style is in perfect symbiosis with the screaming hordes of the Circus Tavern. Rusty tangled Christmas tinsel, messages on greasy chip plates, an atmosphere that is simply inspirational. Keep your Wembley and your Henley. Give me the working-class poetry of darts.

There was certainly poetry on the oche when Phil Taylor played John Lowe in a classic semi-final match. With both players averaging 95 in mid-match, they suddenly exploded into a new gear. The legs went 14, 15, 15, 14, 12, 13, 13, 16, 12, 14 ... simply sensational. It was by far the best sustained session of darts John Gwynne or I had ever seen. 'Heading for Venus, by way of Mars,' I reckoned. Taylor won and the two players embraced in front of an ecstatic crowd.

Bellies and Bullseyes

My main memory of my first gig at the Circus Tavern is of the night before the final. Play had finished at five and we had all been invited back to the club for a New Year's Eve party. My wife Irene was in a splint and on crutches, having broken her kneecap in a fall, but gamely accompanied me to the bash. It was just like New Year at Lynemouth Social Club when I was a youth – give or take some blue rinses and white stilettos. We had a meal, a few drinks and watched a comedian who sang while two lasses with legs like Wigan prop forwards high-kicked and shimmied. Then the fun really started. I began solo-bopping in the aisle to 'Cotton-Eyed Joe' when suddenly six booted, shaven bovver boys surrounded me. I was scared stiff. Then one of the lads linked arms with me and started a kind of do-si-do. 'We are the Catford Skins and we are fans of yours. Dance!' I did.

About one o'clock we left for home and there was more fan 'worship'. Six well-pissed lads with very posh voices guided Irene and I through the snow and slush to our taxi singing the *Jossy's Giants* theme tune. They were all university students. This kind of thing had never happened to me at Frimley Green – and I admit I loved it. Next day I had to lead celebrity guests on to the stage in front of a packed house for a Taylor/Priestley final and we had a team game of darts. I averaged 27 and was roundly booed.

Then three things happened that were of vital importance for the future of WDC darts.

One, Phil Taylor began his dominance of the sport by crushing Rod Harrington 6–2 in sets in the world final.

Two, Barry Hearn walked into the Circus Tavern, resplendent in his role as king of the C1 Sports, and said: 'I love it. I smell money.'

Thirdly, the BDO showed just how petty their campaign against the 'rebels' was by striking Taylor, Priestley, Anderson, Bristow and Lowe from the programme for their Embassy event a few days later. Not content with trying to ruin the careers of the signatories of the WDC charter, Olly Croft wanted to do a Stalin and purge the record. It did not matter that they were past world champions. They were his opponents because they spoke out for themselves or refused to defer to darts' own self-styled 'Guvnor'.

The BDO's use of the phrase 'associating with' WDC people had become a licence for every little witch-finder in every nook and cranny of their organisation. Whatever Croft and his allies in Muswell Hill intended, between the Finchley meeting in spring 1993 and the pre-court case proceedings in 1997 some terrible things were being reported. A darts-playing builder told Phil Taylor that he had been told not to fit Phil's new door. Phil's cousin Jimmy Prince, a Staffordshire county player, was told he must not speak to Phil. Mansfield brewery representatives told Phil that their landlords had been warned not to have exhibitions by Taylor or the other 'rebels'; if they did their pub teams would be banned. Phil did a regular charity darts night for a local hospital's baby care unit, only to have several super league players pull out of the one in August 1993. The BDO had warned them off.

It was the same with other counties. In Scotland, a BDO Scots international playing an exhibition downed arrows and said he would not play on until Jamie Harvey was chucked out. The landlord told him to get stuffed. Just about the most zealous witch-hunter was Fred Page, secretary of Northumberland. He was seen looking in windows at a Rod Harrington exhibition in the north-east and preparing a list of members of the audience who should be banned. I have seen letters from BDO head office warning Page to back off. But he did hound Peter Barron out of Northumberland darts for 'spotting' at a WDC televised tournament. He did this to a man who had served the county as player and official since the age of seventeen.

Freddie Williams, a stalwart of Essex county darts, was forced out for officiating at a WDC event, and John Raby of Hertfordshire received similar treatment.

All this unpleasantness just made the 'rebels' more determined. Some of them mortgaged their homes to raise fees to fight the BDO in court. Players with a bit of money in the bank – such as Harrington, Taylor and Priestley – paid into a legal fighting fund. Tommy Cox, Dick Allix and other agents and manufacturers swelled the fund. And John Raby put in several thousand to keep the campaign for justice going at a crucial stage.

A positive factor as both sides took legal advice was that the WDC prize money, especially from Sky, was increasing year by year. New sponsors were coming in. And such was the solidarity that several top players took their prize money for big events in instalments.

The BDO in their wild arrogance tried to get a world ban in 1994 against the 'rebels' and 'associates'. They should have heard warning bells when Canada and America refused to countenance such a thing. Both the American Darts Organisation and the National Darts Federation of Canada said firmly that the constitution of their countries forbade 'restraint of trade'; it is illegal to stop a man or woman earning a living. When the dust settled in mid-1997 and the BDO were ordered to lift their ban, the grounds the WDC were arguing was that the BDO had been acting 'in restraint of trade'. Perhaps more thought by the BDO would have saved both sides a lot of money. And who can assess the cost in sheer bad blood?

In the middle of 1995 I was in Blackpool, again with the Sky team, for the World Matchplay tournament and was looking forward to welcoming to town my brother Derrick and a Lynemouth posse later in the week. The good thing was that I would not have to smuggle them into our hotel; they were booked into a guest house run by Bobby Hill, a Lynemouth lad, where they would get dinner, bed, breakfast and an evening meal for *ten quid* a go! The Sky team and the players were at the Village, a posh country club-type hotel that had a great golf course. It had only one drawback; it was just over the fence from the zoo. So my beauty sleep was invaded by the roars of randy elephants and hungry lions.

The Winter Gardens was again the perfect venue, with many Scottish fans in with kids and wild Russ Abbot outfits. Star of the first round were my good pals Cliff Lazarenko and Shayne Burgess. Shayne had brought his air gun with him and was living high on the hog, literally; he was out shooting rabbits and hedgehogs and cooking them into pies. He was making a good living from vermin control in Sussex, but sometimes got a shock. Like the time when what he thought was a badger behind a haystack turned out to be a wild boar! Did he run.

When Laz met Shayne in the second round, I really let rip with the patter. 'Shayne is as happy as a hound dog with a year's supply of

209

Bonio', which set the tone for the early play, but Laz triumphed and I yelled: 'Cliff is off and looking for something yellow in a tall glass … and I don't mean daffodils.' This reference to Cliff's liking of a pint or six added a touch of humour. I have drunk in Cliff's company and know his capacity. In fact, in Ireland in 2004 Cliff excelled himself. He was practising at eight in the morning for a match at two. Before the game he had around ten pints of lager and in the commercial breaks he had another four. He lost narrowly and, when walking off stage, he banged his head on a beam. WDC officials decided he ought to go to the hospital and have an X-ray. Cliff was ferried there by Tommy Cox and was waiting in a corridor when a surgeon came past and recognised him.

'Hello Cliff,' said the medic. 'What are you doing here?'

'Banged me barnet, mate. Just in for a check.'

'Come this way,' said the surgeon and led Cliff into a cubicle. 'Oh by the way, have you had any alcohol in the last few hours?'

Cliff did a quick check. 'Yeah … about fourteen pints.'

The medic looked gobsmacked.

Cliff turned to Tommy. 'That's not much for me, is it Tom?'

I have had drinking sessions till late with Cliff and, in a friendship of twenty-eight years standing, have never seen him pissed. No slurring, no Jekyll/Hyde character change, no swearing. Like John Lowe, in his cups he remains a true gent.

On the night before the Geordie posse were due to arrive, Dave Lanning and I went for a curry – and found what we thought was a 'gay tandoori'. Dave had been on the beach all day and was still wearing brief turquoise shorts at eleven o'clock when we finished. We saw a sign saying 'Shalimar Gardens' just along from Yates's Wine Lodge, ran up the stairs and sat down. We got two pints of Cobra and began talking animatedly. Suddenly we got the impression that we were the centre of attention. I snuck a look round and was surprised to see all the tables full of male couples in leather, denim and Freddie Mercury vests. Dave's long pink legs were the object of attention. And, just like years back at the Capricorn Club in Soho we were waxing verbally exotic, to say the least.

'Excuse me while I ring the wife,' I bellowed to Dave like Freddie Trueman. I went to the public phone and pretended to chat to Irene – loudly. 'How's t'kids and t'whippets, love? Can't wait to get back home.'

It did the trick. We got no more glances as we tucked into our biryanis. And every year since, we have taken our custom to the 'gay tandoori'. Last visit, the owner gave me a free bottle of Balti Chardonnay. And in fact, they only have their leather and denim nights once a month.

The next night the Geordies arrived and we had a ball. Richie Stafford and his son Lee, my brother Derrick and his son Robbie, and a couple of others joined Jamie Harvey and me at the Crazy Scot Karaoke Club. Jamie was the star turn and did six numbers, then he hauled me up and we duetted on 'I Belong to Glasgow'. Wisely, thinking of the final, I called it a draw and hit my kip before one. Time was I would have done six numbers. As it was, after a couple of relaxing pints of lager, I had a good night's rest and was chipper for the Matchplay final between Dennis and Phil.

The game was a fitting climax to a great week. Jocky had taken the

Winter Gardens by storm early doors by putting out Rod Harrington. The crowd had cheered on an inspired Keith Deller with 'Things can only get Deller' and John Lowe had been in vintage form. The final would climax thirty-five hours of superb live telly for Sky.

Taylor led the way in the final and Dennis was always two or three legs out of touch. But the drama was maintained by Dennis hanging on grimly. My best line was 'Dennis's darts are going into that 60 at more angles than Hypotenuse ever dreamed of.' I never did know my Hypotenuse from my Pythagoras! Finally Phil won at a canter 16–11 and the players hugged. I knew they would share the £16,000 prize money for first and second. It pleased me to see the cash growing each year and the 'rebels' becoming more convinced they had done the right thing in splitting from the BDO.

After the match the Geordies and I partied moderately. I treated them all to a slap-up Chinese meal and Dave Lanning cracked his 'They'll Try to Sell us Egg Foo Yung' line for the umpteenth time. It still got laughs. I reflected how much cosier I felt with family and colleagues around me. What made me most happy was to see my brother Derrick tucking into food and drink with pals and cracking jokes non-stop. For the last few years he had lived in Lynemouth with my mum, occasionally seeing his two kids Robbie and Regan, who lived in Lowestoft. He had been out of work for a long time and had been spending too much time in the pubs of Ashington, lonely and depressed. Sadly, this was to be his last visit to the darts. He became unwell in July 1996 and died in Ashington Hospital of pneumonia. He was only forty-eight years of age.

Since its inception in 1992 the WDC had pushed to brighten the image and the presentation of darts. Dick Allix and Tommy Cox, now the main driving forces, decided we should mix up the formats of the various 'world' events. So, the world championship was a 'sets' event, with chances to get back at vital junctures, Blackpool was 'matchplay' – legs only – and the World Team (Pairs) championship was designed to add the frisson, so well known to pub players, of the stars relying on not-so-well-known partners. Sadly, somebody forgot to tell the punters and when we started play at the Willows Variety Centre in Salford at one o'clock on Monday, 31 September, 1996, there were only twenty paying customers in the audience. We had to get the bar staff and two blokes painting lines on the rugby league pitch to fill the front rows!

So it was a *sotto voce* Sidney and Dave Lanning who began the spiel when Keith Deller and Jamie Harvey took on the favourites, Taylor and Anderson. Also, the non-atmosphere of the first afternoon seemed to mock the loud rock music and Sky's latest gimmick. The latter was on-screen aggressive slogans, ostensibly by the lads but penned by me. 'We shall fuse the Power and clatter the Cowboy' flashed on-screen as Keith and Jamie walked onstage. I cringed.

But by nine that night, with six hundred Salfordians supping Boddy's and giving it tonsil, the doggerel on-screen did not seem so bad. By Thursday my slogan for Deller and Harvey versus Sean Downs and Gerrard Verrier of USA was 'American Pie are gonna fry'.

The final was another example of the new blood coming through that the WDC were seeking to promote. Taylor and Anderson were taken on by Steve Raw, a great money player from West Durham, and Chris Mason, a tense, emotional player of immense talent. Mason had been watching Embassy videos since he was eight and was a real rough diamond. He had told the papers he had been a bouncer and enjoyed looking for fights. He even admitted driving a car at a bloke who had upset him. This wild streak was later to involve Chris in an eight-month spell in prison for aggravated assault. But despite his wild side, his talent is unquestionable. He and Raw pressed the 'veterans' in the Salford final, and Taylor and Anderson were glad to snidge victory 18–15 in the final.

Funniest moment in the commentary booth was when I was ordered not to use the word 'rug' on pain of sacking. Reason: veteran Lancashire player Jack North was sweating cobs and his curly shellac-black wig was slipping over his left ear. He and his partner Fran Lynch rallied in a match and John Gwynne really went for panto effect: 'Well, Jack's been up the beanstalk – so what's a little leg of 501 to him?' Spot on comment. It would not get a laugh in a playground full of seven-year-olds, but in darts it seems to work.

My week was made perfect when top Geordie actor Tim Healy showed up for a drink with the lads and said on air that my commentaries were worth the price of Sky. What's that about a prophet in his own land? Tim bought me a couple of scoops of Boddys and I replied with a lot of the Broon.

The Sky/WDC tie-up continued to go from strength to strength in early 1997. First it was announced that a million-dollar deal was in place for coverage of the blooming portfolio of WDC events, with talk of a major tournament in Las Vegas. Then came the great news that in June we would be covering the historic *News of the World*

Championships, which carried a £42,000 first prize. There was extra interest as the legal battle between the BDO and the PDC was nearing the High Court stage. In a closely argued letter to *Darts World*, Tommy Cox tried to impress on the BDO that the WDC were accusing them of a vendetta, a very serious matter, and that talks might stop the spending of more money on the case. Tommy stressed that each side was about £80,000 out of pocket with legal costs to date, and that if High Court proceedings began this would escalate to a further £100,000 bill for each side. There was no indication from Olly Croft that he saw the matter as urgent.

With Martin Adams, a BDO stalwart, one of the favourites for the *News of the World* event and Taylor of the WDC in great form, I was licking my lips at the prospect. It was definitely a prestige battle between the rival camps. And, how about this for tension: like always, the *NotW* matches would be the best of only THREE legs! Kamikaze darts, or what?

So Gwynne, Lanning and I were wiping away tears of pure nostalgia as we waited for the first darts to be thrown in front of a packed Aston Villa Leisure Centre. I looked down the list of previous winners and was swamped in memories: Tommy Barrett, twice a winner; Bobby George, twice a winner; Eric Bristow, twice a winner; Stefan Lord, of Sweden, twice a winner. I had to pinch myself because five years earlier at the start of the dispute I honestly thought the game I loved was dead on its feet.

The play was fast and furious and for once I had to play Joe Calm, trying to stop John Gwynne ranting wall-to-wall over the end of matches. 'You're making it fucking radio, mate!' I yelled off mike, but he just rolled his eyes and spouted all the worse. I hasten to add that in the years since John has been less manic.

There was plenty to wax manic and mellifluous about when the semi-finals produced a Taylor versus Adams clash. Going in, Taylor was clear favourite, with a 100 average to Adams' 91. But Adams went the better in leg one and won it. So Phil had to take the next two legs. He produced a titanic leg of thirteen darts: 100, 100, 100, 177 and double 12. Taylor sneered at Adams who had left a show-off 170.

Then Taylor started the last leg with 134. I whispered to the millions, 'Captain Morgan? Torquemada? You name the torturer. Taylor is now dishing out real pain.'

The crowd were silent as Phil left double 4 and 'Wolfie' Adams gasping and toothless – and a ton off the pace. Phil clinched the match and I wound up the spiel: 'It's like being at a convent the night Mother Superior won the Lottery – bad habits breaking out all over the shop.'

The final was a formality. Phil took on Ian 'Diamond' White and slaughtered him over two legs to take the famous trophy. John Gwynne got the punchline spot on. 'Powerus maximus est – Phil is the greatest.'

The WDC champion had won the day. Was it an omen for what was to happen as the four-year bitter dispute reached its denouement?

The end of the dispute came in a rush over four days at the end of June, 1997. In fact the case never started on the floor of the High Court. After three days' debate by barristers for each side, a compromise was reached and on 30 June the Tomlin Order was issued. Its main point was that the BDO lifted their ban on players, associates,

etc and the *Guardian* said baldly: 'the BDO lost its case'. Eric
Bristow echoed the importance of this aspect: 'For the first time in
four years I am free to play in darts competitions all over the world.'
That there had been restraint of trade was *de facto* established. Phil
Taylor, Eric Bristow, Dennis Priestley and Peter Evison raised pints
high in a pub near the law courts to what true grit and collaboration
had achieved. The WDC players were so relieved to get their main
aim that they abandoned any attempt to get damages for four years'
loss of earnings. And the WDC, now renamed the Professional Darts
Corporation was as usual ever eager to spread its wings. A few days
later we were at a packed Circus Tavern for a special 'Battle of the
Champions' on Sky. I went up to the practice room an hour before
Eric Bristow was due to play Alan Evans. Eric was banging in the
180s casually and sipping a pint of Guinness. 'Anybody seen the
cocky Welsh bastard?' I asked jokily. Eric's face blenched. He pointed
to the corner where a small figure, skinny and with thin black hair was
practising. The lips were pursed and the tip-toe style was in evidence.
It was Alan Evans. Thank heavens he had not heard my crack. I
walked over and Alan shook my hand warmly. 'Good to be back. Sid.
I don't suppose you got any new lines. Same old bollocks, eh?' I
agreed. He looked very pale and drawn.

In commentary I recalled the great battles between Alan and
Eric. Sadly, despite the roars of dozens of fans with leeks and
daffodils, Alan went down 3–0 in sets to Eric. There were four brilliant 180s but little else.

Alan had been in poor health with kidney and liver trouble for a
couple of years and in April 1999 he died in Barry, South Glamorgan,

aged forty-nine. He was admittedly self-destructive, but what a talent. He was the cornerstone of the professional game.

In the marquee match at the Circus, Phil Taylor defeated the 1995 Embassy champion Richie Burnett 4–1 in sets with an amazing 114 average.

At Blackpool a few weeks later Phil and Dennis Priestley really rubbed the BDO's nose in it. Before the PDC's World Matchplay, the BDO had organised the British Classic at the Norbreck Castle Hotel and some of their strongest players were there, including Ronnie Baxter, Martin Adams and Ray van Barneveld. Having nowt to do on the Sunday before the Sky event I went along for a giggle with Alan Warriner. Alan and I sat drinking pints of lager in the middle of the hall and were shunned by every BDO official, with especial scowls from the ladies in their maroon trouser suits. One woman growled at me: 'Why don't you stay with yer own lot?' Daft question, luv. Two of 'my lot' were up on the stage taking the BDO lads to the cleaners. Dennis Priestley won the singles and Priestley/Taylor won the pairs! Alan and I were now on our fourth pint of Grolsch and cheering like maniacs. *Darts World* magazine did a cover picture of BDO stalwart Sam Hawkins presenting the cup to Dennis and Phil and his face looked as if he was starring in a castor oil commercial.

And Phil was not done, not by a long chalk. Later that week at the Winter Gardens he played the best week's darts of his life.

He came out in round one like a gladiator and minced Gary Mawson of Canada. The massive crowd of 2,500, in shorts and sun hats, masks and makeovers, were stunned to silence as Phil won 8–0 in legs with an average of 112. At the end Gary sank to his knees, offered up a prayer and kissed Phil's feet. I yelled on commentary: 'It's the nearest thing to a public execution you'll see this side of Saudi Arabia.' It was 100 per cent warranted hyperbole and Giles Smith in the *Daily Telegraph* agreed. He added: 'Let no one say darts isn't a physically complex sport.'

The only two blokes who really tested Phil that week were Rod 'Prince of Style' Harrington, whose nickname I certainly did not make up, and Alan Warriner. Rod, a former schooboy soccer star who played with a young Glenn Hoddle, went down fighting 13–9 to Phil in the semi. Then the Power went berserk against Wozzer in the final; he won 16–11 with an average of 106. It was as if all the pent-up fury of the four-year dispute was being cauterised in a flame of pure tungsten.

At the end there was silver and green confetti tinsel all over the stage and Martin Turner spoke eloquently of what Sky had tried successfully to do with darts: 'Put these genuine working-class heroes together with high-tech presentation and you are on to a winner. It's a simple game played by ordinary-looking people but at a pitch of excellence. What better combination for a sport?'

He might have added that in darts you are never far away from a belly laugh. I always try to do my duty by the fans, and after the Blackpool final I was signing autographs. Then I ran towards the taxi rank with a posse of boozed-up lads after me. I was wearing a new pair of baggy denim trousers and they were slipping down my waist as I ran, clutching at my belt. Suddenly from out of Auntie Maggie's Carousel bar shot a female fan with a large bosom, mini-skirt and very high heels. Just as I reached the taxi queue, she hurled her arms round my neck and began kissing me. I put up my hands to fend her off … and my baggy pants dropped round my ankles! From behind it looked as though we were having sex. There were cries from the fans and a sarky crack from Dave Lanning: 'Surely you can wait till you get her back to the hotel, lover boy.' I shook her off and escaped.

8

The Greatest Dart Player Who Ever Drew Breath

I have to thank my friend Freddie Trueman for the title of this chapter. Many years ago Freddie sat pulling comfortably on his favourite briar pipe and said to the would-be ghost writer of his life story: 'Call it THE LIFE AND TIMES OF THE GREATEST FAST BOWLER EVER TO DRAW BREATH.' The end product was in fact called *Fiery Fred*, but you can't win them all.

I first got to know Phil Taylor and his family well in February 2003, just after he had lost his world darts crown to John Part. I had been commissioned to help Phil write his biography so I made a nostalgic train trip from Leeds to Stoke-on-Trent. I did not intend making many notes on this first trip, nor did I take my trusty tape recorder. I wanted to sniff the animal in his lair, acting au naturel.

As the train pulled into Stoke station I almost shed tears. This is where I landed for many years from 1978 to do the Embassy World Darts Championship. This is where I stood dry-mouthed and nervous in new Farah slacks wondering how many mistakes I'd make on scores and how many scathing letters would find their way into *Darts World*. I waited for a taxi in the shadow of the mullioned and turreted

North Staffordshire Hotel where I had toasted our BBC successes and exorcised our cock-ups with Nick Hunter, my mentor, and the legendary David Coleman.

A few minutes later I was dropped at the large modern detached house in Bradwell where the Taylors had lived for several years. Outside was the Philmobile, a big van that he takes to every exhibition and on the side of which was the famous 'Power' logo. I was made welcome by Phil's wife Yvonne and given a mug of tea. After five minutes' chat, Phil jumped to his feet. 'I've got some nice bits of liver here. I'll do them with some onions and oatcakes. Elevenses.' He dived into the kitchen. It had been all over the papers that Phil had been almost a vegetarian for four months and was scrutinising his every mouthful of food minutely.

'Liver? Onions?' I asked. 'Oatcakes? The press are telling us you are living on rabbit food.'

Phil winked. 'Bit of rabbit food – bit of Potteries food. Got to have a mixture. Lose all my strength if I stuck to salads.'

We sat down and enjoyed the snack. The Taylor living room was spacious with green leather armchairs and a matching chesterfield. Phil showed me his conservatory and I nearly tripped over a set of new-looking dumbbells. 'This what you work out with?' I asked.

'Got them out a couple of times,' he said. 'But I forget they're there.' So much for 'Phil's fitness regime' that the press had extolled, I thought. Maybe our Philip exaggerates his body maintenance mania to the papers a wee bit. Next Phil showed me round the bedrooms upstairs and I came across an impetuous, practical joking, side that might surprise all those who only see his 'business' face when smashing

222

in 180s on telly. He suddenly grabbed something off a dressing table, throttled me with a mighty Popeye forearm and savagely shaved my *eyebrows*! 'New clippers,' he grinned. 'You gotta be smart on telly Sidney; you were looking a bit shaggy.'

In the early afternoon of my first visit, Phil and Yvonne gave me a guided tour of their patch. We went past The Cricketers pub that they ran for several years, then they took me to the bus station in Longton. Again I was damp-eyed as I looked up at the plastic jester sign saying 'Jollees' over a dusty glass door. Had the Taylors ever been at the great darts matches in the eighties? 'No,' said Phil with a sigh. 'We never had the money to go down the pub, never mind chicken, chips and few beers at the world darts.'

Soon we were passing a workingmen's club and Phil got excited: 'That's Ryan Hall Catholic Club where Robbie Williams won all the junior talent competitions. Cocky and confident he was even then.' Then the Taylors took me down streets that still looked part of the Depression of the 1930s. Phil showed me the factory in Burslem where he made toilet-chain handles and we stopped in Blake Street at the first house they'd ever had. Inside, we had tea with Phil's proud mum, Liz, who lives there now, and I was taken upstairs to a working shrine. In a tiny bedroom stood the oche with full lights and scoreboards that he'd practised on since the late 1980s. 'I come back here when I really need to practise hard. John Part has got my title on loan and here I'll graft to get it back.'

On my next visit I saw another side of Phil's character that explains a lot about how he treats darts as his job. I got to his house just before nine o'clock and Yvonne made me a coffee, explaining

223

that Phil was bit busy. After a few minutes he stuck his head out of a small room off the hall and called me in. He sat down at a loom-type machine, called, he said 'a vinyl plotter', and began embroidering badges on to a tennis shirt. On the floor were a dozen or so shirts already neatly done. 'I've got an exhibition in Birmingham tonight and they said they needed team shirts,' he explained. 'So I offered to knock up the shirts at a fair price.' This, remember, from a man who was probably a millionaire by that time. It reminded me of the time I went to see John Lowe at Chesterfield in 1979 when he was world champion. I was shown into the back of his shop where he was carving the plinths for darts trophies. 'Once a joiner, always a joiner, Sid,' said Stoneface.

Phil and I did about three hours taping, then he said he had to be off to the exhibition. 'But you'll be all right, Shaun will take you down the Saggars.' I went in like an apostle approaching Calvary. The Saggars, short for Saggar Makers, where once pottery workers supped, swore and slung hopeful arrows, is a cathedral dedicated to football and darts in general, and Phil Taylor in particular. Landlord Dave Lewis has assembled a Newcastle United wall – everybody up there from Milburn to Shearer – and a Phil Taylor museum. There are shirts, England team pictures and a large portion of Phil's trophies. If you are privileged, one night you can sit in the sports room and watch The Power practise. I sat and supped a couple of Banks' bitters and just dug the ambience. I had to be dragged next door to play pool.

A few days later I joined an exclusive club: I became one of the few people ever to see Phil Taylor drunk.

There was a sound excuse. Phil never had much money when he was in his teens and early twenties, so pubbing was not an option. He now drinks a few before matches: a couple of halves of lager, maybe a glass of wine, or a port and brandy if he's not eaten for several hours. But on St Patrick's Day 2003 we had done great work in taping four hours of material for the book. Yvonne fed us a mixed grill each and off we went at six to a pub. Chris, Phil's son, joined us at the pool table and the local bitter went down a treat. Sadly for me, the pool balls went down a treat for the Taylors. I got only two frames out of a dozen. At about 7.30, having all three of us downed four pints, we started for home – only to meet an Irish ceilidh band booked to play that night. So … Phil and I 'guested' with the band and free drinks flew at us from all quarters. We sang, Phil in warm baritone and me in karaoke kitsch. We did the whole Gaelic emotional range: 'Danny Boy', 'Seven Drunken Nights' and, at least three times, 'The Fields of Athenry', and we drank another three pints each. Thank God it was downhill all the way from the pub to the Taylor mansion. We propped each other up and did not say much. But I saw it as a bit of bonding and so, I reckon, did Yvonne. She packed me off to my hotel in a taxi with a kiss on the forehead.

A few days later Phil came to my house in Pudsey to watch some videos of great matches, but I had a hard job sitting him down. First, he had to inspect all the 100-year-old ornamental tiles in my house. As a lad from the land of Spode and Wedgwood, he knows good ceramics from naff, and I was chuffed when he said the Waddell stuff was top-notch. Then he jiggled with the handles on my French windows. They were loose, due to the last bloke who fixed them putting them on the wrong way round. The Power frowned, took off his jacket and sent me off for a Phillips screwdriver – Phillips what? He replaced the handles in ten minutes and was still looking for odd jobs when I dragged him into the office to work.

Knowing how to work hard and knowing the value of money are key factors in the make-up of the man who has, more than any other single individual, made darts what it is today: a world-wide entertainment sport and thriving business.

I know a bit about poverty. I was brought up in Lynemouth in the 1940s and 1950s, when the miners were at last getting a living wage. My dad never missed a day at the pit and we were well off. But other kids in Dalton Avenue went to school in old cast-off boots and others had raggy shirts. That was nothing to the poverty that Phil Taylor was born into on 13 August, 1960.

From the age of eighteen Phil's father Doug slogged, shifting tons of wet clay by shovel for a tiling firm. In his mid-twenties he was exhausted and took lighter work at a different tiling firm. The wages were rock bottom, as they were throughout the Potteries. Phil's mum Liz helped out working in various porcelain factories. Somehow they scraped together £50 and put it down on a house in Tunstall. It was no palace; the ceilings were caving in and half the windows were boarded up. Phil's dad used to joke that they did not need a window cleaner, they needed a sander.

Things were so tight that when Phil was about five he remembers scavenging council tips for copper wire and selling it for eight shillings a load. He and his mother also scrabbled on pit heaps for coal. Believe it or not, for months the house had no electricity supply, but that did not stop Liz bringing telly into their lives. A set was delivered and a wire was run through the window from next door! The deal was that the lady next door, who paid weekly into a catalogue club run by Liz, was docked a few shillings off her regular payments.

So now when I hear odd players, morose in defeat, say that Phil Taylor 'is only interested in money' I roll my eyes and look the other way.

When Phil was six the family moved into a semi in Mill Hill with electricity and hot water but Liz was as frugal as ever. She cruised jumble sales and bought woollen kids' garments to unpick and re-knit. Her masterpiece was a pair of trousers and a waistcoat for Phil in white with blue flecks. You can imagine what the hard knocks of Abbey Hutton estate, known locally as 'Comanche Country', made of this little kid in woolly keks trotting to his auntie's house. 'They yelled "Sheepdog" and barked at me, but that was all,' Phil recalls.

In his early teens Phil was quite a good bowler in school cricket and tried darts at a youth club. An old man in a muffler and tatty suit watched him for a while and said: 'Keep at it son, one day you'll be world champ.' The road to greatness started in 1967 when Phil was seventeen, at a pub called the Riley Arms, where the darts tradition was deep and the standard very high. It was here that Phil became an apprentice money racer. The star of the Riley Arms was a mercurial bloke in his thirties called Kenny Massey. On a good night he would fling a dart at a double and shake his opponent's hand before it went in. If he was not up to par, Kenny would jam his darts in his pockets and storm off home. But Kenny was not daft when it came to spotting talent. He liked the fact that Phil wound up the stars at the Riley when he beat them, saying: 'If you're so good how come a kid like me can beat you?' Then, as now, The Power was good at the tetchy verbal.

Kenny and Phil paired up in money matches. They would often play for £50 stake money and the split was not down the middle. Kenny would take £45 and give Phil a fiver. 'I never thought it was unfair,' Phil recalls. 'The experience was priceless – and if I had not got sidetracked by girls and discos, I'd have made my pile no trouble.'

So the world had to wait another eight years for the emergence of the Taylor phenomenon. In that time Phil had three different apprenticeships at work needing extreme manual skill. He became a trainee electrician at a local colliery for a few months then signed on to install dust extraction units into factories. But before his most famous job – making ceramic handles – his life in discos bore fruit. He had taken to wearing a white suit with flares and cutting a rug at the Sneyd Arms in Tunstall at the weekly disco. He'd be first on the floor for Mud, the Bay City Rollers and Slade. Then one night he spotted Yvonne Rawlinson, petite, bright-eyed and elegant in a black velvet jacket. He was smitten.

They began courting and, thinking of the future, Phil got a job at Vanroys, a pottery business where he worked on lathes and milling machines. In 1980 he moved to Hackneys doing a similar job. His wage was around £45 a week, making beer-pump handles, insulators for electricity pylons and toilet-chain handles. The work was very precise. If Phil made one mistake in two thousand units he did not wait for the foreman to bollock him, he kicked himself. That is why if he misses a simple double or even a nine-dart finish for £100,000, he bashes his leg with his arrows. This perfectionism was bred in a bleak factory in Burslem.

Despite courting strong, Phil and Yvonne were both living at their parents' houses in 1981 when Phil picked up darts in anger for the second time. At a holiday camp in Devon, Phil easily beat Welsh stars Dap Cairns and Chris Johns.

Still, this did not drive him back to the Riley Arms or give him hopes of representing Staffordshire in the inter-counties darts competition. The Taylors scrimped and saved, Phil did up old cars after work and sold them, and in 1982 they put down a deposit on a tiny house in Blake Street, Burslem. They moved in with borrowed pots and pans. Soon their first child Lisa was born.

I have already described the fateful crossing of the lives of Phil Taylor and Eric Bristow in 1985. After Phil watched Eric in action and said he could beat him, Yvonne bought Phil a set of darts for his birthday in August and darts history began. Phil had a joiner mate make a proper oche alongside the bed in the main bedroom. Yvonne would sit reading magazines as darts whistled above her head. She had to plead with Phil to come to bed. After work he would set himself targets such as six 180s, then bed. He was a complete martinet to himself. He wanted the best out of his talent. As Tommy Cox told me years later: 'Phil is the best practiser I have ever seen. He goes at it hour after grinding hour.' This attitude reaped quick dividends.

Phil began gaining a reputation playing for the Huntsman pub in the super league and had his eye on getting into the Staffordshire county team. In September 1987 the call came to pay for the county

'B' team. The Taylors made the trip to play in London on the cheap. It was the first time Phil and Yvonne had stayed at a hotel. They sat in the bar with halves of beer and made sandwiches with ham, cheese and bits of pork. Despite massive nerves Phil won his match 3–0 and was put in the 'A' team for the next match. For the rest of the season he and Eric Bristow won the man-of-the match awards. The £12 that went with it was peanuts to Brissy, but a golden bonus to the Taylors. And, though he did not show it, Eric was very impressed by Taylor's performances. That season Phil's best win was 3–0 against Glamorgan's Dai Furness in 14, 14 and 16 darts. The occasion meant nothing to the nerveless Taylor; from the start he looked a champion. He also took apart Peter Taylor of Surrey with four 180s in a match.

Then out of the blue, Eric made his move. Early in 1988 he made Phil an offer: he would put up thousands of pounds to sponsor Phil round the world as a darts professional. It would mean Phil taking voluntary redundancy and being technically 'on the dole' for a while, but it was what he wanted. The payback was negotiable. 'Pay me when you win summat,' said Eric. And win he did.

In April 1988 Phil and Yvonne got married at Hanley register office and then the groom shot off to play a county darts match at two o'clock. Only after the match did they have their reception. Then Phil went to Canada to try to prove that Bristow's faith in him was justified. While some of the players drank and had a good time, Eric and Phil went to the pictures and watched Rambo and Schwarzenegger. It worked; Phil beat Bob Anderson 5–1 in sets in the final and got a cheque for $5,000. Eric was in like a rat up a drainpipe to claim the money and his behaviour as Phil's sponsor often rankled. Eric was at the peak of his struggle with dartitis and this may explain his tetchiness, but it became so marked that Phil felt he was being humiliated by his mentor. You rarely see them together at tournaments to this day and when they are in company there is a cold, offhand edge. It baffles me and other pundits, but it is for real.

In the latter weeks of 1989 Eric and Phil practised together for hours in the run-up to the Embassy World Championship. Eric would sip at pints of bitter, while Phil would be in carpet slippers and take nothing stronger than black tea. They played in the Cross Keys at Northwood and even did three hours hard graft on the board on Christmas Day. Then it was off to Frimley Green for the big one.

I still have Taylor's biography form from that historic event. In 'Occupation' it says 'Unemployed Engineer' and Phil was still drawing £74 a week dole. Under 'Ambition' it said 'To beat Eric Bristow in the Embassy final 6–5 in the tie-breaker.' Which fortune teller was he consulting? First, he beat Russell Stewart of Australia then Dennis Hickling of Yorkshire. I noticed in the practice room that many of the established players studiously ignored Phil. On commentary I dubbed him the 'Crafty Potter'.

Next Phil played a blinder against Ronnie Sharp of Scotland and won 4–0. Then he really got us talking when he blitzed Lazarenko 5–0 in the semi-final with a 100.5 average. We all knew about Brissy's dartitis but we thought it was well on the mend. Surely the maestro's nous and big-time flair would pip his protégé? It did not. Taylor wiped the floor with Eric, who buckled after a good start. The score was 6–1 in sets and I will never forget the determination written all over Phil's face; darks eyes flaring, tash twitching, growling heated asides to Eric. He had been taught by Bristow to bully and that's what he did. He later said he was getting back at Eric for the humiliation heaped on him over the sponsorship. In the last set I yelled 'The Crafty Potter is a canny slotter.' Phil kissed the world trophy and the cheque for £24,000. The world should have been his oyster.

Back in Stoke there was a street party to greet the new world champ and Phil got a personal letter from Sir Stanley Matthews. He also got lionised wherever he went. Some folk, grannies even, had put a bet on him to win the world title at 125–1! Legs of lamb, bottles of whisky and boxes of chocolates were left on the Taylors' doorstep. One of Phil's pals had lumped on him so much he'd bought a fancy new car and came round to give the champ a ride. Phil was asked to take the Embassy trophy round to the Crafty Cockney pub for a gala night and the doorman tried to charge him two quid to get in!

The call to England darts colours soon came. Phil was picked to join the crack squad that included John Lowe, Eric Bristow and Bob Anderson. Phil won his games and was declared man of the match. But, and maybe this was an omen of the dark clouds ahead, he fell foul of England team supremo Olly Croft. Phil had splashed out on some red trousers and a spiffy white jacket for the England appearance and Croft was not pleased. He said it was not 'official' gear. Phil refused to get rid of the clobber and thought he might have had his card marked; the England selectors had been known to be draconian with dissenters. But later in the year he made the four-man England squad for the Europe Cup.

He was one of the favourites for the 1991 Embassy World

Championship and practised hard with Eric. But the nerves got him and Dennis Priestley beat him 4–3 in the quarter-final, despite Phil having a 97 average to Dennis's 96.

So the scene was set for the dramatic events of the 1992 Embassy. Phil had completed one half of his darting dream by beating Eric in a world final, now he did the second half: he won a world final 6–5 in a tie-breaker.

I remember commentating on the early Taylor rounds and not being that impressed. He beat Magnus Caris and Per Skau with a mere 93 average. But then glimpses of the greatness to come came out against the very experienced Martin Phillips of Wales. Phil won the match in forty minutes with a 4–0 score-line and a 98 average, followed by a classic against John Lowe. At 4–1 up Taylor seemed to get too cocky, stopped bullying and let John back in to 4–4. Sheer grit kicked in and Phil won 5–4 to book his place in the final. He sat behind the stage and wept for a full fifteen minutes. In later years I was to ask on a Sky trailer: 'Why does The Power bubble [Geordie: cry] all the time?' The answer is a deep passion to excel. The money is great, but the glory is greater.

The final was, up to that time, the greatest darts match ever.

Phil faced the very experienced Mike Gregory, famous as the man who won the Lada Classic twice and so allegedly had *two* Ladas at home! Mike was prone to back trouble because of his awkward action, but also threw slack darts due to anger at making mistakes. I did the first six sets of the final and could not pick a winner. My best line was 'Gregory twisting like a gaffed salmon', and I was not happy that I had to let Tony Green finish the match. Still, I watched with bated breath as the match drew to 5–5 in sets and the players, with Gregory looking the more worried, went to the wire. At 2–2 in legs Mike had two darts at a double to win the title. He missed. Taylor calmly took the score to 3–3 in legs. At 5–4, Gregory again missed a double to win the title. Then Gregory missed with a further three darts. Frustration was written all over him. Taylor never looked back. He levelled the score at 5–5 then took the title with a 13-dart leg.

At the Embassy presentation and reception a couple of hours later I found myself in a hotbed of tension. I had always got on well with Tommy Cox, who was now Phil's manager, and Dick Allix, Eric Bristow's manager. Both men were standing at the back having a drink and I joined them as they discussed the simmering politics of the game. The BDO did not like agents or any idea of player power. 'Olly won't like you talking to us,' said Tommy. As it turned out my future had more to do with Tom and Dick than with the BDO. So did Taylor's.

The 1992 Embassy final should have had the impact on world darts that the 2007 PDC world final between Phil and Ray Van Barneveld did. There should have been more television, more money in the game and more public appreciation of the stars. It did not happen. In fact, the game went into decline, and was then mired in the dispute between the WDC and the BDO. Phil went on to fantastic success on Sky up to 1997.

At the end of 1997 Taylor's wins really rekindled his appetite and took him and the game into a new stratosphere. He beat Brissy's record of five world championships, turned his exhibitions into cabaret nights, practised harder than ever and even gobsmacked Dave

Lanning. 'We never thought we'd see the game of darts *mastered* but now in Taylor we have a master of the game,' said Dave at the 1998 PDC World Championship. How true that was, and what a privilege it has been to verbalise the actions of the master.

Though he did not manage a PDC Grand Slam in 1998 there were hints of great things to come when Taylor hit Rochester for the World Grand Prix. But before Phil got going the 'double to start' rule caused a real panic to our Sky bosses. At nine o'clock the night before the competition started, Dave Lanning and I were having a quiet beer in our hotel. The phone rang and Rory Hopkins invited us down the road to a pub where he and director Andy Finn were having a drink. Ten minutes into our chat I mentioned the double to start. You'd think Andy and Rory had been electrocuted.

'Double to start? Never,' said Rory.

'Yes,' said Dave.

'Which double?' asked Andy.

'Any double they like,' I said with a laugh.

'Fuck,' said Rory. 'We'll have to ring Tommy Cox and get it changed. We'll look awful if we cover the wrong double.'

'Tommy can't change it because the players have been practising double in for weeks,' I said.

There resulted a long phone call and we played double in.

It did not look sloppy and in fact the players were so good at going off on 160 that we had several progressions with a 9-dart in mind. The best of these was by Phil Tayor in the final against Rod Harrington and it is for ever engraved in my memory. In the middle of the match Taylor cracked in 160 and 180 and the crowd in the

Casino Rooms gasped as one. He stepped up looking to win £25,000 if three darts found 161. John Gwynne looked at me across the commentary box which was only thirty feet away from the oche. I went into banshee mode: 'Taylor wants 161 for the nine dart.' The first darts hit 60. 'HE WANTS TREBLE 17!' This was audible ten miles away at Chatham Docks. Phil's dart hit the treble 17 and he glowered at me and said 'Pillock!' Or something like that. I slid on to the floor of the box, sure I'd go down in darts folklore as the loud-mouth who cost The Power twenty-five grand. 'Phil needs the bull for a nine darter,' said John as softly as thistledown falling on new-mown hay. The dart landed in the 25, a millimetre outside the bull.

The crowd went mad. Rod shook Phil's hand. Phil won the match and the title. And a couple of days later I got a phone call from him: 'I'm told you were a bit upset that I heard you shout. Don't you worry, bud. I got the fifty-one when you yelled, but I missed the bull on my own. Don't worry.' So the man who is kind enough and concerned enough to give his winning darts away to kids at the world championship has the heart to boost an over-excited commentator. I call that real class.

A few weeks later the darts cabaret rolled into the Circus Tavern at Purfleet and there were great expectations that Phil would win his seventh world championship. There was also a new positive note in some of the press: they had twigged that Taylor's feats were an exceptional sporting achievement and up there with snooker legends Steve Davis and Stephen Hendry.

The Power bowled into town with all guns blazing. He took veteran Reg Harding to the cleaners 3–0 with an average of 105 and then did for John Lowe 3–1 with a 102 average. It was savage and it was awesome and it inspired me: 'I hear the rattle of a tumbril for Lowe. They're oiling the guillotine and Madame Defarge has put down her knitting.' Kate Battersby of the *Evening Standard* came into the box and was greeted by Dave Lanning: 'You'll love it here with the tungsten tossers.' She did and described her visit: 'At the darts you never met such a friendly crowd. They all tell you how glad they are that you've bothered to come along and after a while you twig that, unexpectedly, you're having a good time. After that there doesn't seem much point in smart-arse one-liners.' I reckon the watershed in press coverage was the 1999 world championship and Taylor's excellence was the catalyst; generally, the papers now treated us as a sport.

Taylor's next victim was Bob Anderson who went down 4–0 to another 102 average from Phil. As our floor manager led Phil off for interview, I could hear Bob yelling in sheer frustration: 'That man is not human – he's a bloody machine.' In the semi-final Phil was given a real game by Alan Warriner but The Power won 5–3. His average was 99 – very slack! In the final Phil easily disposed of Peter Manley 6–2 and his overall tournament average was 99.9. That was Bradman's final Test average and I see fate at work. It's one thing a ranting Geordie screaming that you are a world sporting great, but when the numbers underpin the noise, people take notice. Still, Taylor's seething ambition to have his talent recognised was not being fulfilled. As Ivan Speck commented wryly in the *Daily Mail*: 'Eric Bristow, the man whose five world titles Taylor has consigned to the history book, joked recently that the only hope Taylor had of being recognised in an airport lounge was if Bristow himself was standing next to him.' That was all to change as The Power cranked up the ante and the drama.

During the 1999 World Grand Prix at Rochester I found Phil Taylor in excellent mood at a Chinese restaurant after that night's play. Mick, one of his mates, was commenting on Phil's demolition of Peter Evison earlier that night. Phil had won 9–0 in legs in twenty-one minutes with a 102 average – this with a double to start, so really 110. 'That performance was just for Barney,' said Mick, lapping up won-ton soup. Phil winked and nodded.

Barney was Ray van Barneveld, winner of the BDO world championship at Frimley Green the previous two years, a bloke who some said was better than Taylor. I did not agree, but I certainly knew why Phil had fire in his belly for the contest. As seven times world champion Phil was raking in about £100,000 a year from exhibitions and prize money and he and Yvonne were running a pub in Stoke – a hefty workload. Barney, however, was rolling in clover. After two Embassy wins he had struck a chord with the Dutch sporting public and was estimated to be making around £300,000 per annum, selling more than forty thousand sets of his personalised darts in a single year.

A convincing win by The Power in a head-to-head would show the darting world who was top dog and whose were the best darts to buy.

Thanks to some great spadework by Barry Hearn, whose Matchroom company were the promoters, ably assisted by Tommy Cox, Barneveld had agreed to play Phil in a 'Simply the Best' challenge match at Wembley Conference Centre in early November. The winner would pick up £60,000 and the loser £40,000. Barney was really stepping out on a limb because, as he explained to the press, the BDO did not want him to play the match. They did not want to give the PDC and Taylor publicity. But the Dutchman has a mind of his own and he was eager to cross swords with Taylor.

The match was to have an original format. A giant clock would be set above the oche and it would tick down for exactly one hour. The player leading in legs when time ran out would be the winner. It had been arranged with ITV to cover the match and my Sky contract said that I could not do commentary on such a game. John Gwynne and Eric Bristow were signed up to do the telly, and Dave Lanning and I agreed to do it on radio for *Talksport*. What a laugh we had reading out adverts for 'Charlie's Cars of Ealing' and the like in between the puns, pantomime jokes and the scores.

The atmosphere at Wembley Arena was electric. There were hundreds of orange scarves in the crowd of 3,500 – paying £16 a throw for the privilege of watching – and a deafening chorus of 'There's only one Phil Taylor' from the English fans. At the start, Phil was bouncing like a boxing kangaroo whilst Barney looked as sick as a chip. I told our radio audience how much trouble he'd had from the BDO and how it looked to have sapped him. Ominously Taylor, chucking fast and confident, went into a 9–4 lead and the Dutch fans sounded as though their throats were full of Edam. 'Barney has won the Embassy twice but both times by the skin of his teeth. He is a very good player, but not yet a great player,' I told my audience. Phil looked grim but happy. He went from 10–6 to 16–6 with Dave and I running out of cheeses and Old Masters to drag into the patter. 'It's

Gouda enough for me, this Taylor display,' said Dave. I replied: 'Even Rembrandt couldn't put Ray back into the picture.' Believe it or not we got paid for this schoolyard repartee and the boss of *Talksport* sent us a letter saying we were brilliant!

It was now all over for Barney. He slouched around the stage and slapped his darts in. The British fans started singing 'Walking in a Taylor Wonderland'. Phil was missing nothing and finished winning 21–10 with an average of 103.5 and seven 180s. The phrase 'tortured soul' came to mind as Barney shook hands then got off the stage quick. He told the press: 'I did not have the support of my organisation and that made it tougher. There was a lot of pressure on my shoulders.'

Phil, quite the opposite, was leaping with glee. And the first place he bounded to was the bar, not for a sherbet but to greet the Barney fans. Ray had left the venue and The Power – never one to miss a trick – signed hundreds of autographs and promised to make regular visits to Holland.

The victory over Barney opened the doors for Phil Taylor's talent. There had always been a strong histrionic streak to the lad and he began jazzing up his presentation. In his second world final against Mike Gregory, Phil had worn a special 'Cocky Rat' shirt and he continually varied his themes. He had a sequin period in the mid-1990s that climaxed at Blackpool in a green ensemble – shirt, baseball cap and *cape* – that, along with giant shades, made Snoop Dog look like a vicar. Sadly, he played very badly in the get-up and donated it to a Stoke charity shop. Since then he has specialised in special gear for all the big occasions. On his early visits to Las Vegas, he had a

'God and his Universe' shirt that owed something to Leonardo da Vinci. In Ireland he has the choice of a dozen Kelly Green shirts with purple and gold trim – designed to hook the local fans. And he started the 2007 PDC world final against Ray Barneveld in an orange shirt. That was one bit of shirt psychology that failed miserably.

As landlord of the Cricketers pub from 1994 to 2001, he was never short of ideas to boost trade. He bought his aunt Pat in to do weddings, and ran the disco himself when his darts travels permitted. He used to play hot-and-cold running Mud tracks and drive the punters mad with Black Lace's 'Agadoo'. In the dark days of the dispute he would try anything to liven up his exhibitions, using singers and a disco light set-up. And on a visit to China for his sponsors Unicorn four years ago he excelled himself. He played the dozen best players in the country in front of six hundred invited guests and beat them hollow in double-quick time. Thinking he would give full value, Phil then sang unaccompanied for half an hour, doing 'My Way' and 'New York, New York' and a couple of George Formby numbers, bringing the house down.

But at the 2000 PDC World Championship he needed no flashing lights or loud music. Honed by his crushing defeat of Barney, he arrived at the Circus Tavern bristling for action and was totally on song from the kick-off.

He went through the field like a dose of salts. He beat Mick Manning 3–0 in sets with a 103 average. Then he did for Geordie Graeme Stoddart, Alan Warriner and Dennis Smith. In the final Dennis Priestley managed to take three sets but Phil took his eighth world title with a 7–3 victory. As usual, he broke down in tears at the presentation.

It was during this week that I did my John the Baptist act, screaming to the Sky millions that we were seeing the Messiah. 'Forget Bristow, Forget Lowe,' was my message, 'the Power has taken darts to new planets.' Some of the press thought I was over-egging the pudding. I don't think I was. To my dad and his mining pals darts, snooker, football and cricket were all sports of equal weight and attraction. If brainwashed middle-class journos wanted to pooh-pooh darts because of the bellies, tattoos and beer and not see the skill or the dedication or the work ethic, that was their problem. I went beyond a British context; sure, Phil was up there with Hendry, Davis and Bobby Charlton. But I reckoned the true context was Bradman, Ali and Babe Ruth. Ian Chadband of the *Evening Standard* headlined a vivid piece from the Circus Tavern: 'TAYLOR'S AMAZING GRACE'.

My puns, panting and ranting might get on some folks' wires but it made others sit up and take note. 'Stopping Taylor – that would be like trying to halt a water buffalo with a pea-shooter.' And, of a 180 by Peter Manley with his full-barrelled bomber darts: 'That was like throwing three pickled onions into a thimble.' Where does the exotic imagery come from? Well, I always seem to wax most lyrical in Blackpool. As I've said, my favourite venue was Jollees at Stoke, though the Circus Tavern, Purfleet, has its own unique feel of Essex mayhem. But each summer for one week the Winter Gardens in Blackpool is a cross between the Doge's Palace in Venice and the Maracana Stadium. Here, where Nye Bevan and Hugh Gaitskell fought for the soul of the Labour Party and Thatcher seduced the wets and the blue-rinse brigade, the working-class darts fraternity parades with all their wit and jollity. Each year four secretaries from Essex show up in T-shirts proclaiming that they are 'Tarts For Darts'. The Scots fans wear Russ Abbot red hair and Tammy outfits and in 2000 a team of stag lads were dressed up as Boss Pie Bashers, with rolling pins. It always warms my cockles.

That was the year that I came across a total revolution in the players' drinking habits. On the Tuesday of the Matchplay I walked into the players' practice room expecting to see the usual pints of lager and vodka or brandy chasers on display. Not a pint in sight! Chris Mason was sniffing and sipping a cheeky little Chablis and Alan Warriner walked in with a box of Thresher's finest hock. All right, the lads supped the vino from half-pint glasses, but it marked a culture change nevertheless. Why the change? 'Well,' said Mason, 'It has the desired effect and it's often nicer to drink than flat lager.' Warriner was equally candid: 'I like the taste and it's refreshing.' Next thing you know they'll be asking for skinny lattes to sip during the commercials.

In the middle of the week I chatted to Phil Taylor and for the first time he mentioned retirement. 'I want to pack it in in four years' time and go put my feet up on a beach in Spain,' he said. Chris Mason was passing at the time and said with feeling: 'I hope Phil does bugger off and live in Spain. Then maybe the rest of us will win something.' Since then The Power has cried 'I quit' on several occasions out of sheer emotional pressure, but he has never executed the desire in the cold light of dawn.

He was magnificent on the stage. He took apart a rejuvenated John Lowe 6–4 in legs and then took on wine buff Warriner in the final. It was clinical and totally destructive. At 10–5 to Phil in legs his average was 112 and the final score was 18–12. He banged in nine 180s. John Gwynne and I worked humour into the final:

JOHN: This is not sport – it's pure theatre.

SID: Old Vic – Young Vic – Queen Vic. Rub yerself with Vick if it makes you feel better.

Phil went from strength to strength in the next few months. He completed the PDC Grand Slam by adding the World Grand Prix in Ireland to the world crown and the World Matchplay. The tournament in Ireland was played in Wexford in what I called a 'tent', and what the PDC called a 'pavilion'. A force nine gale nearly swept the structure halfway across the Atlantic on finals night. It made no difference to The Power. He annihilated Shayne Burgess 6–1 in sets in the final then did a passable impersonation of Michael Flatley with the dancing girls in traditional gear. After the final I had a couple of beers with Shayne and he was like a kid at Christmas. He had foraged well for himself in the week, borrowing a boat to catch dabs which the cook at his hotel had fried up for breakfast.

The 2001 PDC world championship had the lot: Taylor in supreme form but fretting at not getting a nine-darter, my Geordie pal Graeme Stoddart losing a set to a *woman* and the press paying even more attention to The Power and his skills.

Stoddy got some stick when he was practising to take on Canadian women's champion Gayl King. 'Have you been to the hairdressers? She has,' shouted one wag. And Gayl did not let her sex down. With the fans going nutty, she took the first set! Graeme gave her a kiss through gritted teeth then set to his task. 'He'll never dare show his face doon the Quayside again if he losses this 'un,' I yelped, waxing Geordie as I often do at times of high adrenalin. In the end Stoddy won and I've never seen a bloke down three pints of lager quicker.

The only man who put up a fight against a rampant Taylor was Les Fitton, a tall whippy lad from Lancashire. Les got one set but then Taylor started to get it together. I stressed the technical side of Taylor's accuracy. In his early career he had used short darts, but later he designed a long, thin dart. This he threw so that it deliberately landed at about ten degrees below the horizontal. This meant he could bounce in the follow-up darts. And you thought this was just a pumped-up pub game. It's not you know, it's a science.

At this tournament Taylor was in such determined mood he did not dress up. There were no sequinned shirts or gimmicks, just brutal darts. In the semi-final he took apart Dave Askew 6–0 in sets and hit fourteen 140s. I talked to him after the match and he was *disappointed*. 'In the form I'm in, the 9-darter will come. But I need somebody to really give me a game. Mark my words, the nine will come when I am in the middle *of a tough game and not thinking about it.*' In a matter of months those words proved prophetic.

In the world final Phil annihilated John Part, the 1994 Embassy champion, in a vicious example of near perfection. He won 7–0 in sets with an average of 107.5 and a 72 per cent check out average. Few sporting stars dominate in this way; there's usually a Coe to an Ovett, or a Bjorg to a McEnroe. There were murmurings, even in our Sky team, of boredom, of viewers getting cheesed off by the Taylor dominance. I pleaded the opposite case: that Taylor was taking the sport to new levels and folk would tune in to see which peak he'd aim for next.

There was a famous blip in Taylor's progression to the heights. It happened in Ireland at the World Grand Prix in Dublin in the autumn of 2001. Dave Lanning and I were on duty for the first-round match between The Power and Kevin Painter. Now, Painter is a very aggressive player, very sure of himself. He knew that he had to hit Phil during early doors in the best-of-three format and he did. Never looking at Phil and never reacting to how near his heels Phil stood, Painter danced to victory 2–1. It was Phil's first defeat in a PDC 'world' event since Manley put him out of the Matchplay at Blackpool in 1999. 'You have seen a slice of darting history,' said Dave on commentary. 'A rare, rare Taylor defeat.'

Some players would have got a monk on and stayed away from the limelight. Not Phil; he was in the bar around midnight as the Sky team unwound. I distinctly saw that he was drinking Guinness and telling jokes. He even bought a round in for Rory Hopkins and the team. I was on my second pint of the black stuff when Rory sidled over. 'What do you think to doing one of the semis and the first half of the final with Phil as your co-commentator?'

I did not hesitate for a second. 'Suits me, Boss. If he talks at the wrong time I'll kick the bugger in the shins.'

'Done,' said Rory.

Next minute a tattooed forearm with the tortion of a pirate's grappling iron grabbed my neck from behind. 'Me and you commentating together, pardner. Good, eh?' It was The Power.

'Yeah. You've got to learn a few little rules …'

'Fuck the rules. We'll have a ball.' Then with one bound he was off to bed.

I had had previous experience of telly commentating with a sporting legend. At the World Pool Championships in Cardiff a few months before, I was told to join Steve Davis to do an important match. I blenched; I was being asked to swap knowledge gleaned in Pudsey pubs with SD, the maestro. A Filipino was playing a Yank and for the first three racks most of the run-outs to the nine ball were prosaic. Then the table looked awkward and SD threw me a nasty curve. Live to millions, he said dryly: 'Beats me Sidney. What would you do here?' There was a gurgle of sarky laughter from the OB scanner. Who said SD had no sense of humour?

I paused for a tick, hanging on a washing line like a holey pair of old keks. 'What I'd do, Steve, is put a little bit of running side on the cue ball – take it off three cushions to pot the two in the middle. Then I'd be dead straight on the three into the opposite bag.'

Short pause by Steve. 'Not a bad idea. Might just work.'

In fact the American played safe, but I had made my point.

There was no gentle sarcasm when The Power came into the box to do the Alan Warriner against Dennis Smith semi-final. He'd bought us each a half of lager to oil our tonsils, so I broke the habits of a lifetime and had a sip. I told him the rules: 'If I rotate my hand keep talking, but if I hold up my finger you should let me in sharpish.' He nodded and off we went.

Phil was brilliant at explaining why certain shots were used to set up big finishes, though he sometimes jumped the gun by yelling:

'This will go in!' and then the player missed. But generally it was good insightful stuff.

Sadly, on the final between Warriner and Roland Scholten, it was my babbling bouncing enthusiasm that caused the bother. I have the habit of jumping to my feet and kicking the microphone wires when there is a brilliant passage of play. Warriner slammed in a 180 and I leapt up screaming: 'Wozzer the Iceman turns up the heat', and my right foot landed on Phil's left. He jumped up too, holding his foot. 'Bloody Hell Sid,' he yelled just off mike. John Gwynne and Dave Lanning came in for the last couple of sets as Warriner steamed to victory, and I helped Phil limp to the bar. 'Next time I'm gonna wear a suit of armour, pal,' he said with feeling.

Next day the *Irish Times* was singing my praises. 'Waddell has become the beloved chronicler of the old pub game of nerves and ale. He is to darts what Johnny Carson was to talk shows and Sinatra to melody.' Phil would have added: 'And what Norman Hunter was to soft shoe shuffling.'

A few weeks later, on the eve of the 2002 world championship the *Independent* summarised the Taylor phenomenon thus: 'PHIL TAYLOR – GREATEST LIVING BRITISH SPORTSMAN.' By the oche in the Mason's Arms, Pudsey, my local, I almost lay down and wept.

At Purfleet in the Skol World Championship, Taylor was imperious: he went through a class field and only dropped two sets. Though his overall average was down to 101, he took Shayne Burgess apart in round two with an average of 111. Shayne said: 'Of course Phil gives you chances to go out – on 170, 161 and 157.' It was Taylor's tenth world championship win and I celebrated in prose that was purple even by my standards. 'Trying to hold Phil is like trying to hang on to the pants of Halley's Comet.'

Next stop for the ever-expanding PDC darts circus was the MGM Grand hotel in Las Vegas for the first Desert Classic Darts tournament. I could not believe the wall of dry heat that whacked me as I walked from the plane at Las Vegas airport. Then there was another wall inside the ice-cool air-conditioned terminal, the clang and whirr of hundreds of fruit machines – before you'd even got your luggage. Then I looked up at a giant video screen and saw ZZ Top, Celine Dion and PHIL TAYLOR! He was chucking darts and dancing and celebrating a 180. Hello USA – we have arrived!

At the hotel I had a kip then went for a wander. There were darters everywhere. I saw Graeme Stoddart at a fruit machine with a two-foot cocktail in a glass shaped like a flamingo. In the Betty Boop bar Tommy Cox's crew were doing their best to turn Vegas into a bit of downtown Whitley Bay, wearing Newcastle United tops and asking where you could get good fish and chips. At a slinky piano bar I joined Cliff Lazarenko for a beer and he told the bloke on the piano I was a dab hand at singing. 'Siddy here will do "Mack the Knife", won't you matey?' I slurped down the drink and made a dash for the door.

I had an early night and met Dave Lanning for breakfast at around ten the next morning. We both fancied a game of pool and suddenly I had a brainwave. One of the old members of the USA Mosconi Cup team, an Italian-American gent, had told me that I would be most welcome at Pool Sharks, run by friends of his in Vegas. I found the address. It was about three miles out in the suburbs.

Just after three that afternoon Dave and I hailed a cab outside the MGM and told the driver where we wanted to go. I thought I caught a ghost of a frown on his face. After ten minutes we both got a bit worried. The suburbs were looking shabby – lots of porno shops and loan sharks' premises. Then the cab pulled up in front of a shop with streaky blackened windows. We got out, paid and the cab shot off. Was the driver shaking his head? Was this a bad idea?

It seemed fine when we got inside. There were about twenty tables, most empty, and one show table in a pit with posh seats around it. The show table was in use by some kids straight out of a Frat house movie: baseball caps on backwards, loud voices, balls smashed willy-nilly. An old man in a muscle vest was polishing glasses behind the bar. I approached him as Dave selected a cue. I explained that my friend had told me to drop in. The old timer's eyes glowed at the name and he extended his right hand for me to shake. I took it and jumped; the man had no thumb. He held up his other hand – no thumb there either. 'Folks call me Thumbs,' and then by way of explanation: 'I fell out with some serious people.' I said no more. Thumbs gave us a rack and some balls and shouted to the Frat pack. 'Get offa that table you punks. These English guys is guests of the house.'

The kids sloped off to an outer table without a murmur. Super Sid and Diamond Dave set up the balls. Elvis came on the juke box singing the praises of the City of Sin and a lass brought us a pitcher of Texas Shriner Bock – Newcy Brown with muscles. 'On the house,

It's 1982 and Jocky is very unhappy with what he reckons is gamesmanship by Sweden's Stefan Lord. Fags and pints were still allowed and Jocky became the Embassy champ at Jollees.

Jocky in his Braveheart period, give or take the blue woad! Raggy mullet, drop of vodka and stand by for brilliant darts. He never drank at home, but did he sup when he met the lads.

BDO world champion at Lakeside, Andy Fordham was to pay for getting to 29 stone and supping 30 bottles of lager in practice. He had to pull out of the great £100,000 challenge against Phil Taylor at the Circus Tavern. He was 5–2 down when he got asthma and heat exhaustion.

Keith Deller was 100–1 against winning the Embassy title at Jollees in 1983. He beat Brissy in a classic final – drinking only milk. Now a key member of our Sky team.

Jocky happy and triumphant not long before he quit the game in 1995. With him is Dennis Priestley, salt of the earth and one of my biggest pals.

There's only one word for Waddell: Just magic

BBC places the accent on darts

By PATRICK O'NEILL

Sid Waddell in regulation gear   Picture: MICHAEL FORSTER

HE'S as Geordie as the Tyne Bridge, with an accent as abrasive as a broken bottle of brown ale.

Sid Waddell, 38, is also the BBC's newest sports commentator.

He aims to do for darts what Eddie Waring did for rugby League, John Arlott for cricket, and Dorian Williams for show-jumping, link the sport with a regional accent which will give it its own identity on television.

Over the next six months, starting with Grandstand on Saturday and ending with the first television - sponsored darts contest in April, the BBC hope to turn the game into a major TV sport.

Dialect

It will be Sid's job to explain the finer points to viewers—terms like beds, segments, tons and on the wire.

'Darts players are now folk heroes,' he said yesterday. 'In the North-East they are treated with the same reverence as soccer stars

Sid was chosen as commentator because of his expertise—he is editor of a book on the game to be published next year—and his instantly recognisable accent.

'Geordie is now a fashionable accent on TV,' he explained. Shows like The Likely Lads and When the Boat Comes In have made it popular. But I'll have to tone down my Geordie accent for the audiences otherwise many of them might not understand me.

'Words, like beds, tons and on the wire are difficult enough with talking about arra (arrows, plays darts together) or muckle canny hoyin (very good throwing).'

So for readers who are not experts on dialect or sport, here's our regional guide to TV commentators:—

John Arlott, the daddy

EDDIE WARING
BORN Dewsbury, manager of Dewsbury in 1936, became the BBC's voice of rugby league in 1951. Disliked by many for 'turning the sport into a TV circus.'

DORIAN WILLIAMS
BORN Aldershot 1914, educated at Harrow. He brought the public school voice to television with his commentary on show-jumping.

JOHN SNAGGE
VETERAN of the BBC, born in London, and broadcast for 40 years covering nearly 40 boat races. Embodies the perfect vowels of official BBC English.

The press have never known what to make of my act. One minute I'm a genius leading a new posse, next I'm mad or have Tourette's. In 1978 the *Mail* compared me to Eddie Waring – bully for that – then the posh papers had me an expert linguist and a piece of 'just magic'. Since 1999 I have been generally regarded as 'The Voice of Darts' and now they all know I ain't mad. But who knows…

Waddell rides into town with a new posse

commen
don as
Fulham,
England
to 1955,
Wimbled
in 1951.

Bill McLaren, Rugby Union. A school teacher from Hawick in the Scottish borders, who despite repeated offers from the BBC refuses to leave his local school. Precise, cultured, articulate Scot.

Waddell lifting English language to new level

The two greatest darts players of all time show affection and respect. Ray van Barneveld was beating all in the BDO hollow so tried the PDC. He has been a sensation since February 2006, and other young Dutch stars have followed his path. Phil Taylor is simply the greatest tungsten tickler there will ever be.

Phil Taylor played a county darts match hours after his wedding. Barney did not go that far, but he and the lovely Sylvia did have a board at the do, so maybe Ray practised a bit in between canapés.

Phil Taylor loves Blackpool and the holiday crowd love him.
Here he is with the World Matchplay trophy. Twelve months
later he shed tears of joy on this stage, having won £100,000
for a televised nine-darter.

Having painted the oches of the darting world purple, Phil and
Barney pose with a painted lassie to publicise the Blue Square UK
Open at Bolton. In summer 2007 Barney put on a Jimmy Savile wig,
took a bow and coasted to the title.

This is me in 1971 with my documentary director hat on. We are on the House of Commons terrace and I am in full *Miami Vice* kit telling Barry Cockcroft to stand straight and talk posh to Lord George Brown.

Two real nutters share the stage at *Celebrity It's a Knockout* in Blackpool in 1980. My style was cramped a bit by the red nose and the attack of gout I was suffering, but the MC was my buddy Stuart Hall, fellow Mincer of the English Language.

Circa 2000, a Sky publicity shoot for darts. Left to right: Big Cliff, Little Sid, Peter Manley, Shayne Burgess and Rod 'The Sheriff' Harrington. Peter got the leather hose on no bother, but had to be shoe-horned out of them.

They could beat Brazil then lose to Blyth Spartans. But once a Toon Looney, your blood is always black and white.

The final shutdown. At long last Dave Lanning, John Gwynne and Stuart Pyke have silenced the loud-mouthed Lip.

I've had a couple of Pukka Pies
And they've brightened up my eyes
The Circus crows begin to sip
And Sid the Banshee will soon LET RIP!!!

I love the fans and they let me know that they appreciate me. Above my desk at home is this wall-eyed cartoon and the line 'Geordie GENUIS'. It reminds my of my privileged position sitting in a plywood box waxing enthusiastic to millions. It sure beats working for a living.

sir,' she said in a honey lilt that would have driven Scarlett O'Hara green with envy. I felt like a pig in parsley.

Two hours later we decided to call it a draw. We took the balls back to Thumbs. He waved away my money and so I bought a couple of T-shirts with the club logo. I asked him for the number of a taxi firm and he looked sheepish. 'They don't really like picking up here. Maybe you could hail one outside.'

Just then one of the Frat boys chased a girl out on to the street. He jumped in a Jeep and she tried to get in. The guy kept accelerating. She was being dragged along the tarmac. It was bedlam. No wonder the local taxis gave Pool Sharks a miss.

After half an hour a woman taxi driver took pity on us. We told her we wanted to go to the MGM Grand. 'Staying at the MGM and hitting a dive like that?' she pointed back to the club. 'You are strange guys.' We looked at each other and nodded.

Back at the darts the Taylor juggernaut marched on. Phil won the first ever Desert Classic and celebrated. Champers? High roller slots? Are you kidding? He tried a quick five bucks on the quarter slots, had a Chinese washed down with black tea and went to see Siegfried and Roy perform a novelty circus act with lions and tigers.

In July 2002 I was on duty at the World Pool Championships in Cardiff. My pal Jim Wych, the former snooker star, fancies himself against the bookies and I was standing with him at the Stan James stall. I suddenly had a whim based on Taylor's fantastic form. I asked Jim to find out the odds on the nine-darter being hit at Blackpool in the Matchplay, which was coming up two weeks later. The bookies said 12–1, Jim scoffed and haggled and the bookies gave me 25–1. I banged on a tenner because I am such a wild child. They said any Sky person could have the same odds at Blackpool.

Now, a bit of deep background. There had been two nine-darters televised in the history of the sport. John Lowe did one in the MFI tournament at Slough on ITV in 1984. John won £100,000 and Dave Lanning, super cool on commentary throughout, won £12,000. In 1990 Paul Lim threw a nine-darter at the Embassy at Frimley Green and won £50,000. It had to happen on Sky sometime.

The night before Phil Taylor's match against Chris Mason in Blackpool, The Power finished practice at about nine o'clock. He switched out the lights on his trusty Dartmate stand and asked a mate of his to pop out for Chinese. He handed the bloke a few tenners. When the food came back, Phil looked at the tenner change and told his pal to 'put it on me getting a nine-darter against Mason'.

When the players came out on 1 August just before eight o'clock, Taylor got an amazing reception from the Winter Gardens crowd. There were cries of 'Give Us a Nine Dart' because all 2,500 fans knew he was in better form than ever. But, as usual, Mace the Ace respected nobody. He started with a 105 average and he and Phil traded blows to 2–2 in legs. Phil now only wanted one thing: to go into the commercial break 3–2 up. Mason hit 135 to start the leg. Phil hit 180. Mace hit a mere 60. Face twisted with effort Phil hit 180 and the crowd went silent. He wanted 141 for a lot of money and history. Dave told me in hushed tones to call it in. Again, I chucked away the thesaurus and let my gut take my tongue. The 60 went in. 'Oooh my goodness,' strangled but clear. 'He's on the 9-darter. Wants treble 19 ...' The dart went in. 'And double 12 for history ... history ...' The dart went in. 'HISTORY!' The last word was a screech of breath like a torpedo hitting the hull of an aircraft carrier.

Cue chaos in the crowd. People by their hundreds waved betting slips; Phil's quest for the perfect nine darts had been well publicised. Our OB scanner was full of screams and laughter because all the Sky lot had been on the bet at 25–1. Mace hugged Taylor who ran to the edge of the stage and checked if his pal had put the tenner on. What a bloke: there was £100,000 in notes waiting for him in the Stan James VIP room in a big cage, and he's checking on a bet for £250! The officials called a five-minute break and we ran the clip a couple of times. Phil was allowed to see but not *touch* his cageful of loot.

The two players came back onstage to a wall of happy sound and the game started again. Phil ended up winning 16–7 and Rory Hopkins told me to clear off and have a beer. I went for my jacket and nearly had a punch-up with a Dutch journalist who was bawling that Sky were a bunch of liars to say this was the first 9-darter on live television. He said Sean Greatbatch had done one months before on a tiny Dutch satellite station. 'Seen by how bloody many?' I shouted. 'This is network mate. Live. Out to millions. Not a tatty tuppeny ha'penny do in a village hall!' He threw his hands up and walked out of the room. OK, technically he had a point, but Sky had a scoop. In fact I did make a crack about the Greatbatch achievement next day. 'Oh for the record, a BDO bloke hit a 9-dart in Holland the other day. No prize – but the other players did a whip-round with a hat and he got a few bob.' Subtle? No – but viscerally satisfying.

I walked on weightless feet to the Gay Tandoori. I was the only customer. I ordered a pint of draught Cobra and the first one did not touch the sides of my pulsing throat. 'I do not fucking believe it!' I told the silk picture of temples and rivers on the wall. My second pint of Cobra came – a sipper rather than a gulper. Poppadoms and dips appeared. 'I don't fucking believe it!' I told them. I was so stunned I even ate the marmalade-coloured dip that I hate. I told the waiter I would have my usual chicken biryani. Halfway down my third pint of Cobra I told the plastic tablecloth: 'I don't fucking believe it!' One hour after sitting down I spooned a sliver of chicken and a dab of rice into my mouth and stopped swearing out loud.

On the last day of the tournament Phil played John Part in a classic final. John is a great counter and was in great form with his scoring. He led Phil 16–15 in the race to 18 legs and it looked all over for Phil. Then the grit took over and The Power won 18–16. Golden glitter snow rained down on him and again he wept.

A few weeks later Taylor arrived in Dublin looking to take the World Grand Prix and complete the PDC Super Grand Slam: all the 'World' standard titles. Needless to say he did it in style. One of his best displays was against Mark 'Boosh' Holden who looks like a bouncer and is fond of pints and Holland's meat pies. Phil's tectonic tungsten was so good that Mark spent the whole match frowning. 'He looks about as comfy as penguin in a microwave,' I opined and my Irish fans voted it Sidism of the year. Next day it was emblazoned on T-shirts.

But Phil kept his real form for the final against John Part. Bouncing and swaggering round the stage – with confidence, not braggadocio – Phil won 7–3 in sets and had an end average of 105. He allowed himself three or four bottles of Bud afterwards and told me he thought we'd be working on the book of his life story soon. He gave the fans a great version of 'Danny Boy' then had an early night. Who or what could beat him in the 2003 world championship? Answer: himself!

9

When Geordie Eyes are Smiling

So why, with all this fantastic form built up over a year, did Phil Taylor not win his eleventh world championship in the early days of 2003?

There are two theories. Phil puts it down to mental tiredness and traces it back to the middle of his two finals against John Part in Blackpool and Ireland. But Eric Bristow and I have a different theory. We reckon that the culprit was the *mirror* in the Taylor mansion in Bradwell. Phil looked in it after the Ireland final, did not like his paunch and went on the rabbit food and exercise big time. No oatcakes, no Chinese meals, no liver-and-onion butties. He was even talking about running in the London Marathon! He lost nearly three stones in twelve weeks and looked gaunt. I think that it affected his balance on the oche; his massive Popeye forearms were out of sync with his reduced torso. So the 'stacking' went adrift, and so did his cover shots at treble 19. A medical expert in one of the papers said that rapid weight loss can also affect the fluid content of the eyes. So maybe that was a factor too. One thing is sure – mere mortals were taking sets off The Power with relative ease from the second round.

Wayne Mardle might bridle at my calling him a 'mere mortal'. He is one of the brightest talents to come along in years. I remember him as a sixteen-year-old doing well in the Haywords Pickles Junior Championships at Frimley Green. Wayne plays on adrenalin and with an Essex crowd behind him and his dad Billy at ringside screeching, he was on song against Phil. He went down eventually by 5–3 in sets but certainly gave Phil a game. 'Eat yer heart out Charles Dickens, this is Greater Expectations,' I yelled as Wayne made a fight of it. I pointed out to the viewers that Phil's average was only 98 and that that 'was not the stamp of a Colossus.'

The game was watched by Alyson Rudd of *The Times* who liked 'Wayne's shiny smock covered in pineapples.' She concluded her piece with a profound verity: 'Take away the voices and darts is dull, but otherwise it is magnificent.' I have always said to anoraks and knockers that darts can be monotone – 180, 140, 180 – and it is up to we voice merchants to joke, extol, bellow or hiss to get over the inherent drama.

In Phil's next match there were more signs of weakness. Dennis Smith was hitting the doubles better in the first half of their game and Phil just managed to find form and win 5–3. His next opponent was Alan Warriner, who had psyched himself up for a real battle. He told the papers that Phil got far too much publicity. I reckon this was a weak attempt to needle Phil. Then Alan went a step further; he took off the mike and walked out of a Sky interview saying he was 'going to sort Phil out'. Though the papers took this seriously, I did not. It was 100 per cent tongue-in-cheek – a page out of the Cassius Clay manual of whimsical wind-ups.

Sadly Alan's mouth was a long way from his trousers. He merely brushed Phil's hand as the opening handshakes were exchanged. Phil needed a mere 95 average to beat him 6–1 in sets in the semi-final. There was another polite handshake at the end.

The final would now be between Phil and John Part. I knew The Power would have a game on his hands. Part had been right on his heels in Blackpool and Ireland and he was, after Bristow, the best counter in the game. His doubles would not be far out. Plus John was playing with a confident swagger. Phil, on the other hand looked pale, irritable and vulnerable. Two years earlier, Warriner's jibes would have meant nothing. And Phil's averages were up and down between 98 and 102; in the past there had been a steady ominous rise as the final drew nearer.

John Part started the final like a Scud missile. He had the lip-curled sneer of a man walking the right line between arrogance and confidence. First leg he did a 121 shot-out. Then, despite averaging 105 to Phil's 110, John took a 3–0 in sets lead. I said: 'John Part is showing more style than Frank Sinatra's hat.' But I knew Phil was often a slow starter. Surely the doubles and cover shots would flow soon. Wrong. Part took the score to 4–1 in the race to seven sets.

With the Circus crowd going nuts Phil fought back to 5–5. In my view, Part went off the boil marginally. Then we were at 6–6 and it was Taylor looking the more fatigued of the two. I banged on about the quick weight loss and the tough game against Dennis Smith. Phil saved the match in the third leg of the final set but had no answer at the death. He missed 121 and John shot 77 to become world champion.

Phil was graceful in defeat. But one small point proved to me that he lacked his usual deadly focus. In his post-match interview he said:

'Let me just say that John has done what Alan Warriner will never do.' Why let Warriner's chelping from the semi-final bug him? As well as physical fatigue, I took that to be a sign of mental tiredness.

I began work on Phil's book in early February but deliberately waited till my third trip to Stoke at the end of the month to talk in detail about the defeat by John Part. I arrived at the Taylor house in Bradwell about ten o'clock and Phil was not around. Yvonne said he was 'doing a bit of work' just around the corner. I thought she meant practising or vinyl plotting a few pullovers, but I was wrong. My taxi dropped me at a small terraced house. The door was ajar and I pushed into a dusty hall, following the strains of 'Mack the Knife' done by a familiar voice. Two ghosts in overalls were whacking at bricks with mell hammers. 'Hey up, Sidney,' said Phil. 'Is this the kind of exercise you approve of?' This was said in a half-sarky fashion. It was a jibe at Brissy and my criticisms of his fitness regime. I said nowt. I watched Phil and Shaun Rutter do a few more minutes bashing and even took out a couple of bags of rubble. 'Doing up this house and another nearby. Might sell them on, make a few bob,' said Phil. Once again I admired the bred-in-the-bone attitude to cash.

Half an hour later we were having oatcakes and strong tea at Phil's mum's and talking about his dad. There were tears in Phil's eyes as he told me about a last-ditch impetuous visit to Lourdes in the hope that that would cure the cancer that was ravaging his father. 'I said get in that bloody car and we'll have you in that water in no time,' said Phil. It did not work.

Next we went to the Saggars and shot a bit of non-combative

pool. At last I asked about the disappointment of losing his world crown. He admitted that the depression had lasted for two weeks but that in a way the defeat had done him good. 'Everybody loves a loser and I've got more fans than ever. They are stopping me in the street, saying get up there and win it back. In fact Party has done me a big favour.' Then his eyes narrowed. 'I admit my fitness regime was not done right. I lost too much weight too quickly. I'm still going down the gym but now it's all measured and supervised.' I changed the subject sharpish. I did not want to get the bum's rush by chirping 'I told you so.'

Back at my hotel in Newcastle under Lyme I played back my tape and began writing up the material. Then at about 6.30 the phone rang. It was Shaun. He explained that Phil had gone off to an exhibition and he was delegated to 'entertain' me on my night in the Potteries. I thought it was a nice touch, especially when Sean insisted on paying for all the drinks and the curry that ended the night. As we chatted I could not believe how many hours Phil was putting in on doing up houses, and how hard he was practising. And the Saggars was full of folk saying Phil would be back with a vengeance.

A few days later he was. He beat John Part in the final of the North American Cup with an average of 105. Then it was on to Bolton and the 'FA Cup of Darts', the new UK Open. Phil smashed through a field of the top 128 in the world and met a rejuvenated Shayne Burgess 18–8 in the final. The crowd of mainly Lancastrians were singing 'The Power Is Back' and one sensed a tide had turned in the affairs of Taylor. He had one aim in life: to get *his* world title back.

At Blackpool a few weeks later Phil displayed a new set of darts that he dubbed 'my arrows of desire'. He showed them to me and I marvelled at the design; the grip was ever so slightly modified so the dart nestled right in Phil's fingers. It is incredible how far back on the barrel those fingers go and how little actual skin touches the tungsten. 'They feel like a glove,' said The Power. However unapt that analogy was, the new darts flew like Achilles' javelins: in his first match at the Winter Gardens Taylor destroyed Les Fitton 10–0 in legs with a 108 average. The final was a stormer, with Taylor just drawing the fire of Wayne Mardle 18–12. Wayne, with dozens of fans behind him in Hawaiian shirts, was at his flamboyant best that week. He made one entrance that Elizabeth Taylor would have been proud of, blowing kisses and air surfing through the crowd. Jeff Stelling, presenting for Sky, offered one of his driest ever cracks: 'Wayne, a lad who just lacks a bit of confidence.'

During the final I indulged in more technical talk, about angles of flight, than usual. Taylor stacked beautifully, but Wayne, when under pressure, hooked his darts into the five when aiming at the 60. I balanced it up with odd jokey bits like: 'Wayne's shirt looks like an explosion in a paint factory.' Giles Smith in the *Daily Telegraph* approved: 'Be thankful for Sky Sports who have cameras everywhere. Without them and the peerless excellence of Waddell, Lanning and Gwynne, darts would seem to be merely a pub game. And we know it is so much more than that.'

I reckon that our Sky commentary team has a mixture of talents that dovetail beautifully. Dave has great timing and an inspired turn of phrase. John is a wizard at statistics and has a great sense of humour; he and I are like comic brokers men at times. Stuart Pyke's voice is full of urgency and he spends hours chatting with the players for background gen. Nigel Pearson has recently joined us and has a voice like a Roman candle – bursting with colour in all directions. Rod Harrington brings the scalpel dissection of a top player and Brissy, when he commentates is, well, just Brissy – part yelling fan, part guru, all gravelly Cockney tonsil. Dave Clark brings attack and journalistic nous to the party and the fans like him. For some bizarre reason they always booed Jeff Stelling when he came on stage for the prize-giving. I reckon it was a back-handed compliment.

In early autumn the Taylor biography was published and Phil and I set off round Britain on a signing exhibition. We did about sixteen shops and he was diligence personified, signing thousands of copies. I remembered the 1982 fiasco with Jocky Wilson's book that I ghosted: the publishers booked Jocky at ten big bookshops and he did not show up at any! And The Power got so carried away with the plugging lark that he went on the *Frank Skinner Show* twenty-four hours before playing in the World Grand Prix in Dublin. I watched his performance on telly in our hotel bar and it was a hoot from start to finish.

Early on Frank said: 'I've been reading your book.'

'I've been reading yours too,' replied Phil. 'Well, no, I haven't. But George has – my driver!'

What an uppercut to the Skinner ego. The studio audience fell about and we all corpsed in the bar while Frank looked as sick as a chip.

His jaw dropped further as Phil told him about Charlie the ghost of the Cricketers pub. 'He flung bottles around and was a right nuisance till one night I looked at him and said, "I'm sick of you Charlie. You pay no bloody rent. Shut up or I'm getting a priest to exorcise you." It worked. I never saw him in my pub cellar again.'

And then Phil excelled himself. At the end of the show he dressed up in drag as Victoria Beckham – in a halter-neck number that displayed nearly all his tattoos – and Frank dressed up as David Beckham. They sang 'Anyone Can Fall in Love' and brought the house down.

When he hit the venue in Dublin, I asked Phil who put him up to the drag singing act. 'Well,' he said with a wink, 'Frank said would I put a dress on and sing. He said it was worth a thousand quid. I said that for that money I would do it *without any knickers!*'

'And did you?' I asked.

He just winked.

At practice that week in Ireland Phil was a revelation; he sipped the odd glass of Chablis and joked with everybody. He went through the field like a dose of salts and prepared to meet John Part in the final. People kept telling him how good he'd been with Frank Skinner. He obviously liked that. There is a very soft spot inside The Power that wants to be liked, loved even; Jocky Wilson had the same deep sensitivity. Taylor's practise had been topped off perfectly by the singing in drag. His mind had put hitting Part very hard to second place for a while. Then John Part did something that touched the Taylor fuse. 'I am the only person who can beat Phil at this moment,' he told Dave Clark. I was in the practice room with Phil when he heard this and his eyes flashed with instant malice. 'Right, Party, it's Boot Hill for you.' He slammed in a 180. It was a spark the size of a flea, but Taylor often needs the merest hint of disrespect to hit full throttle. He did – in one of the most brilliant, brutal displays of darts I have ever seen.

At 2–2 in sets Taylor was averaging a mere 93. This is not bad considering the Grand Prix rules are double to start. But then he went ballistically barmy. He won the next set in 13, 14 and 12 darts. He was averaging 116; straight in, no double, that would have been 124! Phil won the next *nine* legs on the trot. For most of the time his average was between 107 and 112. I told the viewers to 'forget about the Jammy Dodgers and cuppas' and watch the brilliance of Taylor. John Gwynne came out with pure Shelleyan poetry: 'He's picking them off like damsons in September.' No adjectives, no corn, no frills; the instant poetry of commentary from the gut. Taylor had promised us Boot Hill and he delivered a 7–2 burial of the man who had 'pinched' his title.

Then he let his hair down. He had a few more glasses of Chablis and he, Dave Clark, John Gwynne and I led the singing in the Guitar Bar. With dozens of Paddies round us, we sang 'Irish Rover' so loud the glasses of black stuff wobbled on the bar. John treated us to his all-dancing, all-gesturing version of 'If I Were a Rich Man' – think Topol meets Ronnie Corbett. For some reason we also sang 'Do You Know the Muffin Man' and the locals looked at us as if we were from Mars. Then Phil took the lead in 'Mack the Knife' and the night roared on. Dave Clark and I were still singing when the first sparrows twittered. The die was cast for Purfleet and the world championship.

The super-honed Taylor was eager to get through the field and get back 'his' world title. He started the campaign with a 101 average and an easy win against Colin McGarry of Northern Ireland. Then came the straw that made the Potteries camel kick his heels and turn into a bucking bronco. In midweek Phil read in the *Daily Mirror* this piece of wisdom from Peter Manley: 'Taylor is a real crawler who thinks he is a god.' Manley also said that Phil's antics with Frank Skinner had made 'a mockery of the game'. I spoke to Phil later that morning and he reminded me that this was the same Manley who had refused to shake hands after being slaughtered in the 2001 final and was now booed regularly because of it. 'I wouldn't care,' snarled The Power, 'but the cheeky sod was asking my advice in Ireland the other week about how to swing the crowd his way.' But it was not Peter who felt the brunt of the Taylor wrath that week; it was Kevin Painter.

Now Painter and Taylor had, as they say, 'previous'. In Las Vegas a couple of years before there had been a big row over Phil allegedly encroaching on the oche area while Painter threw. Phil was, I noted, standing inside the red exclusion zone which is clearly marked, and thus was in the wrong. Both players exchanged angry words during and after the match. So the 2004 world final was going to be a belter.

Since his defeat by John Part one year earlier, the Taylor fan club had multiplied massively and they were well represented at the Circus Tavern. But they were completely gobsmacked by the end of set five. Playing with fire and finesse Kevin Painter was 4–1 up in sets in a race to seven, and Phil was chewing at his flights like a hungry laboratory rat. It was déjà vu all over again: twelve months earlier he had been 4–1 down to Part.

The players went behind the stage set for a commercial break and I left the commentary box to pee. The scene was like something from

Macbeth. Kevin, glassy-eyed and totally focused, stood stock-still and sipped lager. Taylor lashed at his newly streaked hair and jumped around madly. Between them stood Eddie Cox, a droll Geordie. He is the players' marshal who brings the lads from the practice room and bears the tray with their drinks – which in this case were halves of lager. He is also required at times to be an instant shrink.

'I've had enough of this, I can't take any more,' screamed Taylor. Kevin did not look round. He glared at his darts. 'I'm too old for this kind of pressure,' ranted The Power, a ringer for King Lear, give or take a white beard and a few wrinkles. Gayle Farmer, the PDC Media Manager, was pale-faced and doing calm-down gestures to Phil.

Then a dry Geordie voice cut through the tension: '*I don't hear no fat ladies singin', kidda.*' Eddie winked at The Power and the manic dance of rage became a prowl of murderous intent. I reckon the line was a catalyst for the sensation that followed.

Phil won fourteen of the twenty next legs played. With Kevin twisting on the oche and snarling at bad shots, the score got down to 5–5 in sets. Then, incredibly, after three hours and ten minutes play they were at 5–5 in legs in the last set. Phil started with a sloppy 45, but Kevin could not capitalise. He was wildly off balance now. His first nine darts averaged only 65 per visit and Taylor cashed in. Double five did it for him. He had got his title back. Was he pleased? Well, not exactly. He announced his retirement to the press.

He stayed 'retired' – for four days.

The *Daily Mirror* approved of my non-flashy commentary on the final and suggested I should get a gong from Buckingham Palace for services to darts. They got Phil Taylor to endorse the idea: 'Sid is the real King of Darts and should be rewarded for all those years of hard work.' Since January 2004 Phil has whispered in the ears of Zara Phillips over a cheeky claret and told the *Stoke Sentinel* loads of times that I should be gonged. But I still have not tried on the topper.

I got a nice New Year present from Chris Maume of the *Independent*: 'While the Romans had to make do with Janus to mark the fading of the old year into the new, we have Sid Waddell. With Christianity on the way out, who's to say that in these wild witless times, the Voice of Darts, via the records of his annual missives from Purfleet, couldn't replace Christmas.' He liked my description of the extrovert Alex Roy, all bling and bluster, as 'There's a showman in the gloamin' by the bonny banks of Thames!' I reckon some of these scribes should pay me royalties for filling their columns.

You will notice that for several chapters now I've been very quiet about events down at my old Beeb stomping ground at Frimley Green. That's because I nailed my colours to the PDC/Sky mast and so lost interest in the BDO world championship. Also, many of the Frimley Green stars like Wayne Mardle and Ronnie Baxter had moved over and were playing in PDC events. But in the 2004 BDO championships there was a bloke playing who it was hard to ignore, because he played his arrows at a fighting weight of around *thirty stone*! His name is Andy Fordham. He is the size of Giant Haystacks, has a belly that makes Jocky's paunch look like a six-pack and a shaggy mullet that he can almost sit down on. To complete his perfect CV for Central Casting – Dart Player he admitted to often having twenty or so bottles of lager and a couple of brandies before playing serious matches.

I was among several fascinated telly viewers who watched Andy sweat, shamble and fling his way to the Frimley Green final. As each match progressed his eyes got smaller and redder and a Niagara of sweat drenched his face and shirt. Surely this bloke could not win the BDO final against the fit-looking Mervyn King?

Andy had different ideas.

With hundreds of supporters in Viking helmets going spare, Andy hammered the tight-faced and tense King 6–3 in sets. Then he went back to his pub, The Rose, in Dartford with the trophy, had a few hours' kip, then demolished a monster breakfast fry-up, washed down with a few lagers. Wondrous! The spirit of Leighton Rees, Alan Evans, Jocky Wilson and Cliff Lazarenko was alive and flourishing in a boozer in Kent.

So what did Barry Hearn, ace matchmaker that he is, concoct for the delectation of the darting fraternity? You got it in one: THE SHOWDOWN – TAYLOR VERSUS FORDHAM with £100,000 in the kitty. It was set for November 2004 at the Circus Tavern. We were due to cover it for Sky and I was shaking in my shoes for a week before.

In the months after winning the BDO world championship Andy did manage to trim down a bit – to twenty-seven stone. But he did not change his daily training regime of supping lots of lager while he practised. The Power for his part went all messianic about drink; he seriously proposed that the ban on drinking on the oche become a general ban on players drinking at major events. To echo this and his total dedication, he had a semi-shaven head, like a monk's tonsure, when he hit the Tavern.

The joint was jumping on the Sunday of the big match. I got to the club about two and headed for the practice area beyond the players' bar. I was as tense as a tick and my feet hardly hit the ground as I bounded up the stairs past the garish lap-dancing posters. My stomach was knotted. The bar was bathed in a silver half-light and sitting at the first stool near the door in a misty halo was … Andy Fordham. I mumbled greetings and he gave me a heavy-pawed handshake. I noticed a bottle of Heineken in the other hand. There was over five hours to go before Andy would take on the greatest player ever and here he was on the ale. He was even in his playing shirt. I assumed he'd been practising. Wrong.

Andy excused himself and he went to the toilet. The lad behind the bar was a pal of mine. 'How many has Andy had?' I asked. The lad grinned and picked up a box. 'These hold twenty-four and he's on his eighth. But I reckon he'd had a few at his own pub.'

'Has he been practising?' I asked.

'No. Came in. Asked for Heineken. Sat there. Only been up to go to the toilet.'

It crossed my mind that Andy could afford to treat this as an exhibition match since he got £40,000 even if he lost. But surely pride meant moderation; or did it? It did not.

The big match was due to start around nine after two warm-up matches. I made two more visits to the practice room and only on the second one did I see Andy move from the bar stool. My second visit, at around six o'clock coincided with Phil Taylor buying a mineral water. Andy had gone off towards the toilet. 'Do you know how many drinks Andy's had?' asked Phil. I shook my head. 'Tell him,' said Phil to the barman. He held up the box. There was one bottle left in. 'Twenty-three!' said The Power. He began to wink, stopped and grimaced. He walked off shaking his head. Andy rumbled past me and began to practise.

I went into the commentary box at about half past six and tried to calm down. This was a much harder task than doing five hours on the trot at Blackpool. This match had been hyped for weeks and I wanted to give it the full verbal monty. There was also the childish wish that Taylor would win handsomely and that would be one more poke in the eye for the BDO. Suddenly our floor manager tapped on the booth window and pointed to the stage. I straightened my tie and dashed out to join Eric Bristow and Dave Clark to record a piece for Sky Sports News. I was jangling with nerves and it got worse when the crowd started yelling: 'Sidney, Sidney give us a wave'. I did and the fans got to their feet and cheered me. I blabbered some words to Dave, my mind in a whirl. Then I heard Rory Hopkins's dry voice in my ears: 'Sidney – what are you on? Calm down.' He also said I was dropped from the live interview spot as the head of the show. I returned to the booth and sat with head in hands. I'd been commentating for twenty-seven years and here I was shaking.

By 9.20, however, I had the adrenalin under control. As the players walked out, I let Dave Lanning do the purple verbals. 'In two hours' time who will be rocking and who will be rolling? Who will have the rhythm and who will have the blues?' I replied in kind: 'A whop bam a looma, a whop bamboom! This will certainly be tutti frutti.' It got a laugh from the scanner and I relaxed into my normal scat patter.

Andy did not play like a man who'd had around thirty bottles of designer lager. Phil won set one and Andy pipped him to the second. Then Taylor got going and made the set score 2–1 with a 167 finish. At 3–1 to Taylor Andy began to look in distress. His cheeks were red and lathered in sweat and his eyes were like two dying pickled onions. 'Andy is like a hippo in a power shower,' I yelled. I told the viewers that it was 115 degrees on stage and that Andy was not used to a crucible atmosphere like the Circus. 'He's used to the open acres of the Frimley Green hall with the crowd well back. Here the fans are up yer back like a second skin. They can taste your sweat.'

Andy was looking shattered and he was merely slapping the darts at the board as Taylor took the score to 5–2 in sets and looked sure to get the seven needed for a win. But as the delay for the commercial break got longer, and nobody came out on to the oche, I twigged something serious was up. Soon Barry Hearn was in our studio explaining that the match was over. Andy was in distress and was breathing with difficulty, so it had been decided the match was over with Phil the winner. 'Andy must be allowed the dignity to retire on his stool. I cannot take the risk of him returning only for something more serious to happen,' said Barry.

So ended The Showdown. It was yet another feather in the cap of Taylor and the PDC. And it was a warning for Andy. Sadly, more recently Andy was rushed to hospital in the middle of the 2007 BDO world championships with chest pains. Later, several pints of fluid were drained from his lungs. He did not go back to Frimley Green to play. But if it takes umpteen lagers to make you feel right to play darts, then maybe you ought to change to a less 'volatile business'.

I get volatile on adrenalin; just imagine the bollocks I'd come out with if I tickled my tonsils with a couple of cold Heinekens before start of play.

A couple of weeks after the big showdown between Taylor and Fordham we were back at the Circus Tavern for the world championships. Star of the first two rounds was Top Banana Mark Holden who took out James Wade and Simon Whatley with 3–0 victories. This was remarkable since a year before he had given away his darts and packed up the game due to dartitis. But thanks to £4,000 spent on acupuncture and hypnotherapy he had got back into the big time. Alan Warriner also made the news by arriving in Essex without his darts! His lady Brenda drove north and her mum drove south from Maryport in Cumbria and the missiles were exchanged in Cheshire. And Mark 'Flash' Dudbridge showed world class to get to the final against Phil Taylor.

In Taylor's half of the draw the big story was the allegation by Alex Roy that Phil had used a secret tactic to beat him. 'Over Christmas I reckon he's been stuffing himself with brussels sprouts,' said Alex. 'Phil was farting his arse off against me!' Well, as they say, it's an ill wind – and Phil sailed into the final.

At one stage it looked as though I was going to miss my first final in twenty-eight years of commentating. I felt fine over the first few days but then got a tickle in my throat and a tightness in my chest. So I delved into my hoard of American throat sweets purchased in Las Vegas and doubled them up with my trusty British Proctor's Pinelyptus Pastilles. One of the radio reporters suggested I gargle with tea tree oil and I did, nearly being sick in the process. God only knows what chemicals were churning around in my system by semi-finals night.

Sadly, the cocktail of potions did not work; I had to quit commentating on the semi-final after fifteen minutes and was almost in tears. We had New Year's Eve off and I mooched around my hotel room sucking and gargling and getting ever more depressed. By seven I was able to talk a bit better and was persuaded by Dave Lanning and Stuart Pyke to go out for a beer and a Chinese meal. We started our night in Andy Fordham's pub where the big lad and his wife made us most welcome. I sipped a half of lager and kept going to the loo to test my voice. 'Double four … On the Wire … Unlucky son!' I practised at half bellow into a mirror and a couple of lads who came in looked at me as though I was mad. I zipped up and re-entered the bar.

Over the next half an hour we played pool and I kept my voice down to a whisper. Then I took pity on the two lasses and a lad who had set up their karaoke but could not get any punters to perform. So, before Dave and Stu could restrain me, I was up and giving a half-baked version of 'Your Cheating Heart'. My voice did not break or even scratch once. But I did not risk an encore. Then I sat through a Chinese meal saying very little, but silently repeating my mantra between spare ribs: '*My voice is my trademark. It is a gift. Do not abuse it.*' Back at the hotel at midnight I mouthed along to 'Old Lang Syne' and was in bed with my pastilles at 12.30, having gently whispered 'Happy New Year' down the phone to Irene.

I repeated the pills and the gargling till four o'clock the next afternoon and my voice improved. When I arrived at the Circus I went to the production office and the scowl on Rory Hopkins' face told me I was in trouble: 'Night before the world final and your voice is on the blink and what do I hear – *went on a fucking karaoke.*'

'One fucking song. Only one, honest. Fordham was buying our drinks. Karaoke lot were desperate for somebody to start the ball rolling,' I pleaded.

Suddenly he grinned and took me into a corner. 'You've got a touch of the Circus lurgy like a few other folks and I have. I want you to get into the early sets of this final and *hurl* your voice at it like there's no tomorrow. Go for it and I'll pull you out when you burst.' I shook his hand and prepared for blast-off.

As Taylor and Mark Dudbridge threw their practice darts and the crowd steamed like a hot Irish stew, our director Andy Finn gave me a wide shot that Cecil B de Mille would have wept over. I hurled the battered Geordie tonsils thus: 'What a sight! Circus packed. Even a garter snake smothered in Vaseline couldn't slide in here.' Then Dave and I went to town with every pun and fancy in the book. 'Mark is no DUD-bridge … No flash in the pan this lad, he's fire on the moon …' The peak of our fun came in set two when I picked out top chef Marco Pierre White sitting enrapt at the Ladbroke's table. 'Loves the darts our Marco – so much that he's made a batch of special meat pies for the occasion!' Two minutes later the door of the commentary box opened and a waitress passed in a tray of one dozen hot pies. Nudging Dave to keep spieling, I began to eat one. It was delicious and they put up a shot of me dolloping brown sauce on it. 'No offence to Marco – you know what these chef lads are like – hope he doesn't mind me egging the pudding,' I said, through crumby saucy lips. So after being at the door of despair, the trough of sheer despond, here I was relishing my job and marinading my metaphors. I managed to do five sets, got out, got a pint of session lager, had another Pierre gourmet pie and watched Phil sew things up by taking his twelfth title 7–4.

I was still talking like Darth Vader chewing iron filings five days after the final. The lads in the Mason's Arms in Pudsey were mocking my guttural tones as I played pool with my big rival Keith 'The Professor' Leybourne, who is in fact Professor of History at Huddersfield University and can lay mean snookers on the green baize. Having chewed a couple of pints of XXXX and chilled for an hour or so, I went home. Irene had a message for me. Would I ring a lad called Stuart Theobald in Wisbech; he was a voice coach.

I did just that. It turned out he was a friend of my daughter-in-law and we had a conversation that just about changed my life. Emma knew how worried I was about my voice and she had asked him to listen to me on the telly. He told me he was worried about my rasping tones. 'You could do your voice permanent damage unless you learn to go easy on your vocal chords,' he said solemnly. He went on to explain that he worked with people like university lecturers who he helped project their voices to the kids at the back. He offered to come to Pudsey to work on my dodgy pipes and I leapt at the offer.

So it was that a week later I was lying on my back in my bedroom with Stuart prodding at my ribs and abdomen and teaching me how to breathe properly. The key is maximum relaxation of all body muscles. Once this is achieved the vocal chords – really little buttons rather than strings – relax and don't buffet each other when the person shouts. Once you relax, you do a series of exercises for the mouth and throat. One, the Musical Yawn, loosens the jaw. Two, the Tongue Tango, wobbles the tongue and makes it flexible. Three, the Sinus Tap – fingers tap the sinuses as you make an 'Eeeeeh' sound. Sounds daft? Stick around.

Stuart then made me get off my back and show him my commentary sitting position on a chair. I held a hair curler as a mike and sat like I sit in the booth. He was horrified. 'You're like Lester Piggott in the last furlong of a race. And you're holding the mike like it's a lolly somebody's going to steal from you!' He was spot on. Often, after a long game, I limp out of the box like Quasimodo, tense in every muscle group. 'Chill,' he ordered. 'And no words during the commercial breaks. REST YOUR VOICE!' I winced; I did in fact tend to pepper Dave, John and Start Pyke with nervous jokey patter wall to wall.

I did another hour on the floor working on using my diaphragm better and finally did several tongue-twisters in a single breath. 'Richard of York threw doubles in vain.' 'Herodotus wrote the words but it was Achilles done the deeds.' Then I rounded off the day's work with a Monkey Jive: a shake of every muscle and sinew ending in a King Kong roar.

It may all sound comical, but I reckon it will extend my commentary life by ten years. Sorry folks!

The proof of the pudding came in spades throughout 2005. A new event – the Premier Darts League – was in the schedules and we did it weekly. The best players were in it and the crowds were sensational. Taylor was the winner and my voice rose to all occasions.

When Phil averaged 108 for an 8–1 win I screamed 'He's up there in the sporting pantheon with Bradman, Ali and Jesse Owens.' And when he threw a bag of nails 47 I went into 'death of Caesar mode' 'Oooooh silly ... SILLY Philly.'

I was a new man. Gone the twitchy sleepless nights. Gone the sitting on trains, hissing out darts scores to see if my clack was unblocked. I even chucked my cobwebby packs of Proctor's Pinelyptus Pastilles in the bin.

The story of the 2006 PDC world championship focused on two mighty bellies, one mighty ego and one mighty talent.

The first mighty stomach, and it started just under his bottom lip, belonged to Andy 'The Pieman' Smith of Studley in Warwickshire. Andy is loved by all on the darts circuit and is highly respected. He disposed of Colin Monk and America's Ray Carver then shot off home for a lumberjack's Christmas party! He had been paying into the kitty all year and wanted to make sure nobody got at the pies – mince, pork, mud – before him. I asked if there was ever any fights at the lumberjack booze-ups. 'Not often,' he said, 'but we never take our choppers along!'

The other belly was on the sturdy frame of Peter Manley who pushes it out when he dances onstage to 'Is This the Way to Amarillo'. Pete was involved in a dramatic quarter-final with twenty-year-old Adrian Lewis, full of lip and ego. Adie's talent had become the talk of our sport. He had only been playing for a couple of years but was taking big scalps. He refused to work one Saturday on pain of the sack and he went off and won £3,000 at a darts event. So he packed in work and became a pro. Phil Taylor took him under his wing and made Adie cycle three miles to and from his home in the Potteries for practices. He got the name 'Jackpot' by dropping $74,000 on the high roller slots in Vegas but was refused the money because he was only twenty years old.

Both Adie and Pete were dishing out verbals in the match in time-honoured fashion. But then, well into the action, Manley tossed in a remark, clearly visible on camera, as Adie went for a double. This was well out of order and Adie left the stage in protest. Manley protested his innocence but I reckon the telly evidence was clear. His intention was to put off the opponent. Not good behaviour from the chairman of the Professional Dart Players' Association! In the end justice was done.

Manley won that match but was annihilated 7–0 in sets by Adie's mentor Phil Taylor in the final. I heralded The Power's thirteenth world title in this way: 'If there were skyscrapers in Stoke on Trent, he'd be up there like King Kong – hurling defiance at the universe.'

I am happy to report that there is no bad blood between Adrian and Peter now. In the 2007 Premier Darts League at Wolverhampton the two players shook hands, giggled and pretended to wrestle before their match. Adie won in style and I cried: 'They'll be bashing their Wedgwood in Burslem and lolloping in Longton at the class of this young Stokie.' I reckon Adie will be world champion in the next three years.

I don't know what the Chinese call the year 2006 but if you are Dutch or a keen darts fan it should go down as 'The Year of The Postman.'

In 1991 Raymond van Barneveld was earning a living in The Hague in Holland pushing letters through doors. In 1985 he had been playing darts for a few months and watched the BBC broadcast of the Embassy World Darts Championship final in which Eric Bristow beat John Lowe. He got the bug for the big time. In 1991 he played in the Embassy for the first time and got knocked out in round one 3–0 in sets by Keith Sullivan of Australia. In 1993 he lost to John Lowe but was madly impressed when John took him to the sponsor's hospitality suite and other British pros were nice to him. In 1995 he made the Embassy final, losing to Wales's Richie Burnett.

Then Barney really hit the big time. With a commercial TV station in Holland covering the 1998 Embassy in full, Barney beat Burnett 6–5 in the final to become champion. Thousands of people were at Schiphol airport to greet him. After his defeat in the big clash with Phil Taylor at Wembley Arena, which he lost 21–10 in legs, he pipped Ronnie Baxter 6–5 to win the Embassy again. I watched Ray's progress carefully and reckoned he was a good, if not great player, very emotional and very vulnerable when the pressure was on.

In 2003 and 2005 Barney won the BDO world championship again but looked fragile when losing the title to the young Jelle Klaasen in January 2006. Barney seemed to lack the guts to chase a big game. But this all changed later in the year when he hitched his flag to the good ship PDC and began to play in the Premier Darts League.

On the very first night at Blackburn, I was aware that something very special was happening. Ray came out waving nervously and the crowd went wild. They had clapped and cheered Ronnie Baxter, Ray's opponent who was from the Blackburn area, but it was nothing compared to the rapturous welcome they gave the Dutchman. Ray responded by thumping Ronnie by 8–1 in legs. A week later in Sunderland he blitzed Wayne Mardle 8–4 and did five check outs of over 100, including a 164. On 23 March he took on Peter Manley in front of three thousand frenzied people at Bournemouth and went ballistic.

We were not expecting any fireworks from Barney in his first match. He was playing Phil Taylor later, so we thought the tall Dutchman would not get flying till he faced The Power. But, presumably inspired by the battalions of the Barney Army present, he planted two back-to-back 180s to leave 141 for the magical nine-dart. I told myself silently that Ray had been upstaging Taylor week-in week-out, and that surely he could not swipe the emperor's clothes in front of the league's biggest audience. He did, planting 60, 57 double 12 as clean as sliced Edam.

Over to Ian Chadband of the *Evening Standard*: 'As the most raucous audience that genteel Bournemouth can ever have entertained went as mad as cheese, you could have sworn a small black cabin at the side of the International Centre Hall must have smoke billowing round it. Because inside a small, loud bloke appeared to be in the throes of self-combustion, wailing "I DO NOT BELIEVE MY GEORDIE EYES!!!"' Ian said I turned the feat into a *happening* and I'll settle for that. Again, you will notice, no hyperbole and no shredded thesaurus. Just synchronised viscera from heart to lungs to lips.

A couple of hours later Phil got the chance to put the upstart from Holland in his place but could only manage a 7–7 draw. The biggest crowd ever to attend a darts event in Britain since the *News of the World* at Ally Pally was at its peak in the 1970s cheered both players to the echo. And I realised that our sport had reached new heights: the Barney/Taylor axis was about to blossom.

A few weeks later, as a Barney versus Phil final to the Premier Darts League looked nailed on, Roland Scholten hit top form in the semi-final and trounced Barney by 11–3 in legs at Plymouth. In the final Taylor beat Roland 16–6.

Barney went from strength to strength. In June at the Reebok Stadium in Bolton he captured the UK Open title. He followed up a crushing defeat of Simon Whatley 8–1 in legs with a victory over Taylor. Then he beat Barry Bates of Wales in the final. The tiny bullet-headed little Welshman, by trade a driver for a builders' merchant, had cruised through a class field. He was more excited than any other contestant but ice cool when it counted. His strong accent reminded me very much of the days when Alan Evans would be holding court at Jollees. Lager in one cheek, tongue in the other.

The next stop in 2006 for the darts cabaret was Las Vegas and here Barney shone again. Again he beat Taylor and again he made a final. But on the day the swagger and cool of John Part took the Desert Classic title. The day after, I saw a side of Barney I had not seen before. We were at the airport ready to fly home around one o'clock when there was an announcement that our plane was delayed. Then at about four we got on a plane, but were told to get off since the computer was on the blink. Eventually we were told we had to stay in Vegas that night. I was one who got the long straw. I was told there was a room for me at the posh Luxor hotel. I told Barney and the lads I'd see them later at BJ's, Las Vegas's answer to the darters' and domino players' workingmen's club.

Around nine Dave Lanning and I peered through the neon-tinged gloom of BJs. It was like a scene from *American Graffiti*. Four of the young barmaids had clothes on and the other two were on the 'sexy slinky' shift – they wore nothing but bras, thongs and mesh tights to keep the mainly redneck clientele happily boozing, eating steaks and shooting pool. In the middle of the room sat Barney and his wife Sylvia, having a beer and beaming. The six PDC markers and stage officials, however, looked fed up. It turned out that the Super 8 motel they had been put in was not good. But the Barnevelds were happy as Larry. 'Good steak, good chips and good cheap beer,' said Ray. 'What more can a man or woman ask?' The PDC lot still sneered but Dave and I were with the Barneys on this. We did not let on where we were dossing that night. We sat till late discussing football with Ray, who had just been voted third to Johan Cruyff and Marco van Basten in a Dutch poll to find their greatest sportsmen ever.

On 6 December I began doing interviews for the 2007 PDC World Darts Championships, which were due start on the eighteenth of that month. I sat in a posh Leeds restaurant toying with some goujons of sole and pontificating while Robert Philip of the *Daily Telegraph* attacked a fillet steak and watched the red light on his tape recorder flicker away. In his article a week later he described me as 'making Murray Walker sound as though he is on Prozac'. He approved of my 'gift of combining the erudite with the whimsical, the phantasmagoric with the homespun'. He gave me a whole page. *The*

Times also urged viewers to watch the darts to see if I could top lines like: 'If you had to throw a knife at the wife in a circus, you'd want to throw it like that.' I was not urging wife-targeting, just explaining how Dennis Smith lines up his shots.

The draw had been fascinating, since it made possible a Barney versus Taylor final.

In the first round Ray took on sixteen-year-old Aussie Mitchell 'Moosta' Clegg who showed good form and a belly that was almost Jockyesque. Somebody in the production scanner went on about dinner bells and I rose to the bait: 'Whenever there was spaghetti bolognese on the menu, guess who was first out of the playground when the dinner bell rang?' Giles Smith thought this was not 'tactfully oblique' – I say it was gentle joshing in a kindly way. If senior bellies like Manley's and Lazarenko's are fair game, why not the junior versions? Ray won easily in the end.

Next Ray won a match that Colin Lloyd will want to forget. Colin shot to 3–0 in sets, with the Dutchman nowhere. Then Lloyd seemed to get tied up with tension and the lovely flowing darts started from Ray. He won 4–3. He told the press after the match that he was working hard on a treadmill to improve his fitness and there were hints that he'd been working on his mental approach too. This was to loom very large in the later rounds.

Taylor set the alarm bells ringing early in his quest for his fourteenth world title. He had a 109 average in beating Mick McGowan of Ireland. But then in round three he took on Chris Mason who had been shaking things up in his chats to the press. He dubbed Taylor 'Bertie Big Bollocks' and said Phil, who had just taken delivery of a

Bentley Continental, flaunted his wealth and was always talking about his celebrity friends like the Beckhams. 'Phil is lucky I'm not ten years younger when my bollocks were bigger than my brain,' said Chris, who obviously never did O level biology. Well, I was surprised when Phil responded to a willy-waggling wind-up like this.

Face set, Taylor set about a demolition job on Chris. He won and at the end there were angry words as Mason tugged at Taylor's hand. There were allegations of swearing by Chris. Mason insisted that he had only been swearing because Taylor had taunted him by missing doubles deliberately till the last dart. Hence a couple of remarks like 'No bloody need for that.' Phil told the press shortly after the match that Mason's behaviour was so bad that he felt like packing the game in. He got so het-up he even swore about the swearing himself: 'If the PDC had any bollocks, they'd do something about it.' For my money this overreaction was because he was worried about Barney, not the garrulous gobbing-off of Mason.

While all this serious stuff was going off, there was a moment straight from the boozy past that took me right back to the old days. I happened to be in the backstage area when Wynand Havenga of South Africa, a burly lad with a cheery face, showed up for his game against Peter Manley with a parcel in Christmas wrapping paper. He asked an official to open it for him and it was a bottle of fine brandy! Wynand poured some in a glass and supped copiously. He then did a number on Peter Manley over the next hour and a half, and I went behind the stage again, heading for the toilet. The official held up the bottle – there was about a quarter of an inch of booze left in it! Back in the booth I put on the headphones and listened to Wynand chatting to Dave Clark. I swear he sounded as sober as a vicar after a cup of mint tea; you could not tell that he'd had a single drop.

And then after all the gargling, prancing, lipping and posing we got the final we wanted, one that turned out to be the greatest match I've ever seen.

I'll start with the run-up to what I consider my best commentary ever. My preparations for the 2007 Ladbrokes.com World Darts Championship final began roughly sixty-eight hours before the first dart was thrown. I had put in a long day on the Friday, commentating on the quarter-finals and my dodgy chest was feeling a bit tight as I walked out of the Circus Tavern at eleven o'clock. The mixture of fag smoke and dry ice is not a good environment to be in twelve hours a day, especially if you are asthmatic. And the juxtaposition of icy wind and sleet off the Thames is guaranteed to shake your tubes up a bit. So back at our hotel on the Dartford Crossing I had two slow pints of session lager – five years ago it probably would have been four – and went to bed with a pint of water.

At nine the next morning I got up and did the breathing exercises that Stuart Theobald had designed for me. I cannot tell you how these have totally stopped my fears of losing my voice during a long tournament. At this year's world championship I did fifty-five hours of commentary in ten days – that's like Motson or Tyler doing *thirty* football matches in ten days – and my voice scarcely sounded scratchy at the death.

After doing the exercise I had a bit of a scare while shaving. I felt the right side of my tongue swelling a bit and thought it was the onset of laryngitis. Inspection showed I had snagged my tongue on a jagged bit of tooth where a filling had come out. Still, I went very easy on the semi-final between Phil Taylor and Andy Hamilton. Only when Phil was coasting at 4–0 in sets did I hit the throat after-burner. I told fans in a growl that Hamilton's average of 95 was good enough to win a world title in the mid-1980s 'but it wouldn't give you a cat in hell's chance now.' Phil strolled the match 6–0.

Still, I took no chances on New Year's Eve. Alcohol dries the vocal nodules, so, as my family had a good old Hogmanay knees up in Surrey, I had two halves of lager and an inch of bubbly. I was in bed reading *A Fan's Notes* by quarter past midnight. It stood me in good stead on New Year's Day 2007 at about 8.15. Dave Lanning and I exchanged high fives and Dave said: 'Let rip Sidney and I'll just dance around you...' It was a pleasure to be sat there with the doyen, the silver-tongued old fox, poised to witness a classic between Barney and Taylor.

As it happened I did not let rip till the very end and then I was very parsimonious, patter-wise, by my standards.

The press noticed the change of tone in our veneration of the greatness of the match. In the *Daily Telegraph* Jim White, veteran Sid and Dave watcher, sensed the drama from the kick-off. 'Such was the scale of this game that even Sid Waddell, the Dr Johnson of the commentary box, got mixed up on his way to Dictionary Corner. "Get your Rogetsaurus out now," hissed Sid. "This is indescribable." When Sid is scratching round on his shelves for a synonym you know you are watching something, well, indescribable.' Still, I warned the viewers that this could be 'Kilimanjaro with the top blowing off' then let the match largely speak for itself.

As Taylor approached 3–0 in sets after twenty-five minutes play I began giving strong hints that the match could be over soon. The cocky Taylor had come out in an orange shirt just to get up the Dutchman's nose. I reckoned this was Freudian and not too subtle: 'Phil using the psychological broadsword rather than the rapier.' Taylor sometimes starts slowly but not this time. His average had been as high as 122 to Barney's top of 91, and I feared the worst for Barney. He was missing the 60 bed badly and I epitomised his plight thus: 'If a tiger comes to tea, you don't put sauce on yourself.' I reminded the viewers that a year before in the BDO final against Jelle Klaasen, Barney had failed to chase the game, even though his opponent was paddling along on a mere 90 average. I honestly did not think that Barney had on the night the extra couple of gears he had shown in the Premier Darts League of 2006.

Then something happened.

Raymond had been taking Zen lessons and seeking inner calm at crisis points in games. And, stone me, it began to work. From hitting not one 180 in three sets, he banged in *ten* between set four and set ten. Taylor seemed to be marking time, sitting on a 100 average. He did not think, I reckon, that Ray could get all his marbles – 180s, doubles, high average – together at once. But another main factor in Barney's rally was his pure technique. He stands, like Brissy and Anderson, at six foot one, so is looking straight at the 60 bed. He does not ricochet his darts off others like Phil does; he is the greatest airshot player of all time, better even that the Welsh maestro Alan Evans. So all he had to do was relax and let the Zen ooze.

When Taylor got to 5–3 in sets, I could not see Barney closing the gap. And, I think, nor could Phil. He was, as usual, playing the man and not the board. I reckon Phil felt that even if Barney matched him at 6–6 in sets, his own character and iron will would win. Nobody told Ray that.

He continued to cane the 180s and ended up with twenty-one. I have seen Colin Lloyd win a major match with sixteen 180s but that was leading all the way. To summon up twenty-one in the body of a world final when you've already gone three sets with none is miraculous.

In the deciding set I purred on about the massive respect between the two players. It was deeply felt on my part so naturally a bit of gash Geordie slipped in: 'Respect for Barney oozes from every pore in Taylor, even his *lugs* [ears].' But I stuck to plain effective English when we were down to the last dramatic arrows. 'It's brutal. It's vicious. But in a strange way it is strangely beautiful.'

Taylor hit a killer 180 in the 'sudden death' leg. He must have thought back to 1992 when he bashed Mike Gregory at the Embassy with a 'pulverisational' leg. But Barney hit one in reply. Then Barney sank the winning double. The crowd went wild and the two players expressed their respect and affection for each other. I grabbed a bottle of lager and sat back in the commentary box with a warm glow. What a match. But what a future for darts on Sky: the two best players in the world setting the pace and the pack at their heels. Bliss, to be alive on such a night.

I have watched the tape of the 2007 final several times and in summary I would deconstruct my efforts in this way. It was the opposite of what Nick Hunter, my mentor at the BBC, called 'performance'; at no time was my mood or mania at variance with the sporting action. I had on my hands a brilliant match and I used every verbal and imaginative trick to augment the viewers' appreciation of it. In fact, for once executive producer Rory Hopkins was not yelling at us to big it up but coaxed us to give silence for key shots in the match. It worked. Our audience for the final was, I believe, no less than 4.2 million viewers, and possibly as high as 6 million.

10

Tourette or Not Tourette?

From the very start of my commentating career in 1977, people in the press have questioned where exactly am I coming from, and some scribes have even raised doubts about my sanity. In brief, there have been suggestions that I am mad, or suffering from Tourette's Syndrome – shouting obscenities and squealing random abuse at strangers – and/or under the influence of drink or other drugs. I know of no other sports commentator whose utterances have been put under such scrutiny or who has spawned theories stretching from genius to madness. I feel chuffed and a bit proud – they can get my psyche wrong as long as they get my name right – and now I'll try to put down what I reckon myself.

The suggestion that I have Tourette's did not come exactly as a surprise.

When I was a bright teacher's pet at Morpeth Grammar School I always got told off for gabbling when speaking in public. It had to do with my asthma and my difficulty at being verbally consistent over a long sentence. But I also liked lobbing big words into everyday things like football matches or street games. Again, being Geordie means being excitable and talking fast and often across other people's chat. I admit to being a compulsive gobshite.

But when I coached the shove ha'penny and pool commentators at the *Indoor League* in the early 1970s I knew what I was on about. I had analysed how Eddie Waring, David Coleman and the boxing commentators I listened to on radio with my dad made their impact. You had to have *enthusiasm* for starters, and a little bit of humour helped too. For this latter factor, my role model was and still is Dave Lanning.

I have already detailed some of the fury my voice produced in my early days on the Beeb, so it was good to end my days with them on a bright note. On my last trip to Frimley Green I was greeted with a poem, from Andy, Johnny and the two Daves, all fans:

Like Lee Van Cleef on a bad night,
The man who talks bollocks is back.
I'm telling you it will be a sad day
When he feels his bags he must pack.

He keeps the sport we love on the telly
Without him it wouldn't be right,
Steve Rider's a pain in the belly
And Motson ain't there on the night.

Very nice and in total sync with my theory that the real fans see my enthusiasm for what it is; a reporter/wordsmith with no time to think and getting over his message with all the verbal and imaginative tools he can muster.

But the press began to develop a different deeper theory round about the time of the 1996 WDC World Championship. It took two forks: one, that I might be a genius and the other that I might be raving mad. Giles Smith set the ball rolling in the *Daily Telegraph*. Sky, he wrote 'stole the BBC's darts commentator of sixteen years, Sid Waddell, whispering oche-side genius or prize berk depending on your point of view and hugely entertaining either way.' Giles focused on the Phil Taylor versus Keith Deller match to pick up on some 'vintage Sid'. He liked my reflection on what darting heaven might be like. 'Maybe, John (Gwynne) there is a darts' Valhalla, so we all end up in the sky sitting sipping mead and watching the great ghosts. Might happen.' Would a madman lapse into Icelandic consonantal bouncing metre as used by Thomas Gray in his famous *Elegy Written in a Country Churchyard* to make a relevant point?

The same dichotomy was expressed by Andrew Baker in the *Independent on Sunday*. 'Sid has two modes: hoarse whisperer or screaming banshee. When Taylor notched a bullseye, Sid went ballistic, "That's the best bit of bulling I've ever batted eyes on." Sid did not come down from the stratosphere for the rest of the riveting contest, in one of the most entertaining displays of sustained hyperbole you will ever hear.'

There is a strong hint here of why the Tourette's suggestion was just down the road. The fan inside the reporter is wondering why he cannot rant ad-lib like me, while a nagging doubt is there about the rightful place of such verbal abandon in commentating anyway.

The same chalk/cheese syndrome is there in the people who love to listen to me and the folk who switch off the minute they hear my voice.

My manic histrionic style does not stop when I leave the commentary box. In the early days, the act would continue after work with our Sky team. At each championship John Gwynne and I would set the ball rolling with community singing and next thing you know the whole crew would be ready to 'Climb Up Sunshine Mountain' in the hotel armchairs. John and I peaked in our singing career in the autumn of 1996 at Bognor Regis during the World Pairs Championship. We had just finished a few pints and a few songs and were thinking about our beds when a rugby team from Daventry came into our hotel and began to sing dirty songs. John and I did cameos of more sophisticated rugby songs e.g. 'The Bastard King of England', and then I did my party piece of *The Wild West Show* – featuring a boxing match between a snake and an ostrich – and went to bed with applause ringing in my ears. Next morning at breakfast I was surprised to be given a carrier bag by one of the rugger lads. It contained my *shirt* – flung to the fans in my final moment of triumph.

So keen were John and I to sing at every opportunity that we once forked out forty quid for the privilege. It happened in Blackpool at the Imperial Hotel in 1998. When we got back there after the darts on our first night, we were shocked to find a karaoke set up in the posh cocktail bar, with speakers wall to wall. You had to climb over them to get a beer. Photos of Churchill, Thatcher and Clem Attlee – dating back to when the Imperial was the top conference hotel – frowned down on this sacrilege. Whatever had happened to political chat, the exchange of aphorisms or community singing? So ... John and I had a whip-round, collected forty notes and the karaoke kid took an early bath.

My deep-seated need to let my hair down by singing almost got me the sack a couple of years later. I had put in a particularly hard stint on the Thursday of the Matchplay in Blackpool and was told by the boss Rory Hopkins to hang loose from about eight o'clock. So I dived into an Italian restaurant, had a quick Pepperoni Passion and a couple of lagers. But as I was leaving I was asked to join some PDC directors who invited me to have a couple of glasses of vino bianco. Bad move. I mooched into Yates's Wine Lodge and joined two Scots darts fans, both dressed as Freddie Mercury. Two pints of Grolsch later, we taxied to the Crazy Scot Karaoke bar where Jamie Harvey was in the middle of his act. Spotting me, Jamie hauled me up on-stage, did a duet and left me to my own devices. I really socked it to them. I did 'Your Cheatin' Heart', 'Ain't That a Shame', 'The Wanderer' – twice – and finished with a medley of Rod Stewart hits, backed up by Jamie. More Grolsch flowed.

Around midnight I taxied back to the Imperial and slipped into bed. I woke up to the screams of seagulls and a dry garlicky mouth. I went to the washbasin in the bathroom and took a glass of water. I did not look too bad or feel too bad. Then I spoke to the mirror. I meant to say 'Silly night, Sidney', but all that came out was a dry throaty 'GGGGRRRRRRHHHHH!' I had left my voice at the Crazy Scot. There would be hell to pay.

I did not panic. I shaved carefully, dressed, then slipped down the back stairs. I walked purposefully along the prom to an old-fashioned chemist's shop, one with big coloured bottles in the windows between the packs of unisex passion undies. I pointed to my throat and gurgled my problem to a Hyacinth Bucket lady with a kind face. She beamed.

'I've got just the stuff you need, luv, Proctor's Pinelyptus Pastilles. As used by all the great singers: Gracie Fields, Joseph Locke, Des O'Connor.'

She handed me a small green box lettered in gold. I read off a list of more showbiz greats who swore by the product. 'As recommended by M. Maurice Chevalier, Mme Sarah Bernhardt, Miss Ellen Terry and Sir Henry Irving.' I bought two packets and raced back to the hotel. For the next six hours I gargled with warm salty water and sucked the pastilles, hoping they would not reduce my sense of humour to Des O'Connor's level. By four o'clock I could just about talk. The first semi-final started just after seven. I thought I'd be fit enough to busk my way through the second semi-final. I slid down the back stairs and went into the bar to order some sandwiches.

'Sidney!'

I turned to see Gary Norman, a good friend, and producer of the day.

'How are you doing?' Gary breezed, expecting the usual avalanche of Sidney bonhomie and wit. He had his usual quizzical Cockney grin in place.

'Bit of a summer cold, mate,' I wheezed. 'Taking all sorts of throat sweets. Can I do the second match with Dave?'

Gary's grin dissolved sharpish. He put his arm around me. 'Put a scarf round your throat. Honey and hot water is good. See you down the Winter Gardens. Rest your voice. Don't tell jokes.'

The second semi-final was the most restrained I've ever done in my life. Dave took the lead and I tossed in a few 'brilliants' and 'fantastics'. I was in bed with a good book sucking my pastilles by 11.30. And on the final I was fine. I had learned a life lesson: my voice is like Pele's feet or Darren Gough's right arm. *My voice is my trademark, a gift to be nurtured and never abused.*

Some other people saw a new market potential for Sid's voice. To be precise, Dennis Priestley rang me up and said he'd fixed some exhibitions for the pair of us with Vaux brewery of Sunderland. This was early in 1998 and the money was good: £200 a night for six nights.

'Great idea Dennis and you can count me in, but what exactly do I do?'

There was a long pause. Then Dennis said the immortal words: 'Just show up and be thissen. Piece of piss.'

A couple of nights later he and his driver Dave picked me up at Pudsey for a gig at the Farmers' Arms. I sat in the back and asked where the venue was.

'Near Middlesbrough,' said Dennis. Then he shut his eyes and had a kip. An hour later, at about 7.15, we were in South Bank, a rough part of Middlesbrough, and the driver and I were asking folks where the pub was. Eventually we came across a tatty pub by the river with a sign that said 'Farmers' Arms'. I walked into a tap room containing two old men and a blowsy barmaid. 'Darts? Not here luv. We don't even have a board.'

I ran back to the car and told Dennis the bad news. He pulled a tatty bit of paper out of his pocket. 'Did I say Middlesbrough,' he said sheepishly. 'The pub is in Sunderland!' He had the grace to take the wheel and we got to the right pub just over half an hour later.

There were about two hundred punters and a couple of reps from the brewery. By 8.15 Dave had put up the board and I had a list of fourteen local champions for Dennis to play. We were ready to roll. Then Dennis threw me the chalk and said with a grin, 'You mark.' Ice water ran through my bones. Everybody in darts knows that I can't count. But I did my best. It was not good enough. I was sacked half-way through the first game and replaced by the captain of the pub's ladies' team. So I picked up the mike and began taking the piss out of everything in sight. I scoffed Dennis's red and black sweater 'picked up for a fiver at Matalan' and said of an opponent 'one of the biggest tossers on Wearside'. It went down a storm that night and at all the rest of our gigs. At the end of the night one of the Vaux reps said in my ear, 'I thought it was brilliant the way you pretended to get all the scores wrong.'

I winked solemnly. Once a wide boy...

Because Phil Taylor began to dominate the game so massively from the 1997 World Championship, with only Dennis Priestley giving him a run for his money, I think the press picked me out as the most newsworthy factor in darts. Bruce Millington in *The Sporting Life* reckoned that Eric Bristow and I epitomised the sport: 'The Geordie genius and the Crafty Cockney, apt with the words and both approachable.' Jim White in the *Guardian* was fulsome in his praise of my role in the game over the years: 'More than anyone else it was Sid who had popularised darts.' He was saying that the BDO World Championship at Frimley Green was not the same without me. 'It was the tension between the excited verbosity of his delivery and the silliness of the game that had made him a favourite with lovers of irony everywhere.'

If lovers of irony or lovers of S & M can be persuaded to join the anoraks, students, grannies and all the other punters by my verbals, then that's great by me. But I think that what convinced the press that I'd flipped a fuse was when they thought during the 1997 world championship that I was *making words up*. The background to my efforts to further educate the public in darts technology was simple. Ever trying new means of showing the viewer the lads' skills, Sky had started using 'Flight Cam', a special super-slow-motion device that showed the very odd trajectory of some players' darts after they left the hand. With Lazarenko and Dennis Smith there was no surprise; the darts went in a simple parabola to the target. But with Taylor and Priestley the track was more like the flight of a drunken bumblebee. We brought Phil and Dennis into the video van and showed them the pictures and they were gobsmacked.

Dennis's dart left his hand and went up a foot, travelled to its apex (peak) then it wobbled (I called this a wibble – a new word, but exactly descriptive of the movement) and finally it began the weep (term coined by Swedish scientists who had studied darts in flight). The only trouble was, Sky sat me on a stool like a mad professor and I talked through the shots with a wild-eyed Frankenstein stare. The item was repeated several times throughout 1997 and led, I believe, to the suggestion of Tourette's.

The article in question was written by Chris Maume of the *Independent* and it appeared on 3 January, 1998 just before the final of the world championship between Taylor and Priestley. Up to that point Taylor's progress had been so relentless it was in danger of becoming boring. He had dropped only two sets in eliminating four rivals. Maybe that's why Maume got totally forensic about my commentary. At first he was approving: 'A trip through Waddell's mind is exactly that – trippy man. The Circus Tavern is the setting and Waddell is the ringmaster.' So far, so good. And he liked my description of Rod Harrington, when taking on Taylor, as 'Rod's starting like a jackal out of the woods that hasn't had a meal for a week.'

But then – possibly not knowing about my nerves, my asthma and my dodgy tubes – Mr Maume waxed as clinical as a psychology major: 'Waddell's weirdness is not just to do with the words he chooses (or rather the words that choose him.)...' Just who is strapped to the table and who is wearing the white coat here, I ask. 'His delivery, with its arbitrary whoops and growls and flashes of seemingly Hitleresque ranting is like one of those modern classics or free jazz pieces that explores the whole instrument. Sports presenters learn to break up their sentences to avoid monotony. Waddell does not so much break up as hang draw and quarter them. *You wonder if perhaps he has Tourette's Syndrome.'*

Well, even if it was surrounded by praise for my actual words, the suggestion that I am carrying a verbal disease and thus out of normal control was a worrying one. And things got worse the next day. I went down to breakfast and saw that Rory Hopkins was very upset. He was reading an article in the *Sunday Times*. He looked up at me with sad eyes and said: 'Yesterday the papers said you have Tourette's, now they say you're turning the game into a bloody joke.' He was not being judgemental, but with people saying there were no new stars and that the game was becoming boring with Taylor's dominance, you could do without having your talisman commentator slagged off as well.

The piece was by Peter Watts and it pulled no punches. Here is its most cutting thrust: 'The sport is seen as a joke and Waddell himself is partly to blame. He is a cult figure, which is usually a bad sign, and though some find his enthusiasm endearing, others consider him an *incoherent babbling Geordie* from the genuine entertainment that darts attempts to provide.' Note the fact that Geordie is tossed in as a random insult.

The article ended up by praising the 'Auntie-fied' presentation and commentary of the Beeb's coverage of the BDO world championship.

I did get down in the dumps for a few days, but I knew my style was right for top darts. We earn our money by 'bouncing' the action when it is dull, and by precise vivid gobbets of info when a classic is in progress. Only trouble was, Taylor was now approaching his great era and hardly anybody could give him a game. Thus my frenzied verbals, Dave Lanning's puns and John Gwynne's rants were sometimes seen as ego trips over a parade of Taylor wins. But I vowed that nothing was going to change my style; I would not take lessons from the bland banter of Motson or the silky dry humour of Benaud. I stuck to my blaring flaring own guns and, bugger me, the papers started calling me a genius! The article that set the tone for 'Sid Studies' for the next eight years was this piece in 1999 by Greg Wood of the *Independent on Sunday*: 'WONDERFUL WADDELL,

OUTRAGEOUS SINGER OF ARROWS'. Under that headline, Greg bulled me up to high heaven. 'The big men arrive on the oche and in their wake, one Sidney Waddell, Esq. You pull the curtains, sink into the sofa and allow a stream of Sid to wash over your head. *This* is why you had that wretched dish bolted to the wall in the first place.' Greg reckoned they could do with my patter at the Open golf at the last hole and at Wimbledon for the tennis final.

Greg had hit the nail on the head. My style and that of John Gwynne, ranting, joking, whispery, super tense as the match demands, would not work on football or cricket. There are little or no nuances in darts. There is no off-side, LBW or running of good angles. In darts, 31 with three darts is crap, be it thrown by Phil Taylor or a granny on an exhibition night. Not for us Germanic understatement; with us it is brilliant or it's crap. And how else do you convey quickly your opinion other than by reference to the Bible, Shakespeare or Springsteen? And while commentators like Atherton and Tyler are rarely playing dominoes at midnight with Wayne Rooney or Freddie Flintoff, we spend our down time chilling and supping with the lads. So when we give strong opinions on games we are aiming them sometimes at our pals. Yet, in thirty years on the mike, no player has ever pulled me for criticising him. 'You said I'd be unhappy with that shot,' Wayne Mardle once said to me. 'You should have said I was sick cos I was shit. Why didn't you?'

'Cos I don't want the sack.' I replied.

On the subject of swearing, I have done it twice on air in my thirty-year career and the reaction to both occasions was minimal.

The first time occurred in 1979 when I was talking about

Leighton Rees. The director gave me a close-up of the darts and I said: 'Rees was recently at the British Embassy in Moscow and a Russian bloke wanted to buy his darts. Some chance he'd get ...' I was cut short by the director and ordered to tell the viewers the score. Later that night my father rang up and told that I must not swear on national television! 'Swear! When did I bloody swear on telly?'

'Tonight on the Rees game you called a Russian bloke a *chancy gett*!'

He was right – if I had said it, that is. The phrase means literally 'dodgy bastard son of a bastard' in Geordie and would start a fight in a pub no bother. Thank God nobody but Bob seemed to have misheard it.

The other occasion was at Ayr with Sky in 1995. I used to exchange banter down the talkback with hyper director Martin Turner, and sometimes we swore. And on day one at about 1.25 Martin was bemoaning the small quiet crowd. I pressed my button down – not far enough – and quipped: 'Even mean with their cheers these Jock bastards.' Within seconds a call came from Norma Cox, wife of Tommy, in Whitley Bay. She had heard the crack even though it was muted and mumbled. She must have been the only viewer we had. Nobody else complained and now there is a firm rule that we don't swear on talkback.

There was bit of a kerfuffle at the 2007 World Championship when Phil Taylor in interview with Dave Clark used the word 'bollocks'. Phil apologised, even though it was uttered well after nine o'clock. But I am with Giles Smith who said: 'If you can't say bollocks during a darts programme, when can you say it?'

In 1999 at Blackpool my histrionic talents were employed in a most unusual way.

I thought I'd have nothing to do before the final but peruse my notes and my battered *News of the World* scoring charts. I might even fit in a game of 9-ball pool with Dave Lanning in a cosy little gaff back of the Tower. But Tommy Cox, PDC Tournament Director, and a crafty Geordie who has ways of getting his own way, had other ideas. It was traditional to put on 'entertainment' for the crowd after the third/fourth play-off, which finished at about five o'clock. This year Tommy had brought a rock band called the Cheap Suits, run by his son, down from Whitley Bay. This was to be the biggest gig of their life and they wanted to end with a bang, namely 'Rocking All Over the World', the Status Quo classic. But the band were not strong on vocals so they needed a brash, extrovert lad to join them – right, Tone Deaf Sidney.

There was one small problem: I only knew three lines of the song and I couldn't even remember those properly. Still, if Bob Dylan could mumble a song and Chuck Berry could whoop his way along, then I could busk with the best of them. When I hurled myself on stage I got a big roar of applause. But one table was in complete hysterics. My wife, daughter Charlotte, and my American niece Jessica almost spilt their alcopops – and their sides.

Here we are and here we are and here we go

LA LA LA LA LA LA LA...LO

Yeah, yeah rockin' all over the world.

It would have got the big thumb down from Simon Cowell and Co. but it slayed the darts crowd. We even did the song again for an encore. I slid off the stage sweating like a swamp donkey and flopped in the commentary box. I put on the headphones to hear hysterics in the OB scanner.

Rory Hopkins' voice came over: 'You are sacked Sidney Waddell. I tell you no bloody karaoke the night before matches and now you've screamed a rock song twice – minutes before the final. Collect your P45 from the stage door.'

My voice is my trademark, a gift to be nurtured and never abused.

It was around this time that I started to be invited on to shows and events as a personality, because of the darts, of course, but also in my own right. That great darts fan Johnny Vaughan invited Rod Harrington and I on to his *Big Breakfast* cult TV show to chat about darts and 'mess around on the board a bit'. Little did any of us know that this time it would be Johnny who nearly got his cards. It all went great at first. Rod chatted about the professional game and I discussed some of my greatest lines with Johnny. Then Johnny got a funny manic twinkle in his eye. 'They tell me you two have got a party piece that you do when you've had a beer or two …' I knew what was coming. Johnny had read that some players put a 20p on the tongue of a stooge and knock it off.

I got up and walked to the board. Rod pulled out his arrows. I placed a coin on my tongue and stuck it out. Johnny was the commentator, 'So here on *Big Breakfast* Sid Waddell will risk his Geordie lip …' Rod threw the first dart way too high. The second was too low. I saw the floor manager screaming at Johnny and pointing upstairs. Panic

305

showed in Johnny's eyes. Rod glared at me. He hurled the dart and it hit my tongue, a millimetre below the coin which fell to the floor. Big applause. No blood – thank God no darter ever sharpens his darts.

'Sid, are you OK?' asked a concerned Johnny as some harsh sounding words were being screamed in his lughole.

'Yeth, I thertainly am,' I burbled. 'I curled my thongue up so giving Rod a harder target. Thorry.'

The credits rolled and some men in suits with hard faces began giving Johnny and his producer rock all in a corner. There were murmurs of 'damage assessment forms' and insurance. Rod and I laughed. He said 'Next time Sidney I'm having a couple of pints of lager before the stunt even if it is nine in the morning!'

Next time?

The PDC have always been on the lookout to spread the gospel and early in 2000 Ireland was thought to be the ideal place for a major darts tournament.

The players all love the Irish leisure style. Most of the lads would start an exhibition in England at around 7.30 and be socialising with the bar staff and thinking about a curry around midnight. In the Emerald Isle the star turn would be on his fifth pint of the black stuff and playing number eight out of fourteen punters at that time. There had been big events in Ireland before, and one of them had been visited – partly thanks to me – by the *Loaded* magazine team who took some garish pictures of John Lowe and the lads well gone with ale and doing the naughty version of 'Old McDonald's Farm'. This was in 1995, shortly after I had written a feature for the magazine about Eric Bristow. I put the writers in touch with the lads but did not reckon on the blow-by-blow account of the dreg ends of a boozy night. Mind you, just like the Fat Belly/Even Fatter Belly sketch on the Beeb, I think the *Loaded* piece spread the fan base of the game ever wider.

As a dry run for a big event in Ireland, in February 2000 Tommy Cox's company World of Darts organised the Irish Masters tournament at Wexford in the deep south. Cliff Lazarenko and I were commissioned to commentate on the event for *Talksport* and I looked upon the trip as a bit of a jolly. We would be ferried there free on the Thursday morning, we'd publicise the event on Friday and Saturday and work on Sunday. It did not turn out quite that simple or that cosy …

On the Thursday night I had a couple of pints of the black stuff and did the draw for the event. On Friday morning I went with Peter Manley and his wife Chrissie and plugged the event on a couple of local radio stations. I was wearing an old fleece and a pair of tracky bottoms, since nobody had told me to dress up. Then I was taken to St Mary's Golf Club 'to putt a few shots on the green' for the local telly. Bollocks! In fact there were three men waiting for me in state-of-the-art golf gear and equipment and they'd paid £150 each to charity to go a round with a 'star'. I argued till I was blue in the face. I told them I had pitched and putted but had never held a driver in my hand – ever. It was no good. I was given a bag full of gash clubs to hump round and off we went … for the daftest, sweatiest and definitely the most humiliating four hours of my entire life.

I trekked morosely after my three compadres. I was down to play with a local car dealer and our opponents were a doctor and a local builder. The latter had floral bonnets on the heads of all his clubs and he didn't pull his cart, he just pressed on his remote control and it ran to and from him to order. The other three smashed merry 150-yarders off the first tee and up I stepped. I didn't even have a ball. I was loaned one and took my stance. Once, when doing a weekly column for a Yorkshire sports paper I had taken an hour's lesson from a pro at Adel, and he'd advise me to 'keep your feet comfy and swing through the ball'. I swung the driver through and, stone me, the ball arced beautifully and landed near the rest. There were warm murmurs of approval and the suggestion that I was codding. But the holes got longer and my luck ran out. I had 4, 4, 5 and 6 and then came a downhill section. My drive went 50 yards along the grass and my four attempts at a chip just excavated divots. I could not get the hang of using the wedge. There were no more warm Irish grins or jokes. The trio played on against each other as if I was a passing tramp.

I hacked on merrily, sending balls into the sea and even one sideways into the potato patch of a convent. Word had got back to the clubhouse about the mad determined Geordie rabbit and folk were coming out to see me. John Lowe and his wife Karen were in complete hysterics at the fourteenth. By then I was swearing, swiping madly and in a sheen of muck sweat.

Then there was a welcoming light ahead in the gloom. I fell into the clubhouse and Bob Anderson, winner of the day's prize, led the applause. People came up to shake my hand and my builder pal put three pints of Guinness on a table – from him and my party. 'Sure and 'twas worth every penny of the hundred and fifty quid to see your antics out there,' he said. People kept coming over to buy me a drink and I kept asking for halves. They don't do halves in Wexford.

I woke up with a sore head and blisters on both hands. I watched the first day's play in the tournament and made a few notes for Sunday's matches. Chris Mason was on fire and so was Shayne Burgess. That night I turned down Lazarenko's invitation to down a Magner's or two and had an early night.

At three o'clock the next day we began the oddest broadcast I have ever been part of. About four hundred people were crammed into the disco and I was practically sitting on Laz's knee in the commentary 'booth' – in fact one of the toilets! Above the wash basin was a tiny monitor and I found it easier to stand on a chair and look over the crowd at the action on the oche. And great action it was. In the final Chris Mason showed us a flowering of his amazing talent and just edged victory over Shayne Burgess. After the game I was having a slow pint of the black stuff with Laz and Bob Anderson. Bob had driven Chris Mason from the West Country to Fishguard and we assumed he was taking him home. Not so. Apparently Chris had met a girl, fallen for her and decided he would not return to his wife and kids in Bristol. Wild, impassioned, spur of the moment stuff it might have been, but Chris and Lorna – the lass in question – are still together and still very happy.

I reckon that the year 2000 was the year that my commentating credibility was established all round and some of my press was so flattering that it was embarrassing. The main factor in this sea change was the inexorable drive to greatness of Phil Taylor. He had waltzed the World Championship in January with a record tournament average of 102.5 – Brissy and John Lowe won world titles with 94 – and came to Blackpool for the Matchplay intent on a Grand Slam – World Champion, World Matchplay Champion and, later, World Grand Prix Champion.

Right from day one I was waxing lyrical about The Power. 'If we'd had Phil Taylor at Hastings, the Normans would have gone home.' 'They won't just have to play outta their skin to beat Taylor – they'll have to play out of their essence.' Remember, Martin Amis and John Updike do not work live; polish I ain't got time for. Anyway Giles Smith in the *Daily Telegraph* realised that our Sky team was using molten hyperbole to make extremely valid points. 'It is handy for Phil "The Power" Taylor that his reign as almost certainly the greatest dart player ever to throw tungsten in anger has coincided with the reigns of Gwynne and Waddell, who are so amply equipped to rise to Taylor's achievements and in whom Taylor gets the chroniclers he deserves. Verily darts knows how to throw a party. And equally verily, Sid and John know how to talk it up.' I think Giles could pop into our booth and do a bit of ad-lib patter himself no bother.

Another *Telegraph* man actually showed up in Blackpool that week and asked to come into the box to watch my antics. Martin Johnson was impressed by my style. 'When Sid Waddell gets behind a microphone, dogs start howling, and the cat arches its back behind the sofa.' Hitherto Martin had been of the opinion that I might work on a mixture of hot air and alcohol, but he found out differently. 'Your first suspicion is that Sid himself has rarely found the saloon closed, although he commentates on nothing stronger than bottled water and his own inexhaustible supply of adrenalin. It's not the darts that make tonight's final a must watch, it's Sid.'

I was glad to see that my balls-and-all rip into darts action was seen as no verbal ego trip but as my way of paying homage to great sportsmen.

Nevertheless at one level my 'act' is an ego trip. I try to push my work to the limit every time I am on air. This did not escape the critical faculties of Simon Barnes of *The Times*. In an article extolling Taylor's assassination of Alan Warriner at Blackpool in the 2000 Matchplay final, he called me 'the commentating scene-stealer' and said my determination to be the new Eddie Waring was a bad thing. Eddie was one of my heroes; no mug, steeped in rugby league lore and with a dry wit. I'll take any comparison with him as a mighty plus.

As I've said, some of the praise made me shudder. By the 2001 world championship, even *The Times* had me pegged as 'Sid Waddell, who has enriched television's coverage of darts with his impeccable and faultless tones.' Bit of irony there maybe; I'll buy it literally.

Taylor ripped the field apart to win yet again. He only dropped one set before the final which he took by 7–0 in sets against John Part. His average in the final was 107.5. My best line: 'The tension is as tangible as brown sauce on a sausage butty.' And I was delighted that my sense of humour was now making an impact. 'WADDELL THE STAR IN COMEDY OF ARROWS' ran a headline in the *Daily Mail*, not a paper normally known for its appreciation of working-class sporting sociology. 'Old Auntie Beeb might think that Waddell's presentation of his most unlovely darts heroes to be a touch too down-market, what with his fractured linguistics and all, but he brings to television sport that vital and rare quality – *a touch of natural humour.*'

I thank Bob Driscoll for making the point. Years before when I was at the Beeb, Peter O'Sullivan had been shocked when I said on a chat show that I found much of darts funny and used jokes in commentary. 'Too much money involved in racing for jokes,' he intoned gravely. I think that says more about racing that it does about darts.

Now a surprising statistic that you will not find in the PDC records of match averages and check-out percentages. In the last few days of December 2001 through to the last week of January 2002, I had 14,293 words written about me in the national and local press. Yes, I have all the articles in question and YES I have counted all the words. Juvenile? Insecure? Conceited? Maybe … but it is a fact.

There were major profiles in the *Guardian* and the *Daily Telegraph* – as well as in my old local the Newcastle *Evening Chronicle* – but what pleased me most was a piece in the *Mirror* asking readers if they agreed with me that Taylor was up there in the sporting pantheon with Sir Don Bradman, Muhammad Ali and Tiger Woods. I was delighted that my exaggerations and pun-filled praise of Phil Taylor and his achievements were no longer mocked. The *Sun* called me 'the motormouth commentator regarded as the most entertaining sports commentator on the box. Sid's finest one-liner was a surreal effort from a first round victory for Canadian John Part. "Like they say in the old Canadian proverb, 'When the squirrels march backwards the forest is on fire – and Part is ablaze.'" Genesis: Well, I started with *The Last of the Mohicans* and ended up with Steven King's *Firestarter*... I think.

Ian Chadband gave me a full page glowing review in the *Evening Standard* headlined 'THERE'S ONLY ONE WORD FOR WADDELL: JUST MAGIC'. He particularly like my 'unique brand of combining intellectual references and working-class images.' 'SID WADDELL – DARTS LEGEND' screamed the *Mirror* where Alan McKinlay said I was 'the only commentator who is a bigger star in his chosen sport than the players themselves.'

But my cup ranneth over when I opened the *Independent* to read the latest opinion on Sidney from Chris Maume, the bloke who had suggested in 1998 that I might have Tourette's Syndrome. Now he was singing an entirely different tune. The headline read 'WADDELL LIFTING ENGLISH LANGUAGE TO NEW LEVEL' – you mean like Chaucer, Milton and Will Shakes, Chris? This is how the piece started: 'Every year in early January reviewers of television sport get what amounts to a week off. We have just to sit back with our note-books, watch the darts and transcribe whatever comes out of the mouth of *the great Sid Waddell*.' There followed a couple of dozen of my best lines, for example, of a Shayne Burgess 87 to Taylor's 180 'That's about as much use as a shovel at the bottom of Etna!'

So there's me flogging my tonsils out for love of darts in a hot plywood box while Chris and Co. sip sherry, gobble nuts and crack wise about me! Cushty number, lads.

On 22 January, 2002 I got a phone call from Sky Sports News

that left even the Geordie Lip gobsmacked. I was told that I had been voted Sports Commentator of the Year! The award was organised by Sportscallers.com, a website for sports writers. More than ninety sports broadcasters voted and they put me top of the heap. I was well chuffed. And what illustrious company I was in. John Motson was voted top football commentator and Richie Benaud was inducted into the Sportcallers' Hall of Fame. Chief executive Kel Mansfield said: 'Waddell and Motson and newcomer Lee McKenzie of BBC radio have provided outstanding sports commentary throughout the year.'

Next day I opened the *Daily Star* and found I was the subject of an editorial: 'Voice of darts Sid Waddell has been named Britain's finest sports commentator. It's well deserved. *He's barmy and half the time we don't know what he's going on about* – but you can't fault Sid's passion for his sport. Anyone who claims: "You've got to be fit to play darts" is all right by us.'

On 24 December, 2005, with the 2006 world championship only days old I got the biggest press accolade ever. It came from Chris 'Tourette' Maume in the *Independent* and the headline ran like this: 'SID WADDELL – MAYBE THE FINEST COMMENTATOR IN ANY SPORT ANYWHERE'. This fulsome praise came for my diligent work in a totally non-glamorous match between Denis Ovens and Geoff Wylie. It was slow, grudging and I had to dig deep to hook my viewers. Deep I dug: 'Some games are like Darren Gough doing the mambo. This is like Mr Blobby doing the slow waltz. No rhythm at all. I see Denis as the eighth man in the Magnificent Seven. If Yul Brynner had had Denis there, those Mexicans would have taken a pounding.' Now Seamus Heaney sitting in a quiet loughside croft might do better with his quill and parchment but it gets over in the raw what I meant.

Chris ended the eulogy thus: 'Even a dull game is a jolly holiday with Sid. Long may he reign as the King of Commentators.' There is a good point here. Anybody could wax lyrical on Jocky versus Bristow in their pomp or a Taylor/Barneveld battle now. But it's on Ovens versus Wylie and matches like it that you earn your coppers. Because that's when you have to mine the galleries of your imagination, cull your subconscious and hope what comes out makes a sort of sense.

There was still one shadow lurking in my coverage by the national press. A couple of days after my award, the *Independent* reported that drugs testing was to be introduced to darts. The paper hoped the testing would not be extended to the commentary box. They hinted that lines like: 'He looks about as happy as a penguin in a microwave' might have dodgy origins. Writer Mike Rowbottom wrote 'I fancy mind-altering drugs could be at work here. And losing Sid Waddell is a risk darts cannot afford to take.'

My high profile on Sky Sports has led me down some interesting paths over the years. I was invited on a commentators' special edition of *A Question of Sport* and I did *Never Mind the Fullstops*, a punctuation game show and got bollocked by chairman Julian Fellowes for discussing the modern novel rather than the syntax with my teammate Freddie Forsyth. On *Celebrity Mastermind* I made a right prat of myself by picking far too broad a special subject – Rock 'n' Roll 1956-66, but knowing bugger all after 1960 – and had to 'Pass' twelve times. I came third only because Myleene Klass got only one point on the general knowledge and I redeemed myself a little bit on that round.

But the biggest farce I have ever been involved in was when some bright sparks decided I should become the 'Voice of the Balls' on the National Lottery television show. Yes me. Wor Sid – a lad once described by the *Daily Mail* as: 'The only man I know who makes Eddie Waring sound posh.'

In August 1999, completely out of the blue, I got a phone call from Ginger Productions, Chris Evans's company. They were going to make a new show for the BBC called *Red Alert* and it was going to star Lulu – and me! Could I come to London for discussions with producers Jon Rowlands and David Granger? I agreed in a flash.

A couple of days later we had a meeting in Golden Square in Soho. Rowlands, an extrovert Welshman and Granger, cultured and soft-spoken, painted a vivid picture. They were going to jazz up the National Lottery – the Saturday draw would be in the show – by taking it to the ordinary people of Britain. We would have bin-lid races and *It's a Knockout*-style competitions in the streets of the regions. Top stars like Sir Paul McCartney and Elton John would perform live. Eyes aglow, Jon said he could see me driving a lorry up the M25, the lottery gear in the back and Arnold Schwarzenegger by my side as driver's mate. I pointed out to the lads that I could not drive even so much as a Lambretta, but that did not dampen their enthusiasm one iota. I was also going to be the voice that linked the studio games, commentated on the wacky races and called the actual lottery numbers.

Now, after thirty-three years in television I was prepared for much of this to be radically adapted, but I never dreamed of the fiasco that developed before *Red Alert* limped on to the nation's screens on Saturday 13 November, 1999. At the first rehearsal of the pilot show, held in rooms near King's Cross station, everyone was very upbeat. Lulu seemed a bit unsure about her role in the boisterous games, but Terry Alderton, a comedian who had played goalie for Southend, was brilliant as co-host. There was no sign of my mate Arnie, but I did have a lot of lines in the script put together by the ubiquitous Stuart Maconie. I did the links and set up games like 'Pump Up Your Postie' – punters vying to inflate plastic postmen – with all the gusto I usually gave to Phil Taylor on the oche or Steve Davis on the pool table. I also went off to a sound suite with Jon to voice-over recordings of the lottery balls. I did it in the style of a Geordie bingo-caller, 'Two fat ladies 88, or four double elevens if you're a flashy darts player!' This was all part of 'shaking up the lottery'. My efforts were taken off and studied by the bosses of the BBC and Camelot.

After several rehearsals the team went to the studios at Bray to record the pilot show. We had two weeks to go before the first programme. We stayed at a very posh hotel near the studios and I did not get much sleep; I was quaking with nerves at the prospect of my first live encounter with the lottery balls. I had been practising on old tapes but could not spot the number quickly when the ball was almost upside down. The regular bloke seemed able to do this with no trouble. I walked up the lane to the studios wearing a flat cap and an old overcoat. Suddenly there was a loud beeping and I jumped on to the grass verge. A limo shot past and Lulu waved from the back seat. It stopped at her personal caravan. I got the key to my dressing-room. There was no star on the door.

The long day that followed was a nightmare. For starters, there was no suitable position for me to sit for my voice-overs. I was finally placed in front of two monitors on a table next to the base of the crane camera. I got another table and laid out my script and sat back on a chair to await my cues. All I got was abuse. A grip insisted I was blocking the crane's area of movement. I told him I was not moving. He bellowed into his walkie-talkie. ''Ere this voice-over bloke is getting stroppy. 'E's in the way of the crane!' *This voice-over bloke!* I had come a very long way from starring alongside Lulu and having big Arnie in my lorry.

Once we got going there were horrendous problems with sound. Apart from trying to get Mark Almond and the band sounding right, the engineers had to try to balance screaming contestants and hyped-up audience and live music on the games. It boded ill for my commentating on an outside broadcast of a bin-lid race. Still, I did it with panache and it sounded fine on playback. Then, heart pounding and mouth dry, I went into a shed to try-out on the balls.

I got a very frosty reception from the team who drove the lottery equipment round the country and set it up. They were all pals of the man who had done the voice for ages, and had been dropped on Saturdays for this Geordie. I had a couple of goes and made a couple of mistakes when the balls fell upside down. This did not worry Jon Rowlands, but I thought I caught a sneer from the man in the white gloves. Then I committed sacrilege. 'It would help if these balls were repainted so the numbers contrast more with the background,' I suggested. You would think I had suggested turning Britain into an Islamic republic. I was assured that the balls were sacrosanct: they could not be touched by anyone other than Camelot staff. Repaint them! They looked at me as though I was mad.

Two weeks later we were back at Bray studios at eight in the morning of Saturday 13 November for the real thing. Come hell or high water *Red Alert* would go out to the nation at around 8 p.m. The bosses at the BBC and Camelot had seen the pilot and, apparently, not seen much wrong with it. On the front page of the script I shared billing with Lulu, McCartney and Alderton – 'Voice-over – SID WADDELL' it said in tiny print. But what bothered me more was calling the balls; despite hours of practice I could not get them right when they fell upside down. I sat gloomily in my dressing room. Ginger Productions had spared no expense to make me feel comfortable. On the table was a present – a £3.99 box of Celebration chocolates. Now I knew exactly how Jagger and Britney felt while chilling before a monster gig.

After about three hours of rehearsing, I was very gloomy and almost panic-stricken. McCartney rehearsed two solo numbers and a duet with Lulu. This ate up the rehearsal time. By the time I rehearsed my links and my voice-over on the bin-lid race, the sound crew were being rushed. I was not happy at all at the balance of my voice; I was certain it was being drowned out by the background noise. And the sound on the games, with a manic audience of several hundred, was all over the place. Before I recorded my bits, I mentioned my doubts to the director, but was told to go ahead. It would sound all right on the night. I did my best but was still convinced my voice was being drowned out.

At about six it was decided that we would not go live. We would record the whole show, put it out on tape, and do the lottery section live. With five minutes to go, sitting in the shed by the balls, I felt super calm. Just like when I settled on the starting-blocks all those years ago and the man said, 'Get set ...' I watched the last few seconds of the recording on a monitor. The sound balance was atrocious. Then the red light went on and the balls began to drop. I did not make a single mistake. At the end I got the thumbs-up from a Camelot representative and from Jon Rowlands. In my dressing-room I munched a couple of Celebrations then joined Lulu and her pals in her caravan where we drank pink champagne and did the usual luvvie backslapping. Cracked it, I thought.

Silly me. Over the next couple of days the critics panned *Red Alert* mercilessly, particularly the manic games. On the Wednesday I got a strained phone call from David Granger. He said the BBC felt my accent was too strong and I spoke too fast – I had been their darts commentator for sixteen years so they knew what I sounded like! – and that my voice had been drowned out by the audience and the band – my fault? He said the Ginger team was sorry to see me go. The programme had got only 6.25 million viewers, 1.75 million less than the previous week when Dale Winton had been the host. Obviously Camelot and the BBC had hit the panic button. The papers headlined my departure: 'Away the lad as lottery Geordie gets the chop' said the *Express*. This was the BBC line: 'The programme has an evolving format and Sid just happens to be one of those changes.' They added that *Red Alert* would now run for six shows, not fourteen as originally planned. I vowed I would not in future try to 'evolve my format'. I would stick to talking about big jolly blokes chucking metal at a mat.

So there you have it. In less than ten years I've gone from nutter to genius; hero to zero; madman to national treasure. Drugs? Love of the game and its totally amazing characters is my only drug, and it does, I admit, send me out of my little Geordie head at times.

EPILOGUE

From the Irish Centre to the Dorchester

I suppose in a way this book could be sub-titled 'A Tale of Two Pubs' – with apologies to Charles Dickens.

I walked into the first one at nine o'clock on a bright summer morning in 1973. The Leeds Irish centre was a large workingmen's club, famous as the place building workers flocked to when they got rained off on their sites.

But today was a bit different and a bit special. I was producer of the *Indoor League* and my cast of arm-wrestlers, shove ha'penny champions and darters were due at about eleven – opening time. The darters were the first to arrive. From just after ten they tried to coax beer out of the staff, who were in fact filling hundreds of pints to be started on at eleven. Tommy O'Regan, probably the best dart player in the world at the time, tried to force up the metal grilles when his blarney-soaked tongue failed to impress the staff. I asked him to calm down because I did not want the club committee to chuck us out after all the hard work it had been getting the cameras allowed in.

It amazed me how much the lads and the women players drank and how quickly they supped. But then I saw how accurate they were, given a drop of 'fuel', and within one hour it was clear that the darts was something else. One of the lady players with a very big bosom had 'Watney's Ales' printed in flock on her tight T-shirt. I explained that we were not allowed to advertise and she argued that it was her lucky shirt. It was only with great reluctance that she agreed to play in a plain shirt. The blokes were a motley merry crew. Ron Church, 'The Leaning Tower of Shoreditch', all snaggle-teeth and wearing a moth-eaten cardigan, won a match with a flourish then cut through the crowd like a scythe to get more ale. There was skill, a bit of gentle sledging and players giving victory shouts and kangaroo leaps right into camera.

I was absolutely chuffed to be the 'ringmaster' of the whole show, but I never dreamed where darts would go, or that it would take me with it.

But, thanks to my wheezy gravelly voice and my blinding enthusiasm, I ended up in early January 2007 at the Dorchester Hotel in Park Lane along with the biggest names in world darts. I had the honour of co-hosting the first ever Professional Darts Corporation awards night. My job was to pay tribute to the fourteen players who went out on a limb in 1993 and formed the basis of today's worldwide professional circuit. There was tumultuous applause from the audience of friends, officials and sponsors as I read out the list and each man took a bow.

There was also a massive cheer when I mentioned the work done by Dick Allix and Tommy Cox. The 'rebel' players made the bullets in the long battle against the British Darts Organisation and Dick and Tommy fired them. I believe that the five-year dispute forged a camaraderie that underpins all the achievements of the PDC. Listening to

Epilogue

Bob Anderson talking shop about life on the circuit to Eric Bristow underlines this point. If one pro player gets flu, then all he does is ring up Eric, or Phil or Dennis to fill in at an exhibition. It was magic to see the likes of Cliff Lazarenko and Jamie Harvey in evening dress sipping delicate clarets and cheeky pinot grigios. I regard it as a privilege to have helped put the sport of darts up where it is today.

I ended the night at this poshest of pubs sitting with my wife Irene and Dave Lanning in fancy armchairs in the famous Dorchester Terrace Lounge. All round us swirled a throng of the very rich. Arab ladies having high tea for supper. Sleek City types waving bottles of Cristal and Bolly. *Tout le beau monde* having a ball. Then we got the bill for two halves of cooking lager and a red wine. It was twenty-two quid! Well, you can't have everything.

It was a belter of a night. Nobody fell down and nobody showed their bellies.

The do was a perfect bullseye for a sport that is shooting upward, ever upward.

ACKNOWLEDGEMENTS

On my journey from nervous commentating rookie to senior citizen of the sporting microphone, several people have walked the rocky road with me.

In the early BBC days Nick Hunter had faith in me as a commentator and his coaching was the foundation of my career.

Dick Allix and Tommy Cox stood with me in shady corners at the early Embassy World Championships and wisely marked my card. They were at the forefront of the players' fight for democracy in the sport and both are good friends. Some of their stories provided me with vivid material.

Dave Lanning has been a pal and colleague since 1972. For my money he is the best timer of a line ever, and he and I have bored millions with late night chat about Evans, Rees, Lowe and how they did their unique thing. My other Sky commentating colleagues John Gwynne, Stuart Pyke, Rod Harrington and Nigel Pearson have all contributed to my knowledge of the lore of our game.

The Sky production team has been a fount of anecdote gleaned from good-natured midnight autopsies of our efforts to bring live sporting pleasure to the fans. I'd like to thank Rory Hopkins, Andy

Finn, Lidia Summers, Roger Wilkinson, Dave Clark, Georgina Faulkner and Simon Cole for their input.

I have made friends with thousands of darters in the past 35 years and would like to mention a few who inspired my pen. Alan Evans started the pro darts ball rolling and Leighton Rees carried the torch. The company and chat of Eric Bristow, John Lowe, Bobby George, Jocky Wilson, Cliff Lazarenko, Dennis Priestley and Phil Taylor has kept me up many a night. I regret not a single moment since my darts education increased leaps and bounds – nor my bill for what we Geordies call 'belly powders'.

I would like to thank Andrew Goodfellow of Ebury for seeing the potential in my story and for excellent advice in shaping the chapters. His colleague Ken Barlow also helped in bringing the project to fruition.

Finally, my wife Irene's incisive critiques at various stages have been priceless. She was instrumental in driving the plot when I became somewhat of an averages anorak and was a constant inspiration in making sure I did justice to the sport of darts and my deep involvement with it.

When my manic slipped to depressive she kicked in with big boots.

SID WADDELL
Pudsey, West Yorkshire, August 2007

INDEX

McGovern, Jimmy 174
McGowan, Mick 284
McKenzie, Keith 184, 189, 199–200
McKenzie, Lee 314
McKinlay, Alan 313
McNally, Lord Tom 9
Meade, John 17–18, 19, 26, 27, 89
Mexborough Mafia 182–3
MFI World Matchplay 180
  1984 171–2, 252
  1985 144
MGM Grand hotel, Las Vegas
  249–50, 251
Midland Hotel, Stockport 27, 41–3
Milburn, Jackie 224
Mill, The, Cambridge 2–3
Miller, John 37, 50, 53–5, 56
Millington, Bruce 298
Milton, John 87, 313
Minton, Colin 14, 16
Mitchells & Butler brewery 149
Mitre, The, Cambridge 3, 4
Monk, Colin 278
Monkhouse, Bob 69
Moody, Roger 201
Morgan, Ceri 24–5, 87, 105, 166–8
Morgan, Cliff 2
Morning Star (newspaper) 134
Morpeth 2
Morris, Mickey 39
Mortimer, Sandy 119, 120, 123
Moss, Anthony 75
Motson, John 53, 201, 286, 292,
  301, 314
Mud 228, 241
Murphy, Alex 48

National Darts Association of Great
  Britain 26
National Darts Federation of Canada
  208

National Lottery 316–20
Neighbours (TV show) 178
Nero and the Gladiators 34
Netherton, Brian 7
Never Mind the Fullstops (TV show)
  315
New Walton workingmen's club, Hull
  156
Newcastle City Hall 34
Newcastle United FC 125, 224
News of the World championships 6,
  12, 13, 24, 30, 39, 42, 79, 142–3,
  214–16, 215, 282
  1973 76
  1979 90
News of the World scoring charts 38,
  47, 82, 304
nine-darters 251–3
Norbreck Castle Hotel 218
Norman, Eddie 31
Norman, Gary 296
North American Cup 261
North, Jack 214
Northumberland County darts team
  124
Not the Nine O'clock News (satirical
  TV show) 92–3

Obbard, Phil 38, 39
Observer (newspaper) 11, 91
Observer Sports Monthly 130
O'Connor, Des 296
O'Dea, Terry 64, 68, 106, 113
O'Neill, Jonjo 132
O'Neill, Paddy 58, 90
O'Regan, Tommy 17, 18, 30–1, 323
O'Sullivan, Peter 312
Ovens, Denis 314, 315
Ovett, Steve 245
Owens, Jesse 2, 278